THE CONSTITUTION OF SPAIN

This book provides a critical introduction to the principles and institutions that make up the Spanish Constitution, which was enacted in 1978. It first explains the process of transition from Franco's dictatorship to democracy, in order to understand the historical circumstances under which the Constitution was framed. After offering a theory to justify the authority of the Constitution over ordinary laws, the book proceeds to explain the basic principles of the Spanish political regime, as well as the structure of its complex legal system. Later chapters focus on various institutions, such as the Crown, Parliament and the Government. A specific chapter is devoted to the territorial distribution of power between the State, the regions and local government. The last two chapters deal with the constitutional role of courts, and the protection of fundamental rights. The book includes some reflections on the challenges that lie ahead and the constitutional reforms that may need to be considered in the future.

I0093746

Constitutional Systems of the World
General Editors: Peter Leyland and Andrew Harding
Associate Editors: Benjamin L Berger and Grégoire Webber

In the era of globalisation, issues of constitutional law and good governance are being seen increasingly as vital issues in all types of society. Since
the end of the Cold War, there have been dramatic developments in democratic and legal reform, and post-conflict societies are also in the throes of
reconstructing their governance systems. Even societies already firmly
based on constitutional governance and the rule of law have undergone
constitutional change and experimentation with new forms of governance;
and their constitutional systems are increasingly subjected to comparative
analysis and transplantation. Constitutional texts for practically every country in the world are now easily available on the internet. However, texts
which enable one to understand the true context, purposes, interpretation
and incidents of a constitutional system are much harder to locate, and are
often extremely detailed and descriptive. This series seeks to provide scholars and students with accessible introductions to the constitutional systems
of the world, supplying both a road map for the novice and, at the same
time, a deeper understanding of the key historical, political and legal events
which have shaped the constitutional landscape of each country. Each book
in this series deals with a single country, or a group of countries with a common constitutional history, and each author is an expert in their field.

Published volumes

*The Constitution of the United Kingdom; The Constitution of the United States;
The Constitution of Vietnam; The Constitution of South Africa; The Constitution of
Japan; The Constitution of Germany; The Constitution of Finland; The Constitution
of Australia; The Constitution of the Republic of Austria; The Constitution of
the Russian Federation; The Constitutional System of Thailand; The Constitution
of Malaysia; The Constitution of China; The Constitution of Indonesia;
The Constitution of France*

Link to series website
http://www.hartpub.co.uk/series/csw

The Constitution of Spain

A Contextual Analysis

Victor Ferreres Comella

·HART·
PUBLISHING

OXFORD AND PORTLAND, OREGON
2013

Published in the United Kingdom by Hart Publishing Ltd
16C Worcester Place, Oxford, OX1 2JW
Telephone: +44 (0)1865 517530
Fax: +44 (0)1865 510710
E-mail: mail@hartpub.co.uk
Website: http://www.hartpub.co.uk

Published in North America (US and Canada) by
Hart Publishing
c/o International Specialized Book Services
920 NE 58th Avenue, Suite 300
Portland, OR 97213-3786
USA
Tel: +1 503 287 3093 or toll-free: (1) 800 944 6190
Fax: +1 503 280 8832
E-mail: orders@isbs.com
Website: http://www.isbs.com

British Library Cataloguing in Publication Data
Data Available

ISBN: 978-1-84946-016-3

Typeset by Hope Services Ltd, Abingdon

www.bloomsbury.com

Acknowledgements

I would like to thank the publisher, Richard Hart, and the editors, Peter Leyland and Andrew Harding, for giving me the opportunity to contribute to the 'Constitutional Systems of the World' series. It has been a very rewarding experience to write this book. I am indebted to Peter Leyland and Grégoire Webber, in particular, for their insightful comments on all the draft chapters. They showed me the way to transform the original text into a much better book. It has been a pleasure to work with the team at Hart Publishing. I am grateful to Tom Adams, Mel Hamill and Rachel Turner, for their splendid job when dealing with my manuscript at different stages of production. And it was really fun to offer Putachad Leyland some ideas on Spanish icons for her cover painting.

At Pompeu Fabra University in Barcelona, I have benefited from an excellent environment in which to teach and research. The members of the department of Constitutional Law have always been warmly supportive of my work. I have also found a superb academic community at the University of Texas at Austin, where I regularly teach as a visiting professor at the Law School. I want to express my deep gratitude to all my colleagues and friends in these two institutions.

Alejandro Saiz Arnaiz, Professor of Constitutional Law at Pompeu Fabra University, deserves special mention for having read the entire manuscript with great care. He made many helpful suggestions that I have tried to follow to the best of my ability. He certainly saved me from mistakes of various sorts. The same is true of Luis María Díez-Picazo, former Professor of Constitutional Law and now Justice of the Spanish Supreme Court. He knows that important parts of this book owe much to the many conversations we have had during the years. I have always benefited from his illuminating comments.

Finally, thanks go to my family. My children, Irene, Laura and Marc, are by now fully aware of the amount of work that writing a book entails. I will always remain in debt for their extraordinary patience and love.

Contents

Table of Cases

Supreme Court of Spain

European Court of Human Rights

EU Court of Justice

Table of Legislation

NATIONAL LEGISLATION

Spain

International Treaties and Conventions

1

The Framing of the Spanish Constitution

Introduction – A Tragic Precedent: The Second Republic (1931–36) – A Long Dictatorship – A Negotiated Transition to Democracy – The Constitutional Spirit: The Politics of Consenso – The Constitution as the Embodiment of Shared Values – The Constitution as the Product of a Bargaining Process – Conclusion

PART I: HISTORICAL CONTEXT

INTRODUCTION

ON 20 NOVEMBER 1975, General Francisco Franco died. This event marked the end of a long dictatorship and the beginning of a complex transition to democracy. During three extraordinary years, Spain faced the challenge of creating a new political order. On 29 December 1978, a Constitution patterned after democratic and liberal ideas was finally enacted into law. The new charter was the upshot of an agreement among the major political parties over certain basic rules and principles. It obtained the approval of the vast majority of citizens in a referendum.

For more than three decades now, people have endorsed the Constitution as the fundamental norm of the political system. The governmental structure it lays down, and the rights and principles it designates, are broadly supported by political actors and ordinary citizens of different persuasions. This widespread acceptance of the Constitution has ensured its stability. The main issue that remains to be settled, as we will discuss in chapter seven, concerns the so-called 'territorial problem'. Spain has distributed power between the centre and the regions in a quasi-federal manner. Significant parts of the population in Catalonia and the Basque Country, however, are increasingly unhappy with the existing institutional arrangements. They would like their regions to be awarded a higher level of self-government than they currently enjoy, or to cut their links with the rest of Spain. Whether or not this sentiment will be shared by large majorities in the coming years is an open question. There are also some concerns, as we will see, about the degree of efficiency with which the two levels of government work together to solve common problems. In spite of the territorial controversy, however, the Constitution has taken root, for it has been able to fix many important matters that have historically divided Spaniards (concerning, for example, the form of government, the role of the Church, the responsibilities of the military, and the economic order).

It is important to highlight the relevance of this success from a historical perspective. We must bear in mind that Spain has had many Constitutions in the past.[1] Unfortunately, the more liberal and democratic charters – those of 1812, 1869 and 1931 – were ephemeral. The Constitutions that were less committed to the principles of democratic liberalism, in contrast, lasted longer. This is especially true of the Constitutions of 1845 and 1876, which were in effect for various decades.[2]

Thus, the first constitutional charter Spain adopted (that of 1812) was an advanced document for its age. Indeed, it became a symbol of liberal democracy in Italy, Germany, Russia, and other European countries. It is interesting to note, incidentally, that the term 'liberal' as a political word was first coined in Spain in 1810–12 and began to circulate in Europe in the 1820s to refer to the Spanish rebels of the time.[3] Unfortunately, the Constitution of 1812 was soon repealed by King Ferdinand VII in 1814, and an authoritarian regime was established. Similarly, the Constitution of 1869, a very democratic document, collapsed when King Amadeo I abdicated and a short-lived republic was

---

[1] For a brief description of Spanish constitutionalism, see J Tomás Villarroya, *Breve historia del constitucionalismo español* (Madrid, Centro de Estudios Constitucionales, 1985).

[2] For a classification of Spanish Constitutions along these lines, see F Tomás y Valiente, 'La Constitución de 1978 y la historia del constitucionalismo español' in *Códigos y Constituciones* (Madrid, Alianza Universidad, 1989) 125.

[3] Giovanni Sartori, *The Theory of Democracy Revisited* (Chatham, New Jersey, Chatham House Publishers, 1987) 370.

proclaimed in 1873. More tragically, the Constitution of 1931, a modern and progressive charter that governed life under the Second Republic, died at a very young age, when a civil war broke out in 1936. As a result of the war, a long military dictatorship was established under General Franco, which lasted until his death in 1975.

It is important to say a few words about the experience of the Second Republic and the legacy of Franco's regime, in order to understand the background against which the constitutional framers did their work in 1977–78.

A TRAGIC PRECEDENT: THE SECOND REPUBLIC (1931–36)

Many Spanish citizens took to the streets on 14 April 1931, to celebrate the proclamation of the Second Republic. The new regime came into being in a quick and peaceful way. King Alfonso XIII understood that the victory that the republican parties had just obtained in the municipal elections demonstrated that he no longer enjoyed the support of the people, especially in urban areas. The electoral results were not surprising. Some years before, in 1923, the King had encouraged Miguel Primo de Rivera's dictatorship. The end of that dictatorship in 1930 was bound to mean the downfall of the Spanish monarchy and hence Alfonso XIII had to leave the country in 1931. The popular support that the new republic attracted suggested a promising future. Yet, five years later Spaniards were killing each other in a cruel civil war (1936–39) that was triggered by General Franco's military *coup d'état*. The republican forces were defeated, after hundreds of thousands were killed. A protracted dictatorship was established, which lasted until 1975.

The debate is still open as to the causes of the Second Republic's failure. The international context was certainly not favourable. This was the time of the Great Depression, which led to the rise of fascism in Europe. The impact of the economic crisis in Spain, however, was less serious than in other countries. Much of the Spanish economy was recovering by 1935.[4]

Part of the blame for the downfall of the Second Republic needs to be placed on the constitutional system that political leaders built. The

---

[4] SG Payne, *Spain's First Democracy. The Second Republic, 1931–36* (Wisconsin, The University of Wisconsin Press, 1993) 374.

republican forces behaved in a sectarian way most of the time. They did not work together to find a common ground, in spite of the difficult circumstances they faced. They seemed to underestimate the risks of polarization. In the end, the extreme right embraced fascism, and the anarchists and the left wing of the socialist party resorted to illegal revolutionary activities.

The Constitution, in particular, was not written in a conciliatory spirit. It was a partisan document that did not reflect the political heterogeneity of Spanish society. Conservative interests had remained too uncertain and disoriented to contest the first republican elections of 1931 in an effective manner. As a result, the constituent assembly over-represented the left.[5] The Constitution it produced was ideologically biased, and therefore not well equipped to endure. Thus, when the conservative forces won the general elections in 1933, a tension transpired between their programme and some specific constitutional provisions – concerning, for example, the Church, schools, divorce, and agrarian reform. Life under the Republic would probably have been less polarized if the founding document had been drafted in a different spirit.

The regional problem, moreover, turned out to be intractable. The Constitution established the groundwork for a process of devolution of political power to those regions that wanted to enjoy a measure of self-government. A Statute of Autonomy was first granted to Catalonia in 1932, after a referendum was held in that territory. There was no broad consensus on this move among Spanish political forces, however. The parties on the right were very critical. When the latter won the general elections in November 1933, and the most conservative party (CEDA) eventually entered the government in October 1934, the left reacted in extreme ways. A revolutionary general strike was organized. In Catalonia, Lluis Companys, the President of the Generalitat (the regional government) assumed all powers, and announced the formation of a Catalan State within the Spanish Federal Republic. This illegal action caused the central government to suspend the Catalan Statute of Autonomy, and to arrest Companys – who was later sentenced to prison. When the left won the general elections in February 1936 and came into power again, regional self-government was restored in Catalonia, and the devolution process was extended to the Basque Country and Galicia. A referendum had already been held in the Basque Country in 1933, but it was not

---

[5] Ibid 378.

until October 1936 that the Statute of Autonomy was finally enacted into law. A referendum was also organized in Galicia, but its Statute was sent to the national Parliament just a few days before the Civil War started. Self-government was never introduced in that territory. During all those years, the regional problem was not approached in a constructive manner by some key political figures. The extreme positions tended to prevail over the more moderate ones.

To make matters worse, the electoral system that was established under the Second Republic was not well designed. Too many parties were represented in the national Parliament. This fragmentation caused a high level of governmental instability, which made it difficult for public policies to be defined and implemented consistently.

A LONG DICTATORSHIP

In spite of all its shortcomings, the Republic was still supported by many people when the military rebellion started on 18 July 1936. It is unlikely that General Franco would have won the war without the help he obtained from Mussolini and Hitler.

This does not mean, however, that it was only through brutal repression that the dictatorship was able to maintain itself after the war. The regime was actually sustained by the more conservative sections of Spanish society, who were afraid of the revolutionary left. The Catholic Church, moreover, was an important ally that Franco could rely upon. There had been violent waves of anti-clericalism under the Second Republic, and the Church was grateful for the dictator's protection. The regional question also played a part: some sections of Spanish public opinion believed that the unity of the country had been broken as a result of the process of regional devolution that had started under the republican Constitution. Franco played to such sentiments when he decided to dismantle the self-government that had been granted to Catalans and Basques during the Second Republic, and to persecute regional languages and cultures.

The dictatorship was a long one, however, and it had to evolve through the years. Historians usually distinguish two main periods. The first period starts at the end of the Civil War and reaches the late-1950s. During this time, Franco's dictatorship exercised extreme brutality against anyone believed to be an 'enemy of Spain'. Indeed, large numbers of people went into exile, while others were executed or imprisoned. These were very hard times. This was also the period of Spain's isolation from the rest of the world. The dictatorship became an anomaly after the victory of the Allies in the Second World War. Restoring democracy was the order of the day in Western Europe.

The second period, from the late-1950s to 1975, was milder in comparison. In 1953, in the context of the Cold War, the Spanish Government signed various economic and military agreements with the United States. It also renewed its relationship with the Vatican, through a new Concordat. The economy, moreover, gradually opened itself to the international markets. The gross domestic product grew dramatically in the 1960s, causing a substantial expansion of the middle classes. The regime also carved out some spaces for individuals and groups to exercise limited freedoms. A new law enacted in 1966, for example, abolished the prior censorship of the press. Political parties, however, were still illegal.

In spite of the progress made during this second period, the dictatorship was a regressive step in Spanish history, all things considered. The country suffered a great loss during the first years. It was not until 1952, for example, that the level of industrial production that had been achieved in 1930 was finally recovered, in *per capita* terms.[6] The degree of misery was staggering for a long time. The country went backwards, breaking the trend towards modernization that had started at the end of the nineteenth century. It was not until the 1960s that the regime abandoned the failed policies of 'economic autarky' that were initially adopted. By opening its doors to outside markets, the country finally benefited from the great economic performance of post-war Western Europe. But if Spain had been a democracy, it would have been better off. It would have received funds, for example, from the Marshall Plan launched by the United States to help reconstruct Europe. And it could have entered the European Community: Franco's application for membership in 1962 was rejected on account of the authoritarian nature of the regime.[7]

The dictatorship, moreover, was not sustainable in the long run. It created the conditions for its own gradual decline. The economic mod-

---

[6] JLGarcía Delgado, 'La economía' in JLGarcía Delgado (ed), *Franquismo. El juicio de la historia* (Madrid, Temas de Hoy, 2005) 169.

[7] R Carr and JP Fusi, *Spain. Dictatorship to Democracy* (London, HarperCollins, 1981) 175.

ernization in the 1960s led to a great expansion of the middle classes, as has already been noted. Once the years of misery were over, citizens were less eager to accept severe restrictions on their liberties. The floods of tourists that started to come to Spain every summer, in particular, helped change prevailing moral attitudes. The influence of the Catholic Church began to diminish as a result of modernization. In the 1960s, moreover, a generation that had been born after the Civil War came of age. Young citizens looked to the future, not to the past that the dictatorship always invoked in its official discourse.

In reality, even the Catholic Church started to distance itself from the regime. Since the Second Vatican Council (1962–65) had embraced human rights and liberties, Franco's dictatorship found itself in an embarrassing position. Cardinal Vicente Enrique Tarancón, a liberal Catholic who had participated in the Vatican Council, became President of the Spanish Episcopal Conference in 1971. He sought to disentangle the Church from the State, in order to foster the reconciliation of all Spaniards. In Catalonia and the Basque Country, moreover, some relevant members of the Church sympathized with nationalist sentiments. The Bishop of Bilbao, for example, was put under arrest for publishing a pastoral defending the use of the Basque language. And the Abbot of Montserrat – a monastery that symbolizes Catalan culture – publicly denounced Franco's dictatorship in *Le Monde*.[8] There were also criticisms from the outside. The Archbishop of Milan (who was later to become Pope Paul VI), for instance, protested against the government's execution of Julián Grimau, a Communist leader, in 1963.

In Catalonia and the Basque Country, the opposition to the dictatorship was reinforced by nationalist discontent. Franco had dismantled the institutions of self-government that the Second Republic had created in those regions, as has already been noted. The local languages were marginalized from public life. The struggle against the regime adopted a violent form in the Basque Country. A terrorist group was founded in 1959: ETA (Euskadi ta Askatasuna, which means Basque Homeland and Liberty). Its criminal activities posed serious problems to the dictatorship. In 1973, for example, ETA killed the President of the Government, Luis Carrero Blanco, whom Franco had recently appointed to guarantee the maintenance of the regime in the future.

[8] Ibid 150–56.

A NEGOTIATED TRANSITION TO DEMOCRACY

So the dictatorial regime that was in place when Franco died in 1975 lacked legitimacy in the eyes of an increasing number of people. The transition to democracy was not an easy process, however. The leaders of the political groups that had defended the Republic were in exile, distant from the new realities in Spain. The leaders that were emerging in Spain, in turn, were scarcely known by the people.[9] It was difficult, moreover, for the democratic opposition to organize itself effectively in a common front and citizens were not intensely mobilized. To a large extent, this was a legacy of the dictatorship, which had instilled political apathy among the people.

In such circumstances, the opposition realized that it was too weak to destroy the dictatorship. It needed the complicity of those players within the regime that were in favour of a democratic transformation. Only a gradual and negotiated transition to democracy was feasible.[10]

An important figure came to perform a surprising role in this process: King Juan Carlos. Few people expected he would serve the democratic cause. We should bear in mind that Juan Carlos was crowned in 1975 by virtue of the laws of the dictatorship. It was Franco himself who had chosen Juan Carlos in 1969 as the future head of state. The dictator disliked Don Juan de Borbón, Juan Carlos' father, who had been critical of the regime. So when Franco died, Prince Juan Carlos was proclaimed King, after taking an oath of allegiance to the fundamental laws of Franco's regime.

The President of the Government at that time was Carlos Arias Navarro, a member of the establishment with a terrible authoritarian past who was unwilling to propose any real political reforms. In April 1976, *Newsweek* attributed to the King certain statements that were very critical of the President. Arias finally resigned, and the King decided to appoint Adolfo Suárez, a relatively unknown figure who had worked

---

[9] R Dorado and I Varela, 'Estrategias políticas durante la transición' in JF Tezanos, R Cotarelo and A de Blas (eds), *La transición democrática española* (Madrid, Sistema, 1989) 265.

[10] Santiago Carrillo, the leader of the Communist Party, was aware of the weakness of the democratic forces. He believed that the only path to democracy was a negotiated reform – what he called a *ruptura pactada* (negotiated break with the past). See his *Memorias* (Barcelona, Planeta, 1993) 622–23.

within the apparatus of the dictatorship. President Suárez soon expressed his resolution to make important changes, and he turned out to be the engine of Spain's successful transition to democracy.

The King thus played a democratic role that the opposition had never anticipated. Santiago Carrillo, who was then the leader of the Communist Party, has written:

> Within the democratic opposition, at least amongst the men with whom I had talked so far, there was no trust in the Prince, and there was even a very negative impression of his intellectual capacity. We were still looking for the hinge that would facilitate the transition from dictatorship to democracy, ignoring that the hinge was already there in the proper place and that it had been placed there by the last person we would have expected: Franco himself.[11]

As soon as Suárez started to give signals that he was earnest in his plans to establish a democratic order, the political opposition became eager to negotiate. Suárez knew that the illegal parties in the opposition expressed the democratic legitimacy that the regime lacked, and that for any transformation to be successful he had to come to an agreement with them. Meanwhile, some sections of society were mobilizing themselves. Workers, for example, were striking extensively.[12]

Suárez was in a difficult position, though. He had to reach agreements not only with the democratic groups in the opposition, but also with the most recalcitrant representatives of the status quo. For his proposed reform to be approved, in particular, he needed to obtain the consent of the Cortes, the undemocratic Parliament that Franco had created in order to give his regime some appearance of constitutional legality. The members of this legislative assembly —the so-called *procuradores* — were loyal to the dictator.

The *Ley para la Reforma Política* (Law for Political Reform)

The reform launched by President Suárez was articulated in 1976 in a *Proyecto de Ley para la Reforma Política* (Project of Law for Political Reform), which sought to amend the fundamental laws of Franco's regime. For the valid amendment of such laws, it was necessary to

[11] Ibid 613.
[12] JM Maravall, *La política de la transición: 1975–80* (Madrid, Taurus, 1981) 23–27.

obtain the approval of the Cortes and of the people themselves in a referendum.

The *Proyecto de Ley para la Reforma Política* proclaimed the principle of popular sovereignty and guaranteed fundamental rights. It also established that the legislative power would be bestowed upon a bicameral Parliament (Cortes), which would consist of a Congress and a Senate to be elected by universal, direct, and secret suffrage. The King, however, was authorized to appoint up to one-fifth of the senators. Moreover, it provided for the possibility of enacting 'Laws of Constitutional Reform', which could be proposed by the Government or by Congress, and would be enacted into law if approved by Congress and the Senate, as well as by the citizenry in a referendum.

Fortunately, on 18 November 1976, the old Cortes voted for this new Law. To a large extent, the *procuradores* were moved by some of the arguments that President Suárez' ministers had advanced during the parliamentary discussions. In particular, the Government had insisted that this was the reform that the King wanted, and that since Franco had asked the *procuradores* to support Juan Carlos as his successor, refusing to vote for the reform would ultimately be a betrayal of Franco's will. In addition, the fact that the King would be entitled to appoint one-fifth of the senators led some *procuradores* to believe that they could easily get a seat in the new Parliament without having to participate in popular elections. In any case, the old Cortes committed political suicide: they gave the green light to a law that would eventually dismantle the dictatorship.

The Law for Political Reform was then submitted to the people, by means of a referendum that was held on 15 December 1976. The political parties in the opposition were still formally illegal and did not have a meaningful participation in the campaign. Some of them encouraged abstention in protest for the undemocratic character of the referendum, but in fact they accepted the Law as a good instrument for introducing democracy in Spain. The turn-out was 77.72 per cent, and 94.2 per cent voted yes. President Suárez's programme for reform was thus made into law. This was his first victory.

The Democratic Elections of June 1977

The next step was to establish the conditions for the democratic elections, to select the members of the newly created Cortes, the bicameral

Parliament. Suárez reached an agreement with the political parties in the opposition concerning the details of the electoral system, the rules for financing political parties, the criteria for having access to public media, etc.

Importantly, Suárez agreed to legalize all political groups, including the Communist Party, which had led the opposition to Franco's regime. The most conservative forces were appalled by the decision. The Minister of the Navy, Admiral Pita da Veiga, resigned in protest, and the Consejo Superior del Ejército (the Superior Council of the Army) issued a note criticizing the decision. The Communist Party, in order to allay the fears of the most conservative people, reacted by appearing in public with the national flag that represented the monarchy, instead of the flag that Spain had had during the Second Republic. This gesture was aimed at convincing public opinion that the Communist Party would act in a moderate and responsible manner.[13]

Once the political parties had been legalized, and the electoral rules had been established, the Spanish people were convened to vote on 15 June 1977.

At first it was uncertain whether President Suárez would participate in the elections. In May he announced that he would, since he wanted to obtain the democratic legitimacy that he lacked. He became the leader of a coalition of political parties of the centre and moderate right (Unión de Centro Democrático, UCD). Suárez could offer this coalition his personal charisma and the advantage of being in power.

A multitude of political parties were created and ran candidates for Parliament. The elections witnessed a high level of popular participation: the turn-out was 79.11 per cent. Fortunately, the Spanish electorate was able to act in a rational way, and the political landscape that resulted was simplified. The main parties that emerged were the following. On the right: AP (Alianza Popular). Towards the centre: UCD (Unión de Centro Democrático). On the left: PCE (Partido Comunista de España) and, more moderate, PSOE (Partido Socialista Obrero Español). In the elections for Congress, these parties obtained the following results: UCD: 165 seats; PSOE (together with its Catalan branch: PSC): 118 seats; PCE: 20 seats; AP: 16 seats. Some other smaller parties obtained seats too. Importantly, the nationalist parties from Catalonia and the Basque Country were represented in Congress: Pacte Democràtic per

---

[13] Carrillo (n 10) 659–60.

Catalunya: 11 seats; Esquerra de Catalunya-Front Electoral Democràtic: 1; Partido Nacionalista Vasco: 8; Euskadiko Ezquera-Izquierda de Euskadi: 1. There was no regional or nationalist party representing Galicia, however, or any other territory.

The new Parliament was a democratic institution in the middle of a sea of dictatorial power structures. A Constitution would have to be approved to eliminate those structures. Congress thus appointed a Parliamentary Commission on Constitutional Matters. Seven members of the Commission were asked to draft a first version of the constitutional text.[14] These were soon called the *padres de la Constitución*. After a long process of negotiation and discussion in both Congress and the Senate, the Constitution was finally approved on 31 October 1978. It was then ratified by the people in a referendum that was held on 6 December, and was finally promulgated by the King. It became part of the legal system on 29 December 1978.

That democracy did not come to Spain through a popular revolution, but through political negotiation, is reflected in the legal structure that governed the process of transition. The Constitution of 1978 was enacted according to the process that had been stipulated in the *Ley para la Reforma Política,* which itself derived from the old fundamental laws that structured Franco's regime. The fact that the old legal forms were respected shows that a revolutionary break with the past was not politically feasible. At the same time, however, the regime was not strong enough to preclude a democratic transformation. The final product of the process, the Constitution of 1978, expressly repealed the basic laws of the previous regime (including the *Ley para la Reforma Política*).

THE CONSTITUTIONAL SPIRIT: THE POLITICS OF *CONSENSO*

There was something special about Spain's 'constitutional moment' of 1977–78. Political parties were able to reach a broad agreement about the fundamental rules of the new political order, an agreement that was made possible by the enormous spirit of conciliation, generosity, and

---

[14] This smaller group (*ponencia*) included three representatives of UCD (Gabriel Cisneros, Miguel Herrero Rodríguez de Miñón, and José Pedro Pérez-Llorca); one of PSOE-PSC (Gregorio Peces-Barba); one of Minoría catalana (Miguel Roca i Junyent); one of PCE-PSUC (Jordi Solé Tura) and one of AP (Manuel Fraga).

public service that those parties exhibited.[15] Several factors pressed in that direction.

First of all, both the right and the left, as well as nationalist parties from Catalonia and the Basque Country, were present in the new Cortes. The political plurality of Spanish society was thus reasonably mirrored by Parliament. The victorious party (UCD), moreover, only garnered a relative majority of the seats (47.14 per cent). To enact a Constitution, therefore, the support of other groups would be needed.

Spanish citizens, moreover, expressed their preference for moderation. The majority of voters on the right chose UCD over AP, while those on the left preferred PSOE over PCE. Even the more conservative right (AP) and the more radical left (PCE) avoided extreme positions. Manuel Fraga, the leader of AP, who had served as a Minister under Franco (and as an Ambassador in the UK), was willing to convert old Francoists into conservative democrats. He had a great admiration for British democracy, which he viewed through conservative eyes. He played a crucial role in 'civilizing' the extreme right. Santiago Carrillo, on the other hand, was a moderate communist. His book *Eurocomunismo y Estado*, published at a crucial moment in Spanish politics (1977), expressed his commitment to democracy, which he did not regard as a mere instrument for the establishment of socialism. The Communist Party in the Soviet Union criticized the book for being too heterodox, while Manuel Fraga praised it! Moreover, Carrillo was the first Secretary of a Communist Party to be invited to visit the United States. (He was there in 1977, invited by Yale, Harvard and John Hopkins universities).[16]

Secondly, history had taught some lessons. Many Spanish people still remembered the Civil War, and were aware that no democracy can flourish in an extremely polarized environment. Things had to be worked out in a conciliatory manner. This spirit of accommodation was especially present among the seven members of the special committee (Ponencia) that wrote the first constitutional draft. At first, for example, PSOE obtained two seats in the Ponencia, but it decided to give one of them to the conservative right (AP), so as to broaden the political agreement on

---

[15] In fact, they were able to find common ground, not only for purposes of adopting a Constitution, but also for defining the necessary policies to stabilize the Spanish economy. Such policies were articulated in the *Pactos de la Moncloa* of 1977.

[16] Carrillo (n 10) 685–90.

which the Constitution should rest.[17] This gesture on the part of PSOE showed that the left had no spirit of revenge. There was even friendship, in the end, among the seven Congressmen. In October 1977, for example, Carrillo gave a speech in Madrid, before the members of an exclusive club, and it was Fraga who introduced him with pleasant words.

Thirdly, these were difficult times for Spain. The economy was suffering as a result of the oil crisis that started in 1973. Inflation was high, and unemployment rose. More threatening for the immediate future were the violent actions by terrorist groups, ETA in particular. The Constitution was being discussed while 30 people were killed in 1977, and 99 in 1978.[18] Most victims were members of the police and the armed forces. This caused all democratic parties to worry that the situation might get out of control. It was imperative to work together to reach a broad consensus on the rules and principles that the new Constitution should embody.

There were, inevitably, moments of tension within the constitutional committee. At a certain point during the debates, a coalition seemed to emerge around the centre-right (AP, UCD and Minoría Catalana), against the left (PSOE and PCE). The PSOE's representative, Gregorio Peces-Barba, abandoned the debates in protest. When President Suárez learned about this, he intervened to make sure that from then onwards the agreements would shift towards the left.[19] Fortunately, the final text was primarily based on the agreement between UCD and PSOE. The agreement was almost entirely accepted by PCE, and partially so by AP. As a result, the Constitution was supported by the vast majority of the members of Parliament, both in Congress (94.2 per cent yes; 1.8 per cent no; 4.1 per cent abstentions) and in the Senate (94.5 per cent yes; 2.3 per cent no; 3.3 per cent abstention).

There was a cost to the process, however, in terms of transparency. The real negotiations and discussions did not take place within Parliament, but in restaurants and private offices and homes, where the leaders of the major parties met secretly. Julián Marías, a philosopher and senator appointed by the King, protested against the absence of

---

[17] G Peces-Barba, *La elaboración de la Constitución de 1978* (Madrid, Centro de Estudios Constitucionales, 1988) 20.

[18] Carr and Fusi (n 7) 237.

[19] S Gallego-Díaz and B de la Cuadra, *Crónica secreta de la Constitución* (Madrid, Tecnos, 1989) 46–62; and Peces-Barba (n 17) 123–33.

'parliamentary spirit' at the constitutional stage. The basic agreements were being struck outside Parliament.[20]

Not surprisingly, given the broad consensus political parties reached, the Constitution was ratified by the vast majority of citizens in the referendum. Of those who turned out, 87.87 per cent voted yes, while 7.83 per cent voted no. The Constitution was a clear success. The turn-out in the referendum was low, however: 67.11 per cent (which was lower than the turn-out of 79.11 per cent in the general elections of June 1977). Part of the abstention was politically active, however: the Basque nationalists of PNV encouraged abstention because they were not happy enough with the degree of self-government they had obtained under the new Constitution. Less than half of the Basque electorate (46 per cent) voted in the referendum. In part, the abstention in the rest of Spain also reflected a certain measure of *desencanto* (disenchantment) that prevailed among the people. Some citizens did not like the secret politics of *consenso*.[21]

PART II. THE FOUNDATIONS OF THE CONSTITUTION'S AUTHORITY

We have examined a set of historical events that led to the enactment of the Constitution of 1978. All those things happened more than 30 years ago, however. As new generations of Spaniards enter democratic politics, the question concerning the Constitution's authority needs to be posed. Why should this charter prevail over ordinary legislation enacted by current majorities in Parliament? As we will see in chapter three, the framers decided to make it difficult for the Constitution to be amended in the future. The Constitution is technically *rigid*, to preserve the basic political choices made in 1977–78 against the contrary decisions made by ordinary majorities during normal politics. Why this rigidity?

We need to distinguish two basic rationales to support the Constitution's authority. One is linked to its expressive function: the constitutional text reminds ordinary citizens and politicians – and tells the rest of the world – what are the shared principles and values that

---

[20] Gallego-Díaz and de la Cuadra (n 19) 85–86.
[21] On this point, see F Rubio Llorente, 'El proceso constituyente en España' in *La forma del poder. (Estudios sobre la Constitución)* (Madrid, Centro de Estudios Constitucionales, 1993) 24; and Maravall (n 12) 81.

define the political community. The other rationale has to do with the need for some fundamental issues to be settled through a bargaining process, before political life can develop in a normal way. Let us explore these two justifications with some detail.

THE CONSTITUTION AS THE EMBODIMENT OF SHARED VALUES

The Spanish Constitution expresses a widespread commitment to democracy and fundamental rights. These were the values the democratic opposition to Franco had struggled for. And these are also the values that the vast majority of citizens nowadays endorse. The Constitution is not felt by the living generation to be an imposition from the past, when it enshrines democracy and basic rights.

To a large extent, what has made it possible for the Constitution to resist the passage of time is its non-partisan character. Because the text adopted in 1978 was not written to serve the programme of one section of the political spectrum, but was instead meant to express a set of principles that were held dear both by the right and by the left, the Constitution has not been eroded as a result of the shifts of power in ordinary politics. Indeed, it has proven to be a charter under which both the centre-right (after the general elections of 1979, 1996, 2000 and 2011) and the centre-left (after the general elections of 1982, 1986, 1989, 1993, 2004 and 2008) have been able to govern comfortably. This is in contrast to the way things developed under the Second Republic. As has already been pointed out, the republican Constitution was too biased in favour of the political programmes espoused by the left. The framers of the 1978 Constitution agreed that that had been a mistake they should not repeat.

The Bill of Rights the framers wrote, in particular, obtained ample support. Except for some clauses that were hard to negotiate, as we will see later, there was a deep commitment to link Spain to the culture of rights that prevails in Europe. It is true that the left was more insistent than the right on including a *long* list of liberties in the constitutional text.[22] But this does not mean that the parties on the right were less committed to their protection. Actually, in 1977, more than one year before the Constitution was enacted, the UCD Government signed several

[22] Gallego-Díaz and de la Cuadra (n 19) 30–31.

international instruments: the International Covenant on Civil and
Political Rights; the International Covenant on Economic, Social and
Cultural Rights; Conventions 87 and 98 of the International Labour
Organization; and the European Convention on Human Rights. The
centre-right was clearly sensitive to the need to safeguard fundamental
liberties. The Constitution that was finally agreed upon embodied values
that were then shared, and are still shared, by different political forces
and social groups throughout a broad ideological spectrum.

In order to reinforce the protection of democracy and rights, the
Constitution expresses a common will to connect Spain to international
organizations. This common will has to be understood against the background of Spain's isolation during the dictatorship. None of the 'fundamental laws' adopted under Franco made any reference to international
law. This was in contrast to the very advanced character of the
Republican Constitution of 1931 in this regard, article 78 of which had
constitutionalized Spain's membership in the Society of Nations.[23] The
Constitution of 1978 restores this internationalist conception when it
mentions the Universal Declaration of Human Rights in article 10.2.
The Constitution provides that this document must be taken into
account when interpreting the rights and liberties enumerated in the
Constitution. It also refers interpreters to the international Conventions
ratified by Spain in the field of rights. In addition, the framers had the
European Community in mind when they wrote article 92, which ena-
bles Spain to enter international organizations that exercise powers delegated by Member States. Once more, the great value accorded to this
provision has to be read as a reaction against the dictatorship. As was
explained before, the European Community had closed its doors to
Franco's Spain. Democracy was associated with the country being able
to participate in European organizations. Both the left and the right
were in agreement about this, and they still are. The Constitution does
not really constrain democratic politics in this regard. It expresses a
'supranationalist' commitment that is shared across the nation. It was a
unanimous Congress, for example, that on 26 June 1985 voted for the
law that allowed Spain to enter the European Community. All deputies
that were present in Congress that day (309) voted yes. And they rose up
for a long and strong applause.[24]

---

[23] A Remiro Brotons, *La acción exterior del Estado* (Madrid, Tecnos, 1984) 12.
[24] See *Diario de Sesiones, Congreso de los Diputados*, Pleno, núm. 222, 26/06/1985.

The constitutional framers were of the view that the new democracy they were in the process of creating would be fragile if Spain remained isolated from the rest of the world. Indeed, events were soon to reveal the initial weakness of the democratic system. The Constitution had barely celebrated its two-year anniversary when, in the evening of 23 February 1981, a group of military officers led by Lieutenant Colonel Antonio Tejero forced their way into Congress. At that moment, a vote was being taken to elect Leopoldo Calvo-Sotelo as President of the Government. Tejero and his officers started to shoot in the air. The deputies were held hostage in Congress. The King gave a nationally televised address that night denouncing the rebellion and insisting that all measures had been taken to stop it. The deputies were finally liberated next day. The new Government, under the presidency of Leopoldo Calvo-Sotelo, soon decided to apply for Spain's membership in NATO, and stronger efforts were made to make it possible for the country to join the European Economic Community. Democracy at the domestic level, it was correctly believed, would be more secure if it were constrained by international and supranational rules and institutions.

THE CONSTITUTION AS THE PRODUCT OF A BARGAINING PROCESS

We have seen that there was broad agreement on democracy, basic rights, and supranational law, among the political parties that wrote the Constitution in 1977–78. Since that agreement is shared by the different parliamentary majorities that have emerged over time, no real tension arises between the Constitution and ordinary democratic processes. Things get more complicated, however, with respect to other parts of the Constitution that do not express shared convictions, but bargains struck after a hard process of negotiation. Why should those agreements bind future majorities in Parliament? What is the argument to support the authority of the Constitution over ordinary laws in this connection?

The case in favour of the Constitution can be made to rest on two complementary ideas: first, there are democratic virtues to the efforts made by representatives to accommodate different views and interests; second, there are contexts in which constitutional constraints liberate future majorities. The argument is as follows.

The principle of majority rule should govern democratic life in ordinary times. If we required decisions to be made unanimously or by a super-majority, we would be giving a veto power to the minority that favoured the status quo. If we want to treat the opinions of everyone on an equal basis, the principle of majority rule must operate. This argument in favour of majority rule, however, does not deny that decisions that are reached unanimously or by a super-majority, through a process of sympathetic accommodation, are extremely valuable from a democratic point of view, when the issues at stake are of profound importance. From this perspective, the conciliatory exercise that Spanish political parties engaged in 1977–78 is to be celebrated on democratic grounds.

This connects with the other part of the argument: a Constitution is often needed to stabilize democratic politics. Democracy cannot operate in a social and political environment that is constantly polarized over certain fundamental matters. A Constitution that resolves some controversies through a set of agreed-upon rules can facilitate, rather than frustrate, democratic government. As Stephen Holmes has argued, a Constitution can be democracy-enabling and democracy-stabilizing:

> If we can take for granted certain procedures and institutions fixed in the past, we can achieve our present goals more effectively than we could if we were constantly being side-tracked by the recurrent need to establish a basic framework for political life.[25]

This argument is perfectly applicable to Spain. The framers of the Constitution of 1978 understood that some historically divisive issues had to be settled. And the settlement had to be respected by future majorities in Parliament. Some examples can be mentioned to illustrate this point.

With respect to the form of government, for instance, there was division of opinion between the left and the right. The left was mostly republican, while the right was in favour of preserving the monarchy. A solution was designed that most people found acceptable. On the one hand, the monarchy was maintained. The left agreed that King Juan Carlos had played a crucial role in Spain's transition to democracy, and it came to the conclusion that the issue of monarchy versus republic was

---

[25] S Holmes, 'Precommitment and the Paradox of Democracy' in J Elster and R Slagstag, *Constitutionalism and Democracy* (Cambridge, Cambridge University Press, 1988) 216.

of secondary importance. As Santiago Carrillo said, 'by searching for the Republic we may end up losing democracy'.[26] On the other hand, democratic qualifications were introduced so that the King would no longer enjoy the powers exercised under Franco's laws. The monarch would have moral authority (*auctoritas*), but no effective political power. This equilibrium was possible because the issue concerning the monarchy was part of a larger constitutional package. Interestingly, polls indicated that if a separate referendum on the preservation of the monarchy had first been held, the people would have voted yes. The republican parties would therefore have lost a bargaining chip at the constitutional table. Because no such referendum was organized, the parties on the left were able to reduce the power of the King (and obtain additional benefits too), in exchange for their acceptance of the Crown.[27]

Similarly, the regional problem was addressed in a conciliatory spirit. Spain had been a centralized polity since the eighteenth century. At the end of the nineteenth century, the two most economically advanced regions in Spain – the Basque Country and Catalonia – expressed their will to be granted some measure of self-government. The Second Republic tried to give an answer to this problem by awarding Statutes of Autonomy to the regions that wished to have them, as was already explained. One of the causes of the Civil War was the lack of agreement on this issue. Franco abolished the Statutes of Autonomy that had been enacted, and during 40 years Spain was once again a strongly centralized state.

During Spain's transition to democracy, it was clear that working out an acceptable solution to the regional question was at the very top of the political agenda. Actually, before the Constitution was enacted, President Suárez had already struck an agreement with Josep Tarradellas, the 78-year-old exiled President of the Generalitat (the Catalan Government that had existed under the Second Republic), to establish a provisional local government in Catalonia. Tarradellas returned in triumph to Barcelona on 23 October 1977 to preside over the reinstalled Generalitat. Self-government was also restored in the Basque Country, after the deputies and senators from that region negotiated with the Government in Madrid. An interim body was created in the Basque

---

[26] Carrillo (n 10) 674.

[27] C Powell, *Juan Carlos of Spain. Self-made Monarch* (St Anthony's/Macmillan, 1995) ch 7.

Country under the presidency of Ramón Rubial, a historic socialist leader.[28]

So the constitutional framers had to organize a process of devolution of political power. Article 2 of the Constitution, after announcing that the Spanish nation is one and indivisible, recognizes the right of self-government (*autonomía*) of the different regions and *nacionalidades* that make up Spain. The term *nacionalidades* is rather ambiguous. It seems to refer to territories that are special, because of their cultural or linguistic specificities, but which cannot be considered to be nations. The inclusion of this expression in the constitutional text is a revealing example of the delicate balances that had to be struck when the Constitution was written. Article 3 is also based on a difficult equilibrium when it provides that *castellano* (Castilian Spanish) is the official language of the State, which all Spanish citizens have the duty to learn and the right to use. The article also establishes, however, that the 'other Spanish languages' will also be official within the respective territories, in accord with their Statutes of Autonomy. All these general principles figure in the Preliminary Title of the Constitution. Title VIII then specifies the system of norms that regulate the territorial structure of the State, although many issues are left open to future political negotiations. As we will see in chapter seven, the Constitution has not been able to completely settle the territorial problem, but it has at least improved things on this front. In spite of some current criticisms, the quasi-federal structure that the Constitution has given birth to is a stable one. There is no significant political party at the national level that really wants to eliminate it.

The Bill of Rights also includes some articles that were the result of a bargaining process. The Constitution, for example, includes the right to private property, but it establishes that the scope of this right is to be defined by the social function that private property must serve (article 33). The Constitution protects individuals against takings without just compensation (article 33), but it also imposes a constitutional duty to pay taxes under a system that is based on the principle of fiscal progressiveness (article 31). Likewise, it guarantees the right to free enterprise within a regime of market economy, but it also constrains this right by authorizing the Government to intervene in the economy in different ways in order to serve the public interest (articles 38, 40, 128, 129, 130

---

[28] Carr and Fusi (n 7) 234–35.

and 131). Although the differences between the right and the left are less pronounced now than they were in 1977–78, the Constitution does rule out certain economic programmes that ordinary majorities may wish to implement. But these constraints have been useful: they have reduced the stakes of ordinary politics when it comes to social and economic issues.

A similar pattern emerges with regard to the right to education. Here the left and the right had different views about how to organize schools. The right basically wanted to protect private schools, especially religious ones, while the left defended the centrality of public and secular education. Since they could not agree on any specific solution, they chose to enumerate the rights and goals that ought to be accommodated in the future. Article 27 thus provides that parents can decide the kind of moral and religious education their children will receive. The aim of education, however, is the free development of one's personality under the principles of democracy and rights, which means that the right of parents has limits. Similarly, private individuals are granted the fundamental right to create schools, but teachers, parents and students are entitled to participate in the administration of those schools that are subsidized by the Government. The State, moreover, shall inspect and regulate the educational system as a whole. Interestingly, the inclusion of a reference to human rights Treaties in article 10.2 of the Constitution helped pacify the debates over the school system. The more conservative forces thought that those Treaties helped reinforce the protection they wanted private schools to enjoy under the new Constitution.[29]

Similarly, with respect to the position of the Catholic Church, a solution had to be worked out through negotiation. The more conservative parties wanted to secure the central role of the Church, while the left was against. They finally agreed to hammer out the principle of religious neutrality (the State has no religion or church), subject to this qualification: 'the state shall take into account the religious beliefs of Spanish society and shall therefore cooperate with the Catholic Church and the other religions' (article 16). This was not a solution everyone could be fully satisfied with, but it occupied a middle ground between the various positions at war.

---

[29] A Saiz Arnaiz, *La apertura constitucional al Derecho internacional y europeo de los Derecho Humanos. El artículo 10.2 de la Constitución española* (Madrid, Consejo General del Poder Judicial, 1999), 15–34.

In sum, as a result of these bargaining efforts, the Constitution has performed a pacifying function. Ordinary majorities in Parliament are constrained by a collection of fundamental rules that were adopted in 1977–78. Such constraints have proven to be useful to stabilize the democratic regime. Different political majorities in Parliament can thus pursue their own programmes in the many fields that are left open by the Constitution, while enjoying the stability that such constraints make possible.

CONCLUSION

When read against the background of Spain's troubled constitutional history, the text of 1978 is a great achievement. This Constitution has laid down the foundations for a democratic system that is committed to the rule of law and fundamental rights. These foundations have been tested by more than 30 years of ordinary politics, and they have revealed their strength. The secret of the Constitution lies in the conciliatory spirit with which it was written. *Consenso* was the magic word that was in everyone's mouth at the constitutional stage. The various political parties that obtained parliamentary seats in the 1977 elections were aware of the extraordinary task the people had entrusted them with: the establishment of a democratic regime that would endure. The memory of the Civil War and of the long dictatorship that came after it was very present in Spanish society. A collective resolution was made that never again should a democratic political order collapse as the Second Republic did in 1936.

As we will see throughout this book, the Constitution of 1978 is not a perfect document. Some of the pieces in the governmental system it defines need to be reformed. Certain constitutional amendments will have to be considered in the future, in order to improve the performance of various institutions that have not worked as well as it was originally envisaged. Political parties have been reluctant, however, to discuss possible changes. Because it was hard to negotiate several important matters when the Constitution was adopted, the feeling prevails that it is better to leave things as they are. Amending the Constitution has thus become political 'taboo' in Spain, as we will see in chapter three. This has some interesting consequences for the theory of constitutional interpretation. Before we consider that, however, we should obtain a general view of the political system that the Constitution establishes. This is the purpose of the following chapter

FURTHER READING

Carr, R and Fusi, JP, *Spain. Dictatorship to Democracy* (London, Harper-Collins, 1981).

Colomer, JM, *Game Theory and the Transition to Democracy: The Spanish Model* (Aldershot, Edward Elgar, 1995).

Gallego-Díaz, S and de la Cuadra, B, *Crónica secreta de la Constitución* (Madrid, Tecnos, 1989).

Gunther, R, Montero, JR and Botella, J, *Democracy in Modern Spain* (New Haven, Yale University Press, 2004) chs 2 and 3.

Maravall, JM, *La política de la transición: 1975–80* (Madrid, Taurus, 1981).

Payne, SG, *Spain's First Democracy. The Second Republic, 1931–36* (Wisconsin, The University of Wisconsin Press, 1993).

Peces-Barba, G, *La elaboración de la Constitución de 1978* (Madrid, Centro de Estudios Constitucionales, 1988).

2

An Overview of the Spanish Constitutional System: Basic Principles

Spain as a 'Social and Democratic State Under the Rule of Law' –
A Parliamentary Monarchy with Limited Mechanisms of Direct
Democracy – The Constitutional Relevance of Political Parties –
Quasi-Federalism: The *Estado de las Autonomías* – Conclusion

IN THIS CHAPTER, a general picture of the Spanish constitutional system will be offered. We need, first, to say something about the kind of State that Spain wishes to be. The very first article in the constitutional text proclaims that Spain constitutes itself as a 'democratic and social State under the rule of law' (*Estado social y democrático de Derecho*). This is an important clause that points to different dimensions of political morality, which need to be understood as forming part of a coherent whole.

We will then examine the basic features of the specific system of government that the Constitution sets up. Spain is a parliamentary monarchy, one in which the King exercises no political power. There is, moreover, a tight connection between the executive branch and the legislative assembly: to be appointed, the President of the Government needs to obtain the support of a majority in Congress. There is a formal separation of powers between the Government and Congress, but there is, in practice, a concentration of political power in the hands of the ruling majority. The checks on the latter come from the political parties that are in the parliamentary opposition.

Another characteristic of Spain's political organization is the distribution of authority between the centre (the State) and the regions (the Autonomous Communities). Each region has its own Parliament, which can issue laws covering specific fields. The so-called *Estado autonómico* (autonomic State) or *Estado de las autonomías* (State of autonomies) that the Constitution has given birth to is a form of federalism. But it has its own idiosyncratic elements, as we will see.

In this chapter, we will also examine some details about political parties and the mechanisms of direct democracy. Since these elements are present on all levels of government (national, regional, local), it is useful to cover them here.

SPAIN AS A 'SOCIAL AND DEMOCRATIC STATE UNDER THE RULE OF LAW'

Article 1 of the Constitution proclaims that Spain constitutes itself as a social and democratic State under the rule of law. It then announces that the 'superior values of the legal system' (*valores superiores del ordenamiento jurídico*) are liberty, justice, equality and political pluralism. This is arguably the most important provision in the entire document, for it defines the kind of political community that Spain is to become.

The clause mentions three normative components of the State. These elements are analytically different, but they must be understood to form a coherent whole. The superior values of liberty, justice, equality and political pluralism are connected to those normative components, and must also be read in a harmonious way.[1]

The Rule of Law

We start with the rule of law, a principle that is more specifically formulated in article 9.1, which proclaims that 'citizens and public powers are subject to the Constitution and the rest of the law'. Article 9.3 then details some of the normative consequences of this fundamental principle.

The basic idea is that the different branches of government must abide by the law when carrying out their tasks. The apparatus of the State works more efficiently, and the rights and interests of individual citizens are adequately protected, if the law is observed.

---

[1] For an influential and early treatment of this constitutional clause, see ÁGarrorena Morales, *El Estado español como Estado social y democrático de Derecho* (Madrid, Tecnos, 1984).

When the framers hammered out the principle of the rule of law in the Constitution, they did so against the background of the dictatorship. An underdeveloped form of *Estado de Derecho* had been constructed during the 1960s, as part of the efforts undertaken by the Francoist regime to modernize the apparatus of the State. Some new laws had been enacted at that time to allow courts to check the legality of administrative acts in a more or less independent manner.

The Spanish Constitution, of course, embraces a much more ambitious conception of the rule of law. The individual rights to be protected include many rights and liberties that the dictatorship repressed. Title I of the Constitution enumerates those basic rights. All the institutions of the State, moreover, are to be constrained by legal standards. In addition to the public administration, the Government and the Parliament must abide by the law. The Constitution, in particular, lays down rules and principles that political institutions must observe, and that courts are authorized to enforce.

For the rule of law to be realized in practice, certain technical requirements need to be met. The law, for example, must be organized in a hierarchical structure, so that the large collection of rules that are generated by the institutional machinery of the modern State do not lead to chaos. The rules occupy different ranks, and those at the top prevail over those at the bottom (*lex superior derogat inferior*). There is a connection here between the rule of law and democracy. The democratic ideal can supply some criteria to arrange the different rules. If a State is properly structured along democratic lines, the highest norms in the legal system should be the ones that are produced through procedures where popular participation is most intense. Thus, legislation enacted by Parliament should prevail over administrative regulations, to the extent that the former is the product of a more deliberative and participatory political exercise than the latter. And if the Constitution is ratified by the people in a referendum, there is a democratic case in favour of its being assigned the highest authority.

That the law needs to be structured hierarchically does not mean, however, that *lex superior* is the only principle that can be employed to resolve conflicts within the legal system. The traditional criteria of *lex posterior* and *lex specialis* are also to be used, of course. In modern legal systems, it is a standard principle that the more recent norms must prevail over older ones. It is also the case that the more specific legal provisions are usually preferred over the more general ones. Other criteria, such as the 'principle of competence', must do their work too, when conflicts arise. Thus, as we will see in chapter seven, the 17 Autonomous Communities that exist in Spain have a constitutionally protected sphere of autonomy. Courts confronted with a normative collision between a State law, on the one hand, and a law enacted by a Community, on the other, have to decide which of the two levels of government is competent to regulate the matter under discussion. There is no hierarchy between State law and regional law. If the State law is found to intrude upon the legislative authority granted to a Community, it is the latter's law that must prevail.

Another technical requirement that needs to be satisfied for the rule of law to be honoured concerns the accessibility and the clarity of the law. It is very important that the laws be accessible to the public. Individuals can only plan their actions, and can only check the performance of the State, if they have access to the existing laws. Article 9.3 of the Constitution proclaims, in this regard, the 'principle of publicity'. The law must be published in an official gazette in order for citizens to learn about it. The basic instrument in Spain for these purposes is the *Boletín Oficial del Estado,* which is available through electronic means.[2] The principle of publicity is connected to another requirement that is not explicitly mentioned in the Constitution, but is implicit in it: the law should be expressed with clarity. Citizens must be able to understand what the law provides. The Constitutional Court, following in the steps of the European Court of Human Rights, has held that the clarity requirement is an ingredient of the rule of law idea. It is of particular relevance in the area of criminal law.[3]

Another important ingredient of the rule of law concerns the temporal effects of the laws. Article 9.3 of the Constitution prohibits the retroactive effects of laws that establish sanctions, unless the new laws are less severe than the ones that existed at the time the relevant facts occurred. This constitutional provision also bans the retroactive application of laws that restrict 'individual rights'. The Constitutional Court has interpreted the expression 'individual rights' narrowly, however. It has said that it primarily refers to the fundamental rights protected in Title I of the Constitution (see STC 112/2006). The expression does

---

[2] On the principle of publicity, see P Biglino Campos, *La publicación de la ley* (Madrid, Tecnos, 1993).

[3] On the principle of clarity in criminal law, see V Ferreres Comella, *El principio de taxatividad en material penal y el valor normativo de la jurisprudencia* (Madrid, Civitas, 2002).

not cover, therefore, all rights granted by ordinary legislation. As a result, the democratic branches can introduce new laws to bring about important social transformations. The democratic and social components of the State mentioned in article 1 of the Constitution press here against a broad reading of the non-retroactivity clause.

To make sure that all these requirements that define the rule of law are duly respected by governmental bodies, mechanisms of judicial review must be set up. Different courts have different responsibilities in Spain when it comes to checking the actions and omissions of public institutions, as will be explained in later chapters. An important division of labour is established between the Constitutional Court and the rest of the judiciary ('ordinary courts'). While only the former can declare the unconstitutionality of statutes (or other norms that have the same rank as statutes), any court is empowered to check the validity of administrative regulations, which have a subordinate rank. A specific branch of courts ('administrative courts'), moreover, is specialized in reviewing the legality of the decisions made by the Government and the public administration, as we will see.

The power of judges to review the decisions of the executive and legislative branches does not stop when the latter are given discretion to exercise their powers, since they must always act on the basis of reasons that are connected to legitimate public goals. Article 9.3 points to this idea when it lays down the principle of 'public accountability' and the 'prohibition of arbitrariness'.

Article 106.2, moreover, guarantees the right of individuals to obtain compensation from the State, if the public institutions wrong them. (Article 121 also guarantees compensation when courts cause damage). As we will see in chapter six, a controversial string of precedents established by the Supreme Court has dramatically expanded the scope of the State's liability for damages caused by public authorities, including the legislature.

The Social State

The second component of the kind of State the Constitution defines is the 'social' principle. Again, the framers' insistence on this principle has to be understood in a historical context. Franco's dictatorship had performed very badly in terms of social benefits and economic justice. In spite of the great economic growth that began in the 1960s, which allowed Spain to become the world's tenth-ranking industrial power, the regime was based on a very regressive and limited tax system, which made it impossible for the State to ensure basic equality in social matters. Thus, in 1975, when Franco died, only 9.9 per cent of Spain's GDP was devoted to the provision of social services, as compared with a European Community average of 24 per cent. Expenditure on public education, in particular, was extremely low. The social security system was a little better, but lagged significantly behind other European countries.[4]

As soon as the new democratic regime was established, public policy was redirected. A progressive tax system was adopted, and public spending on social services was largely expanded. The victory of the socialist party (PSOE) in 1982 was an important moment in this evolution, but the very first Government under UCD in 1977 had already worked in the direction of realizing the principles of the social state. It had reformed the tax laws, corrected some of the more glaring deficiencies in the education system, and increased the provision of social-protection services.[5] There is, after all, a connection between democracy and the social state. If political parties compete for the votes of large majorities of citizens, they have to offer programmes that guarantee the provision of a certain level of social benefits. If people can strike and demonstrate in the streets to protest, moreover, the Government is more likely to pay attention to their worries. The absence of democracy and liberties under Franco allowed the State to be insensitive to the social needs of many citizens.

Because Spain is defined as a social State in the Constitution, the Government is expected not to remain passive vis-à-vis the economy and civil society. As article 9.2 of the Constitution proclaims, public institutions must promote the conditions that ensure real and effective liberty and equality for individuals and the groups they belong to. It is their task, the article goes on, to remove the obstacles to the full enjoyment of liberty and equality, and to facilitate the participation of all citizens in political, economic, cultural and social life. The clear assumption here is that there is no intrinsic justice to the workings of the economy

---

[4] R Gunther, JR Montero and J Botella, *Democracy in Modern Spain* (New Haven, Yale University Press, 2004) 337–41.

[5] Ibid 354.

and civil society: there are normative deficits in terms of real liberty and equality, and it is the responsibility of the State to enact policies that make up for such deficits. As we will see in chapter nine, the Constitutional Court has used this article to uphold several measures of affirmative action in favour of women and other discriminated groups.

Consistent with the general task the Constitution charges the State with, a list of social rights and principles are mentioned in Title I, concerning education, social security, health, culture, decent housing, among others. The public administration, through a large network of civil servants, has a key role to play in the provision of many services. The dignity and the basic liberties of the beneficiaries of public services need to be respected, however, and this may require the establishment of various procedures to ensure that the interests and views of the beneficiaries are properly taken into account.[6]

The mechanisms to guarantee most of the social rights enumerated in the Constitution, however, are weaker than those that generally apply to fundamental rights. Article 53.3 provides that the 'social and economic principles' included in Chapter III of Title I of the Constitution shall animate the legislation to be enacted, as well as judicial and administrative practices, but cannot be directly enforced by courts. The capacity of the judicial branch, therefore, to make the political branches comply with those social and economic principles is rather limited. This does not mean that the incorporation of the social State principle in the Constitution has no consequences. Citizens can invoke the Constitution when criticizing the Government for its social failures. The social and economic rights allow courts, moreover, to uphold legislative measures that might otherwise be questionable. A measure that restricts private property or market freedoms can be more easily justified if the social goal being pursued by the measure is itself a principle that the Constitution explicitly requires the Government to satisfy.

The Constitution, moreover, guarantees workers certain fundamental rights that are subject to the general regime of full protection, such as the rights to belong to trade unions, to strike, and to collective bargaining (articles 28 and 37).

As far as the economic system is concerned, the Constitution recognizes the right to free enterprise in the framework of a market economy

---

[6] On this issue, see JM Rodríguez de Santiago, *La administración del Estado social* (Madrid, Marcial Pons, 2007).

(article 38). The economic system, however, is amenable to several forms of State intervention.[7] Thus, the State can set up economic plans, and it can create public enterprises. It can even reserve for the State certain resources or services, thus establishing State monopolies. Private property, in turn, has limits. The Constitution explicitly provides that the 'social function' of property can justify the imposition of limits on this right (article 33). There is ample room for flexibility in this area, however. The Constitution excludes certain radical measures, but different Governments can put in practice very different economic programmes. This flexibility made it unnecessary for Spain to amend its Constitution in order to become a member of the European Economic Community in 1986. The requirements that European Community law imposed in economic and social matters were easily accommodated within the Spanish Constitution, which is quite capacious in this field.

The Democratic State

The third dimension of the State is democracy. Because this feature was completely absent under the dictatorship, the constitutional framers made many references to it in the text.

Democracy means, first, that the different organs of the State owe their existence to the people. They are there, and they have the structure and the authority they do, as a result of a democratic choice. The Constitution provides that 'national sovereignty is vested in the Spanish people, from which the powers of the state derive' (article 1.2). The fact that the Constitution was enacted by a popularly elected Parliament, and that a referendum was held to obtain the people's approval, makes it possible to assert that all governmental institutions exist by virtue of popular will.

This idea has some consequences when it comes to the Crown. The King is not elected by the people or by any democratic branch. But the very existence of the Crown as an institution rests on the democratic choice that the Constitution embodies. Because there are no exceptions to the proposition that all State institutions derive their existence from

---

[7] See, generally, M Bassols Coma, *Constitución y sistema económico* (Madrid, Tecnos, 1988).

the people, there is no limitation on the power of the people to dismantle the monarchy through a constitutional amendment. The Constitution
explicitly provides for the possibility of amending the articles dealing
with the Crown – although it imposes a very burdensome procedure, as
we will see.

That Spain is a democratic State means, secondly, that the laws are
'the expression of popular will' (as the Preamble of the Constitution
announces). There must be an institution, therefore, in charge of legislation, the members of which are elected by citizens. This is the central
role of Parliament. There is a bicameral legislative assembly at the State
level – the Cortes Generales, which consists of Congress (Congreso de
los Diputados) and the Senate (Senado). And there is a unicameral
assembly in each Autonomous Community. The statutes produced by
these institutions have a special democratic dignity because of their
source. Democracy also requires that the other branches of government
bear some connection to popular will: mechanisms must exist for those
in office to be accountable to the public.

Whether the people should have a direct say in the production of
laws is a controversial question. Given the complexity of modern states,
it would be unreasonable to allow citizens to discuss and adopt laws
directly on a regular basis. A division of labour between the people and
their representatives seems necessary. There is room, however, for
mechanisms to be introduced, to register the unmediated will of the
people in particular matters. As we will see, the Spanish Constitution
includes some procedures of direct democracy, but they are subject to
many limitations.

To make democracy possible, citizens must of course be granted the
right to vote and to stand as candidates. Article 23.1 of the Constitution
establishes that 'citizens have the right to participate in public affairs,
directly or through representatives freely elected in periodic elections
by universal suffrage'. This right, article 13.2 specifies, is reserved to
Spanish citizens, except for the possibility of allowing foreign citizens to
vote and to stand as candidates at municipal elections, in accordance
with the principle of reciprocity.[8] European Union law, in particular,
grants European Union citizens the right to participate in the municipal
elections in the Member State in which they reside.

---

[8] The more specific regulation of this right is to be found in arts 176, 177, 210,
210*bis*, *Ley Orgánica 5/1985 del Régimen Electoral General* (hereinafter: LOREG).

The right to vote can only be exercised by those who have come of age, which the Constitution fixes at age 18 (article 12). Those who are incapacitated or confined in a psychiatric hospital cannot vote.[9] In the past, the punishment of some crimes included the suspension of the right to vote. This is no longer the case, under current ordinary law.[10]

The laws facilitate and protect the exercise of the right to vote. Citizens, for example, do not have to register: they are automatically included in the *censo electoral* by the relevant public authorities (the local councils and the consulates). And it is possible for citizens to send their vote by mail, if they expect to be absent on election day. The laws, moreover, establish a set of administrative bodies that guarantee the fairness of the elections. The 'electoral administration' is made up of so-called Juntas electorales and Mesas electorales, the members of which are selected in ways that ensure their independence from the political branches. Some members are appointed by the judicial branch, others by common accord of the political parties, and still others by lot. Their decisions, moreover, can be reviewed by ordinary courts and the Constitutional Court.[11]

A PARLIAMENTARY MONARCHY WITH LIMITED MECHANISMS OF DIRECT DEMOCRACY

While the 'social and democratic State under the rule of law' is the abstract type of government the Constitution defines, the more specific form of political regime the Constitution chooses is a 'parliamentary monarchy', as article 1.3 proclaims.

This means, first, that Spain is not a Republic. The Head of State is a King (or a Queen), who is not elected by the people or by any democratically elected institution. The monarchy, however, is of the 'parliamentary' sort. This means that the Head of State does not have real political power. The power is in the hands of the President of the Government and his or her Cabinet, together with Parliament.

---

[9] See art 3, LOREG.

[10] See arts 32–57, *Código Penal*.

[11] Interestingly, the Constitution explicitly establishes that the validity of the electoral credentials of the members of the national Parliament shall be subject to judicial control (art 70.2). This is in contrast to the situation in other countries, where parliaments have the exclusive authority to verify the validity of the electoral qualifications of their members.

That the regime is 'parliamentary' also implies a distinctive form of distributing power between the executive and the legislative assembly. Instead of the checks and balances that characterize presidential systems, the parliamentary form of government results in a fusion of the executive branch and the party (or coalition of parties) that has a majority of seats in the legislative chamber. In Spain, the President of the Government is selected by the lower house: Congress. He is in fact the leader of the political party (or coalition of political parties) that has obtained the majority of parliamentary seats in that chamber. To remain in power, moreover, the President needs the continuing support of his party (or coalition of parties) in Congress. If he loses such support, he can be removed, as we will study in chapter five.

That Spain is a parliamentary system does not mean that there is no space for some forms of direct democracy. The Constitution lays down some procedures to permit the direct participation of citizens. Their scope is limited, however. The framers in 1977–78 thought that it was necessary to strengthen the role of political parties in a scheme of representative democracy, given the legacy of the dictatorship. Franco's regime had insisted on the dangers of political parties. They were said to be responsible for the lack of unity of citizens, and for the weakness of the Government. In contrast, various referenda had been held during the dictatorship, to capture the people's will. Because such referenda had not taken place in conditions of freedom, they were criticized by the democratic opposition. When writing the new Constitution, the framers reacted against the practices and understandings of the dictatorship. They chose to make political parties and representative institutions the centre of gravity of the democratic system. The avenues for direct popular participation were designed to be narrow.

Popular Legislative Initiatives

A first mechanism of direct democracy is the popular initiative. Citizens are allowed by the Constitution to present legislative proposals to be considered by the national Parliament (article 87.3).[12] This is a very limited form of participation, however, since a majority of members of

---

[12] The law that regulates popular initiatives is *Ley Orgánica 3/1984, reguladora de la iniciativa legislativa popular.*

Congress can decide at an early stage not to take the proposal into consideration, which means that the proposal will not be discussed any more.

The Constitution establishes various conditions and restrictions for the exercise of the initiative. First, it requires that at least 500,000 signatures be collected. This number represents a very large portion of the population, much larger than in Italy, for example, where 50,000 signatures are sufficient.[13] It would be unconstitutional for a statute to reduce this number, since the Constitution clearly wants 500,000 signatures to be the minimum.

Second, popular legislative proposals cannot involve certain matters. They cannot deal with taxes, international affairs, and pardons. Nor can they propose an amendment to the Constitution. The Constitution goes so far as to exclude issues that must be covered by an 'organic statute'. As will be explained in chapter five, an 'organic statute' is a special type of statute that the Constitution requires for the regulation of certain matters. Among the matters that are reserved to organic statutes are the fundamental rights mentioned in articles 15–29 of the Constitution. This means that no popular legislative proposal can be advanced that touches upon any of those rights, such as religious freedom, the right to association, the right to life, the right to education, the right to privacy, freedom of speech, the right to judicial protection, to name a few. It is objectionable that citizens have been denied the possibility of triggering the legislative process in such cases.

In practice, Congress has so far rejected to take into consideration all the popular proposals that have been submitted to it, with the exception of a proposal that was presented in 1996, dealing with procedures for forcing owners of apartments to pay their debts to the community of property-owners. Two parliamentary groups tabled their own legislative bills on that matter, and the three proposals were discussed together. A new law was finally adopted.[14]

With respect to regional politics, all Autonomous Communities have allowed citizens to submit legislative proposals. The requirements to be fulfilled differ from one Community to the other, but they tend to be rather restrictive. In practice, however, citizens have used this mecha-

---

[13]   Art 71, Italian Constitution.

[14]   All the information about the history of the various popular legislative proposals can be accessed at www.juntaelectoralcentral.es.

nism of direct democracy more often at the regional level than at the national level. A larger number of proposals have been presented, and a higher percentage have been taken into account and finally enacted into law. The Canary Islands, in particular, is the region where the procedure has been most successful so far. At the local level too, citizens are granted the right to present initiatives.[15]

Referenda

A different and stronger form of direct democracy is the referendum. The Constitution provides in article 92 that the President of the Government, having obtained the authorization of an absolute majority of the members of Congress, may submit 'political decisions of special transcendence' to the people. The question posed to the citizens must be of a general character. No specific statute, therefore, can be submitted to the people.

This form of direct democracy, however, has been cabined to make sure it does not erode representative democracy. First of all, the referendum is not legally binding. It is merely *consultivo*, as article 92 says. Second, the law that regulates the referendum has organized it in such a way that political parties are actually the leading voices in the campaign.[16] The referendum has thus been 'rationalized', to prevent political parties from losing their centrality.[17]

So far, Spanish citizens have been asked to participate in this type of referendum twice: in 1986, to decide whether Spain should remain in NATO (North Atlantic Treaty Organization); and in 2005 to approve Spain's ratification of the Treaty Establishing a Constitution for Europe. In both cases, the majority of citizens voted 'yes'. The reasons why people were called to the referendum were different, however.

In the first case, the problem originated in 1981: in the aftermath of the failed *coup d'etat,* a new UCD Government presided over by Leopoldo Calvo-Sotelo announced that it would start negotiations for Spain to

---

[15] Art 70*bis*, *Ley 7/1985 reguladora de las Bases del Régimen Local.*

[16] See *Ley Orgánica 2/1980, sobre regulación de las distintas modalidades de referéndum.*

[17] For a description and criticism of this 'rationalization' of referenda, see P Cruz Villalón, 'El referendum consultivo como modelo de racionalización constitucional' in P Cruz Villalón, *La curiosidad del jurista persa, y otros estudios sobre la Constitución* (Madrid, Centro de Estudios Políticos y Constitucionales, 1999) 255.

enter NATO. The main party in the opposition, PSOE, was very critical of this unilateral move. It argued that a larger consensus was needed before Spain could make a decision that would be so hard to reserve in the future. The opposition asked the President to call a referendum on the issue.[18] The President refused, however, and Spain became a member of the alliance in May 1982. This led the PSOE leaders to promise that, if they were installed in the Government after the next elections, they would call a referendum to decide on Spain's withdrawal from NATO. The socialists indeed won the elections in October 1982, but they soon realized that it was in the best interests of Spain to remain in NATO. They therefore had to change their strategy: they were now in favour of Spain's membership, but they decided to keep their promise to organize a referendum on the issue. They included some 'conditions' on Spain's membership, however. Those conditions were that Spain would not form part of the military structures of the alliance, that no nuclear arms would be placed in Spanish territory, and that the United States' military presence in Spain would be gradually reduced. During the referendum the PSOE campaigned in favour of 'yes', while the main party in the opposition (the conservative right, AP) recommended citizens to abstain. A majority of the people who participated voted yes (52.54 per cent). This was probably the most difficult moment during the first socialist Government. (Years later, in 1999, Spain finally entered the military command structure of NATO, after obtaining the authorization of an almost unanimous Congress: 91.5 per cent of deputies voted in favour of a more intense involvement with the alliance, thus neutralizing one of the conditions that had been mentioned in the referendum).

The referendum that took place in 2005, in contrast, was far less controversial. Under the presidency of José Luis Rodríguez Zapatero, Spain had signed the Treaty Establishing a Constitution for Europe. The Government decided to hold a referendum, as some other countries had also announced they would do. It was clear that there was large support for the Treaty in Spain. Both the PSOE in the Government and the main party in the opposition (PP) were in favour. After a rather monotonous campaign, the result was unsurprising: a vast majority of voters

---

[18] Many scholars were of the view that, in the absence of broad parliamentary agreement, there was a strong case for a referendum. See, eg A Remiro Brotons, *La acción exterior del Estado* (Madrid, Tecnos, 1984) 91.

(76.30 per cent) expressed their endorsement of the new Treaty. (The Treaty ultimately failed, as a result of the negative votes in the referenda that were later held in France and the Netherlands).

In addition to the non-binding referendum described so far, the Spanish Constitution requires referenda in some other cases, with binding results. At the national level, referenda are sometimes required to amend the Constitution, as we will see in the next chapter.

In the regional sphere, referenda are also sometimes required to enact and amend the Statutes of Autonomy – the legal instruments that organize the political system of each Autonomous Community.[19] These referenda have a 'constitutional nature' to a certain extent, since they relate to the basic charter that structures the regional institutions.

There is some controversy about the possibility of holding non-binding regional referenda on other matters. The Constitution is silent on this, and so is State legislation. The Parliament of the Basque Country once passed a law to regulate and call a referendum on the future status of this Community, but the Constitutional Court ruled it invalid. The Court held that it is for the central Parliament to regulate and authorize regional referenda (STC 103/2008). In 2010, the Catalan Parliament adopted a law regulating regional referenda, which the central Government challenged through an appeal to the Constitutional Court. The case is pending at the time of writing. What seems clear, in any case, is that the Constitution establishes that it is for the State to authorize any referenda (article 149.1.32 is explicit in this regard). As we will see in chapter seven, this is an extremely important point, since it entails that any referendum that may be held in the future to ask Catalans or Basques (or the citizens of any other region) whether they want to secede from Spain, for example, can only be authorized by the central Government.

At the local level, referenda can also be organized. Again, it is the State that has the power to authorize them. The local entities cannot call referenda on their own authority.[20] In addition, it is worth mentioning that in small municipalities, the local government can be run by the citizens themselves. This is the so-called *concejo abierto* (which is referred to in article 140 of the Constitution).

---

[19] See arts 151, 152, and *Disposición Transitoria* 4 of the Constitution.
[20] See art 71, *Ley 7/1985, reguladora de las Bases del Régimen Local*.

THE CONSTITUTIONAL RELEVANCE
OF POLITICAL PARTIES

When it comes to giving life to the democratic system, the Constitution emphasizes the key role of political parties. Article 6 proclaims that political parties express political pluralism, help form and manifest popular will, and are fundamental instruments of political participation. In addition, it provides that political parties can be feely created, and that their activities are free, within the limits imposed by the Constitution and the laws. Their internal structure and functioning must be democratic. A specific statute on political parties develops this article through more specific regulation.[21]

Article 6 figures in the Preliminary Title of the Constitution, where the most important principles are mentioned. The framers wanted to emphasize in this manner the key role that political parties were to perform in the constitutional order.

Political parties, indeed, are the main players in the elections. It is them that produce the list of candidates to the different parliamentary seats. Citizens cannot choose candidates from different lists – the lists are 'closed'. Nor can citizens alter the internal order of candidates – the lists are 'blocked'. (The only exception to this rule concerns the Senate, as we will see). All this gives political parties an enormous power over individual representatives.

The law also allows *agrupaciones de electores* (groups of electors) to participate in the elections, but they are not permanent associations: they are mere collections of citizens who present candidates for a particular election, at a particular district. As a matter of fact, they are absolutely marginal.

Not only are political parties the key players. The system of political parties as a whole has become quite stable, after the troubled beginnings in the first years of democracy.[22] On the left, the main party is PSOE, which was founded in 1879. It competes with a smaller coalition of parties, Izquierda Unida, which is dominated by the Communist Party (PCE). On the right, a single party now occupies all the space: PP. During the first years of the democratic regime, UCD (more to the centre) and

---

[21] See *Ley Orgánica 6/2002, de Partidos Políticos*.

[22] For a detailed view of the evolution of the party system in Spain, see Gunther, Montero and Botella (n 4) 198–279

AP (more to the right) competed for the conservative vote. After the collapse of UCD in the 1982 elections, which the Socialists won, AP became the main party in the opposition. After various changes (including its name: PP), it finally became the only party on the centre-right. It is important to note that public opinion has evolved towards the political centre, and the two largest parties (PSOE and PP) have moved to capture the moderate votes. There is actually no extreme or anti-system party at the national level that has gained seats in the Cortes Generales. In the recent years, a new party has appeared at the national level: UPyD (Unión Progreso y Democracia), which is not easy to locate in the ideological space, and which is particularly critical of the *Estado autonómico*.

In addition to these national parties, there are regional parties that are also represented in the national Parliament. The most important ones are CiU (Convergència i Unió), from Catalonia; PNV (Partido Nacionalista Vasco), from the Basque Country; and CC (Coalición Canaria), from the Canary Islands. In practice, the Governments are either in the hands of PSOE or PP. When these parties do not obtain an absolute majority of the seats in Congress, they often rely on regional parties to get the necessary support for the investiture of the President of the Government and for the passage of the laws.

At the regional level, PSOE and PP are also the parties that have traditionally governed most Autonomous Communities. Catalonia and the Basque Country are two important exceptions, however: CiU (in Catalonia) and PNV (in the Basque Country) have had the regional government in their hands most of the time.

Restrictions on Political Parties: Internal Democratic Structure, Gender Parity, Militant Democracy

Because of the centrality of political parties in Spanish democracy, the laws have subjected them to certain restrictions, which have increased throughout the years.

As has already been noted, the Constitution provides that political parties must have a democratic internal structure. This is a rather vague requirement, which the Law on Political Parties has not fleshed out in a sufficiently detailed way. That Law establishes, basically, that there must be a general assembly where members of the party can participate, either directly or through delegates. The assembly must be empowered to take the most important decisions. The organs that govern the party, in turn, must be elected by secret ballot. The members of the party have the right to participate in its activities, and are entitled to run as candidates for the various party offices. There are certain procedural guarantees, moreover, against the sanctions that the party may impose on its members. Overall, the Law establishes a relatively open-ended scheme, which gives much room for parties to choose their own structures and decision-making procedures.

In connection with this, it is worthy of note that the Socialist Party (PSOE) has sometimes used primaries to elect its candidates for prime ministerial posts both at the national and regional levels, as well as for mayor at the municipal level. The primaries were first introduced in 1997, and attracted much public attention. The experience was not very encouraging at first, however, since important frictions arose between the candidate who won the primaries for Prime Minister, Josep Borrell, and the General Secretary of the party, Joaquín Almunia, who had also participated in the primaries and lost. A deep crisis developed in the party when Josep Borrell finally resigned in 1999, as a result, to a large extent, of his conflicts with the party's apparatus. Almunia then became the candidate to the Presidency of the Government in the 2000 general elections (which he lost). In spite of these troubled beginnings, the socialists have recently insisted on using the primaries to nominate their candidate in the next general election.[23] Primaries have also been held in IU (Izquierda Unida): in 2007, Gaspar Llamazares, the coordinator of this coalition, was challenged by some of its members. Primaries were then organized, which Llamazares won.

In addition to the requirement concerning internal democratic structures, political parties must observe other legal restrictions. They are not totally free to make up their lists of candidates, for example. The law imposes gender parity in all types of elections. In particular, a minimum percentage of 40 per cent is required for both sexes. Since the candidates in the first positions in the lists are the ones most likely to get parliamentary seats, the law requires that the 40 percentage apply to every five candidates down the lists.[24] This statutory provision was challenged by PP, then in the opposition, through an appeal to the Constitutional Court.

---

[23] On the socialist experience with the primaries, see R Blanco Valdés, *Las conexiones políticas* (Madrid, Alianza Editorial, 2001) 85–112.

[24] See art 44*bis,* LOREG.

The latter upheld the law, as a legitimate affirmative action measure to ensure gender parity in political institutions (STC 12/2008).

Another set of restrictions concern the goals political parties can seek, and the means they can employ to achieve those goals. A special chamber within the Supreme Court has jurisdiction to ban parties that violate these restrictions. Some of the grounds for banning a party are not controversial, such as helping terrorists through financial means, for example. Other grounds, however, are arguably too restrictive. A party that engages in speech that 'excuses' the exclusion that people suffer on account of their ideology or beliefs, for instance, or that 'legitimizes' violence as a political method, or that 'minimizes' the impact of terrorism, may be declared illegal. Some forms of radical speech may end up being suppressed as a result of this law.

In September 2002, the regional government of the Basque Country challenged the law through an appeal to the Constitutional Court. The Court upheld it (STC 48/2003), relying in part on the jurisprudence of the European Court of Human Rights.[25] Soon afterwards, the Special Chamber of the Supreme Court, on application of the Spanish Government, declared the illegality of Herri Batasuna, a nationalist party from the Basque Country.[26] What triggered the Government's application was the party's failure to publicly condemn a terrorist act that had been perpetrated by ETA in Santa Pola (Alicante) in the summer. There was further evidence, which the judges were provided with, that Herri Batasuna had cooperated with ETA in various ways. Given that additional evidence, the final outcome reached by the Supreme Court was easy to justify. Actually, the Constitutional Court was unanimous in upholding the decision after a constitutional complaint was filed (STC 5/2004). The European Court of Human Rights, which heard the case, was unanimous too. The European Court actually made it clear that the decision to ban the party would have been acceptable, even in the absence of that additional evidence. For it is not against the European Convention, the Court held, for a political party to be outlawed for refusing to condemn terrorist crimes committed by others.[27]

---

[25] The Constitutional Court explicitly cited the European Court of Human Rights judgment of 31 July 2001 in *Refah Partisi v Turkey* App no 41340/98 (2002) 35 EHRR 3.

[26] See decision March 27, 2003

[27] Case of *Herri Batasuna and Batasuna v Spain* App nos 25803/04 & 25817/04 (ECtHR, 30 June 2009) para 88.

The problem, however, is that the Law on Political Parties includes too broad a definition of the activities and goals that are prohibited, well beyond what was necessary to capture Herri Bastasuna or any other party that is linked to terrorist groups. Arguably, the law could generate a chilling effect on speech – especially on speech uttered by marginal political parties.

It bears emphasizing that a significant evolution has taken place in this field of Spanish constitutional law. During the transition to democracy, the understanding that prevailed was that any political party should be allowed to participate in public life, no matter what its programme or discourse was, provided it was prepared to respect the rules of the game and therefore abstained from using violent means to achieve its goals. That the Communist Party had to be legalized, for example, no matter its programme, was part and parcel of the idea of an open democracy. The Constitution was also thought to protect the parties on the extreme right that celebrate Franco's dictatorship, for instance, or those that are in favour of regional secession. Actually, when the Constitution was being framed, proposals establishing some form of 'militant democracy' were rejected.[28] The first statute that regulated political parties, enacted in 1978, reflected this original understanding. Most scholars, moreover, insisted on the open character of the Constitution, which can be amended in many different directions, thus making it possible for anti-system political parties to pursue radical programmes.[29] In 2002, the current statute was adopted, which deviated from the conception that had prevailed until then. It imposed restrictions that go beyond the prohibition of using violence: certain goals are excluded (those that are incompatible with democracy and rights), and certain forms of speech are prohibited (those that are not sufficiently critical of terrorist actions, for example).[30]

It is worth mentioning that the law also specifies that those who have been elected through a political party that is later banned by the courts will lose their parliamentary seats, unless they make a declaration repudi-

[28]   R Blanco Valdés, *Los partidos políticos* (Madrid, Tecnos, 1990) 124–41.

[29]   The most important doctrinal work in this regard was I de Otto, *Defensa de la Constitución y partidos políticos* (Madrid, Centro de Estudios Constitucionales, 1985).

[30]   For a critical comment on the law, see V Ferreres Comella, 'The New Regulation of Political Parties in Spain, and the Decision to Outlaw Batasuna' in A Sajó (ed), *Militant Democracy* (AJ Utrecht, Eleven International Publishing, 2004) 133.

ating the actions that have led to the judicial decision outlawing the party. If they later say or do things that are in contradiction with such declaration, they lose their seats.[31] This may turn out to be a significant restriction on parliamentary speech.

Financing Political Parties

In light of the importance of political parties for the well-functioning of a democratic system, the laws provide for the availability of public funds to support their activities.[32] These funds come from several sources. Political parties receive money from the government to partially cover their ordinary expenses. The amount each party receives depends on the number of votes and seats it obtained in the previous elections. Public funds are also distributed to cover their expenses during the elections, the amount depending on the number of seats and votes obtained. Parliamentary groups (which mirror political parties in the legislative assemblies) also receive public funds. Parties are also guaranteed free access to public media during the elections, in accordance with the number of votes they garnered in the last elections – though parties that run for the first time are also allotted some free time. All these rules have been criticized on the grounds that they are biased in favour of the largest parties.[33] If only the votes obtained by the different parties counted for purposes of getting public funds, the rules would treat all parties equally. Instead, under the existing rules, the parties that obtain parliamentary seats get extra funds, and the votes that matter are only those that have made it possible for a candidate to obtain a seat in a particular electoral district.

In addition to public funds, political parties can obtain regular contributions from their members. Spanish parties have low levels of membership, however, in comparison with other European countries. There are various reasons for this. According to some political scientists, because Spanish parties were created in the era of public financing, incentives for the recruitment of members were weak. The relatively elitist politics of *consenso* during the transition, moreover, and the legacy

---

[31] See art 6.4, LOREG.

[32] See, generally, *Ley Orgánica 8/2007, sobre Financiación de Partidos Políticos*, and art 121–34, LOREG.

[33] For a critical view of the system, see Blanco Valdés (n 23) 76.

of 40 years of dictatorship, helped demobilize the citizenry. And the fact that parties emerged in an era that is dominated by personalistic campaigns conducted through television has also played a role.[34] It is important to bear in mind that nearly all the parties that participated in the first democratic elections of 1977 were new – they had no tradition of recruiting members and mobilizing citizens. The main exceptions were PSOE and PCE at the national level; PNV in the Basque Country; and ERC (Esquerra Democràtica de Catalunya) and UDC (Unió Democràtica de Catalunya) in Catalonia. But even these parties had suffered organizational discontinuities as a result of the repressive actions by the dictatorship.[35]

Political parties can also receive private donations, within certain limits. Donations, for example, cannot be anonymous, and there is a limit to the amount each person can give (€100,000). No money can be accepted, moreover, from private enterprises that are under a contract to provide works or services to governmental institutions or public enterprises. On the other hand, foreign citizens, as well as legal persons, are allowed to donate funds. The law establishes, moreover, a favourable tax treatment for the resources political parties collect.

To check the legality of their funding, political parties are under the supervision of the Court of Audit (Tribunal de Cuentas), a special tribunal that we will study in chapter six. The sanctions that this institution can impose on political parties can be challenged through a direct appeal to the Supreme Court. This supervision has not prevented parties from breaking the law, however. Several parties, including the two largest ones (PSOE and PP) have been involved in scandals concerning illegal funding, such as the Filesa and Naseiro scandals in the 1990s. Criminal sentences have been imposed in some cases on the individuals in charge of the moneys. The belief is widespread in society that the practices should be changed, but it is not clear what types of reform ought to be adopted to improve the system. Proposals are currently being discussed, for example, to impose limitations on the money that political foundations can receive – since such foundations are very close to political parties. Limitations are also being considered on the amount of debt owed by political parties that banks are authorized to condone.

---

[34] Gunther, Montero and Botella (n 4) 238–39.
[35] Ibid 215.

QUASI-FEDERALISM: THE *ESTADO DE LAS AUTONOMÍAS*

The last feature of Spain's political organization that we should mention in this overview relates to the territorial structure. In chapter seven, we will study the details of the devolution of political power to the Autonomous Communities. But a few preliminary notes will be useful at this juncture.

As was already explained, the constitutional framers in 1977–78 decided to open a process to decentralize the Spanish State. As a result of this process, 17 Autonomous Communities have been created, each of which has its own democratic Parliament and executive branch.

An important set of legal instruments that have been used in this context are the Statutes of Autonomy (*Estatutos de Autonomía*). These are the norms that give birth to the different Autonomous Communities. Each Statute gives the corresponding Community its name, defines its territory, specifies the powers that are transferred to it, and regulates its basic political structure.

The *Estado de las autonomías* (State of autonomies) that has thus been constructed is similar to a federation. But it deviates from standard cases of federalism in several important aspects. It is an instance of what is sometimes called a 'unitary State that is decentralized in regions', or a 'regional State'.[36] Here are some of its distinctive traits:

First, the distribution of competences between the State and the regions is not established in the Constitution, but is deferred to the Statutes of Autonomy. The Constitution merely defines some criteria for the distribution, but it is each Statute of Autonomy that determines which powers are actually ascribed to each region.

Second, the Autonomous Communities cannot freely frame and revise their own government. The Statute of Autonomy that fixes the basic institutions of the Community requires the consent of the national Parliament for its approval and modification.

Third, the Autonomous Communities have no meaningful participation in the process to reform the Spanish Constitution. They merely have the right, like some other institutions, to propose a constitutional

---

[36] M García Pelayo, *Derecho constitucional comparado* (Madrid, Alianza Universidad Textos, 1984) 242–44. For a historical and comparative study, see P Biglino Campos, *Federalismo de integración y de devolución: el debate sobre la competencia* (Madrid, Centro de Estudios Políticos y Constitucionales, 2007).

amendment for Congress to discuss. But the decision whether to enact the reform is made by Congress and the Senate. Sometimes a referendum is required for the amendment to be valid, as we will see, but the result depends on the votes of the Spanish people as a whole, regardless of their distribution throughout the territory.

Fourth, the Autonomous Communities hardly participate in the political process where the national will is formed and expressed. The Senate, in particular, is not structured in the right way, nor does it have the necessary powers to protect the interests and competences of the regions, as we will see.

Finally, as part of this introductory picture, it should also be noted that the regional distribution of power in Spain affects the executive and the legislative branches, but not the judiciary. Both ordinary courts and the Constitutional Court are part of the national set of institutions. The Autonomous Communities do not have their own judiciaries.

CONCLUSION

We have seen in this chapter that Spain is defined in the Constitution as a social and democratic State under the rule of law. This is the kind of State that the framers of the Constitution, working against the legacy of Franco's dictatorship, wished Spain to be. The State should be bound by the law, in order to safeguard the interests and rights of individuals. The law must be generated through procedures that register the will of the people and their representatives. And the State should play an active role in society and the economy in order to guarantee real liberty and equality for all individuals and groups.

These abstract ideas are to be translated into practice through a particular institutional arrangement: a 'quasi-federal parliamentary monarchy'. The Head of the State is a monarch, but one that exercises no real governmental powers. The system is parliamentary, not presidential, to the extent that the President of the Government needs to obtain the support of the majority in Congress. There are some rather limited forms of direct democracy (popular legislative initiatives and referenda), which complement the representative scheme that is basic to the system. Political parties, however, are the key players in the institutional game. And there is a vertical separation of powers between the centre (the State) and the regions (the Autonomous Communities). This territorial distribution of political authority is similar in many respects to the distribution we encounter in federal polities. It exhibits some distinctive features, however, which we will explore in more detail in chapter seven.

With all this background in mind, we must now turn our attention to the Constitution as part of the legal system. We will discuss, in particular, how the Constitution opens itself to the future (through the amendment process), as well as to the external world (through clauses that make reference to international and supranational law).

FURTHER READING

Aragón, M, *Constitución y democracia* (Madrid, Tecnos, 1989).

——, *Estudios de Derecho Constitucional* (Madrid, Centro de Estudios Políticos y Constitucionales, 2009).

Bassols Coma, M, *Constitución y sistema económico* (Madrid, Tecnos, 1988).

Blanco Valdés, R, *Las conexiones políticas* (Madrid, Alianza Editorial, 2001).

——, *La Constitución de 1978* (Madrid, Alianza Editorial, 2011).

Cruz Villalón, P, *La curiosidad del jurista persa, y otros estudios sobre la Constitución* (Madrid, Centro de Estudios Políticos y Constitucionales, 1999).

de Otto, I, *Defensa de la Constitución y partidos políticos* (Madrid, Centro de Estudios Constitucionales, 1985).

Ferreres Comella, V, *El principio de taxatividad en material penal y el valor normativo de la jurisprudencia* (Madrid, Civitas, 2002).

——, 'The New Regulation of Political Parties in Spain, and the Decision to Outlaw Batasuna' in Sajó, A (ed), *Militant Democracy* (AJ Utrecht, Eleven International Publishing, 2004) 133–56.

Garrorena Morales, A, *El Estado español como Estado social y democrático de Derecho* (Madrid, Tecnos, 1984).

——, *Derecho Constitucional. Teoría de la Constitución y sistema de fuentes* (Madrid, Centro de Estudios Políticos y Constitucionales, 2011).

Gunther, R, Montero, JR and Botella, J, *Democracy in Modern Spain* (New Haven, Yale University Press, 2004).

López Guerra, L, Espín, E, García Morillo, J, Pérez Tremps, P and Satrústegui, M, *Derecho constitucional* (two volumes) (Valencia, Tirant lo Blanch, 2010).

Pérez Royo, J, *Curso de Derecho Constitucional* (Madrid, Marcial Pons, 2010).

Rubio Llorente, F, *La forma del poder. (Estudios sobre la Constitución)* (Madrid, Centro de Estudios Constitucionales, 1997).

3

The Constitution and the Legal System

⟶⊶⊷⟵

The Nature of the Constitution as a Legal Norm – The
Constitution and Time: Constitutional Amendments – The
Constitution and Space: International and Supranational Sources
of Law – Conclusion

I
N THIS CHAPTER, we need to focus on the Constitution as a
legal norm. As we have seen, the Constitution establishes the basic
governmental institutions, and places some substantive limitations
and requirements on them. The Constitution does this in its 'legal capacity', as we may put it. The Constitution is, after all, part of the law, and
its provisions must therefore get enforced by the apparatus of the State
– including, of course, courts. The Constitution, however, exhibits
some distinctive features as a legal norm. We have to investigate some
of them here. In addition, we must deal with two important issues in
this chapter: how can the Constitution be amended? And how does the
Constitution interact with international and supranational sources of
law? In other words, how does the Constitution deal with the passage of
time (amendments), and with the existence of a broader space that is
occupied by States and international organizations with which Spain
needs to interact?

THE NATURE OF THE CONSTITUTION AS A LEGAL NORM

The Constitution as Law: Direct Effect

The Constitution is, of course, part of the Spanish legal system. This
entails an important consequence: as any other norm in that system, the

Constitution must be enforced by courts. Its provisions are directly applicable, even if the legislature has not issued any detailed regulations to specify or develop their content.

This may be a trivial proposition to hold, but the truth of the matter is that during the early years of the Constitution's existence, many ordinary judges in Spain were reluctant to include the latter as part of the law they had to interpret and apply to decide controversies. They saw the Constitution as a 'political document' that was external to the law. As soon as the Constitutional Court was established in 1980 and started to lay down decisions, it had to react against that understanding. It emphasized the 'normative force' of the new fundamental charter. The Constitution is *law*, and courts must apply it directly, without having to wait for the legislature to intervene. If the Constitution recognizes the right to conscientious objection to the military service, for example, judges must guarantee the core of this right, even if Parliament has not yet passed a statute regulating the conditions and the procedures to exercise such right (STC 15/1982).[1]

This general principle of direct applicability needs to be qualified in some cases, however. The Constitution explicitly provides, for example, that the economic and social principles mentioned in Chapter III of Title I can only be enforced by courts in accordance with the pertinent laws and regulations (article 53.3). It is clear, then, that such principles have no direct effect. In addition, the very structure of some constitutional norms is such that the legislature's intervention is necessary. Article 125 of the Constitution, for instance, recognizes the right of citizens to participate in the administration of justice through the institution of the jury, in those criminal cases and in the manner that the legislature stipulates. This clause is of such a nature that, inevitably, judges need to wait for the legislature to provide for the regulation of the jury. Only then may courts decide whether a case must be sent to the jury, and how the jury is to be formed. Thus, the jury did not come into existence until 1995, when a statute regulating it was finally passed by Parliament.

Apart from these exceptions, the general rule is that constitutional clauses enjoy direct effect and must be applied by judges, as legal provisions normally are.

---

[1] An influential book that highlighted the nature of the Constitution as law was E García de Entería, *La Constitución como norma y el Tribunal Constitucional*, 4th edn (Madrid, Civitas, 2006).

The Constitution, however, is not merely part of the legal system. It exhibits two features that make it special: it is the supreme norm, and it structures the legal system as a whole. These are analytically distinct ideas, which need to be examined separately.

The Constitution's Supremacy

No article in the Spanish Constitution explicitly proclaims that the Constitution is the supreme law of the land. Article 9 establishes that citizens and public institutions 'are bound by the Constitution and the rest of the law', but it does not say that the Constitution is superior to 'the rest of the law'. The supremacy of the Constitution is implicit in the institutional arrangement it lays down, however. Title X of the Constitution, in particular, establishes the procedures to amend the Constitution. Since these procedures are more burdensome than those that are employed to enact and modify ordinary legislation, a hierarchy is hereby implicitly affirmed.

This is in keeping with the decision to create a Constitutional Court. Title IX regulates this specialized tribunal, the most important function of which is to review the constitutional validity of legislation enacted by Parliament. As we will study in chapter eight, the Court can strike down statutes (or other norms of equivalent rank) that it finds inconsistent with the Constitution. This clearly indicates that the Constitution is supreme over statutes. Ordinary judges, in turn, must certify a question to the Constitutional Court, if they believe that a piece of legislation is unconstitutional. The Constitutional Court has a 'monopoly' in the field of legislative review.

Administrative regulations are, of course, subordinate to the Constitution too. They must therefore comply with it, as well as with ordinary legislation. This is especially important where statutes give broad discretion to the regulatory powers of the executive branch. In those circumstances, the Constitution plays as key role, in terms of constraining the exercise of such powers. Even if a regulation meets the existing statutory requirements, it may still be found to offend constitutional values. When it comes to administrative regulations, any court can check their validity.[2]

---

[2]   Art 6, *Ley Orgánica 6/1985 del Poder Judicial.*

The Constitution as the Norm that Structures the Legal System

The Constitution is not only the highest norm of the legal system. It has an additional characteristic: it organizes the sources of law. That is, it establishes which organs, following which procedures, under what kinds of constraints, are authorized to issue which types of norms. And it orders these different sorts of norms into a systematic whole – defining the relationships among them.

Any modern legal system that is based on a Constitution is likely to exhibit at least three normative levels: the Constitution, statutes enacted by Parliament, and regulations issued by the executive branch. This simple picture is sometimes expressed in the form of a pyramid: the base is occupied by regulations, the middle rank is occupied by statutes, and the Constitution stands at the apex. There is a hierarchy within the pyramid, which means that the higher norm can always repeal the lower norm, whereas the latter must respect the former for it to be valid.

This portrait is useful as a starting point. Legal systems tend to be more complicated than that, however. In the case of Spain, the sources of complexity are related to several factors. First, special statutes – so-called 'organic statutes' – are required to regulate certain matters. The constitutional framers wanted the future laws on those matters to be based on a broader parliamentary consensus than simple majority. Second, the process of devolution of political power to the regions required the enactment of Statutes of Autonomy, as we have seen. These Statutes are a special type of law. Third, the executive branch is allowed, under certain conditions, to issue legal provisions that have the same rank as statutes. Fourth, Parliament issues its own standing orders or by-laws, which need to be protected from external interferences. Such legal instruments have a special nature, which makes them different from ordinary statutes. Fifth, local governments enjoy a constitutionally protected sphere of autonomy, which both the State and the regional parliaments must respect. The regulations adopted by the local institutions exhibit distinctive features. Sixth, Spain is open to international and supranational developments, and rules need to be articulated to coordinate external and domestic legal sources.

So the legal system is an intricate network of norms. The image of a simple pyramid with three stages belies the complexity of the legal order. As we examine different political institutions in various chapters of this book, we will have the opportunity to examine the different types of law with some detail. In this chapter we focus on the Constitution and international Treaties.

It is important to stress this structural function of the Constitution, given the traditional role of the Spanish Civil Code in this field. Indeed, the Code was for a long time the basic document where the sources of the legal system were defined. This was true in other European countries too. Article 1 of the Spanish Civil Code provided (and still provides) that the sources of the Spanish legal system are 'laws, customs and general principles of law' (*leyes, costumbres, principios generales del Derecho*). This is a very sketchy definition of the sources of law. There is nothing wrong with it, but it needs to be interpreted in light of the Constitution, which is now the most important legal instrument where the elements of the legal system are fixed. The importance of the Code is that it recognizes two sources (customs and general principles of law) beyond those that the Constitution explicitly mentions. These extra-constitutional sources are legitimate, since the Constitution (in article 149.1.8) authorizes the central government to 'determine the sources of law', which implies that there may be other sources of law beyond those specified and regulated in the Constitution.[3]

THE CONSTITUTION AND TIME: CONSTITUTIONAL AMENDMENTS

As has already been noted, the Spanish Constitution is more difficult to amend than ordinary legislation. We must now examine with some detail what the requirements are to amend the text, and what problems have arisen in practice – or may arise in the future – as a result of them.

Constitutional Rigidity in the Service of *Consenso*

We saw in chapter one that the Spanish Constitution was the product of a broad agreement reached in 1977–78 to settle some important issues that had historically divided Spaniards in tragic ways. The framers were all of the view that the Constitution that embodied that settlement

---

[3] I de Otto, *Derecho constitucional. Sistema de fuentes* (Barcelona, Ariel, 1988) 86.

ought to be rigid. A transient parliamentary majority should not erode the basic decisions that the document expresses.

Article 167 thus establishes a relatively burdensome procedure to amend the Constitution. A super-majority of three-fifths of both Congress and the Senate is initially required. If that super-majority is not obtained, a Joint Commission made up of members of Congress and the Senate must try to agree upon a text. If the new text is not approved by three-fifths of each parliamentary chamber, Congress can enact it by a two-thirds super-majority, provided that at least an absolute majority of senators voted for it. (Absolute majority means that those in favour are more than 50 per cent of the total number of senators).

It is worth stressing that the crucial role that political parties played at the initial constitutional stage is replicated in the amendment context. It is basically a new pact among political parties that can lead to a reform. The Constitution does not allow the people to initiate the process of constitutional amendment: only the Government, Congress, the Senate, and the regional parliaments can propose a reform (article 166). And a referendum is not necessary for the valid enactment of the amendment, unless 10 per cent of Congress or 10 per cent of the Senate ask for it.

In fact, the only two amendments that have been introduced so far were enacted by Parliament exclusively. No referendum was called. In 1992, the constitutional text was modified to allow citizens of the European Union to stand as candidates in municipal elections. Without the amendment, it would not have been possible for Spain to validly ratify the Maastricht Treaty, which granted that right. In its original version, the Constitution permitted non-Spaniards the right to vote in municipal elections, but not the right to stand as candidates. Changing the Constitution was thus necessary. More recently, in 2011, a constitutional reform was enacted to impose certain limits on public debt and public deficit. Article 135 of the Constitution was modified to reinforce Spain's compliance with public deficit and public debt limitations established by European Union law. This amendment was introduced in the middle of financial turmoil in Europe, to send the message that Spain would be committed to fiscal discipline, along the lines of the new Treaty on Stability, Coordination, and Governance in the Economic and Monetary Union (signed on March 2, 2012), which requires State parties to incorporate a golden rule of budgetary equilibrium in their Constitutions, or in norms that are of equivalent permanence. Not only were the people excluded from this constitutional reform. The two main parties (PSOE and PP) quickly agreed on its terms, and it was enacted by the Cortes Generales in just a few days.

Interestingly, during the constitutional debates in 1977–78 it was the more conservative right (AP) that was in favour of expanding popular participation, making the referendum compulsory in all cases. The other parties (especially those on the left) argued that it was dangerous in Spain to enlarge the institutions of direct democracy, since they might undermine respect for the parliamentary system. They were concerned about the fragility of political parties and representative institutions in a country that had suffered 40 years of dictatorship.[4]

The Constitution, however, includes an exceptional rule to govern amendments of a special kind. Article 168 establishes a special procedure to enact a 'total revision' of the Constitution, or a partial one that affects certain clauses: those of the Preliminary Title (which includes some of the most basic principles of the constitutional system), those that guarantee a special sub-set of fundamental rights (those enumerated in Section 1, Chapter II, Title I, that is: articles 15–29), and those that regulate the Crown (Title II). An extremely difficult process needs to be followed in such cases: first, Congress and the Senate have to approve the general proposal by a majority of two-thirds each. Second, Parliament has to be dissolved immediately, and general elections called for. Third, the new Parliament has to ratify the decision to initiate the reform. Fourth, the reform has to be approved by two-thirds of the members of each house. Fifth, a referendum has to be held, to obtain the support of the majority of citizens.

This is indeed a very burdensome procedure. The framers, apparently, sought to immunize certain constitutional choices against repeal.[5] They were not very careful, however, when it came to identifying the matters that deserved this extra protection. They could have said, for example, that the existence of a monarchical form of State is protected by the special procedure of article 168. Instead, they covered Title II as a whole, with all its minor details about the structure and functioning of the Crown. In contrast, they left aside the principle of human dignity, which article 10 solemnly proclaims to be one of the foundations of the

---

[4] J Pérez Royo, *La Reforma de la Constitución* (Madrid, Publicaciones del Congreso de los Diputados, 1987) 131–35, 142–50 and 159–60.

[5] Ibid 156–57, 190 and 202; and P de Vega, *La reforma constitucional y la problemática del poder constituyente* (Madrid, Tecnos, 1985) 148.

political order. The framers, moreover, included a sub-group of fundamental rights (those that figure in articles 15–29), but they did not distinguish between restriction and expansion of rights. Article 15 of the Constitution, for example, abolishes the death penalty in general, but allows criminal military law to impose it in the event of war. That law can, of course, decline to establish the death penalty, as is currently the case. But if a proposal is made to reform the Constitution in order to eliminate the exceptional circumstance where capital punishment is permitted, why should the extraordinary procedure of article 168 be imposed?

In any case, it is important to emphasize that, although there are two procedures of constitutional amendment, the Constitution as a whole has turned out to be very rigid as a political matter. Even if the formal requirements of the easier procedure (that of article 167) are not hard to fulfil in theory, a political practice has developed that avoids any real talk about constitutional reforms. Changing the Constitution has become political taboo. The fear exists that any revision of the text – even if the matters involved are relatively marginal – may end up generating big divisions of opinion among citizens and political groups, of the kind that the framers of the Constitution tried to settle in 1977–78. In this regard, it is extremely revealing that the only two amendments that have been adopted so far were 'forced' on Spain by its membership in the European Union. As was already indicated, the 1992 amendment was necessary to make it possible for Spain to validly ratify the Maastricht Treaty, and the 2011 amendment was required to enshrine the rules on fiscal austerity that were expected from Spain to deal with the crisis of the euro. No 'internally driven' reform has been adopted after more than three decades since the Constitution was enacted.

This reluctance to reform the Constitution has had some repercussions on interpretive practices. The constitutional text has sometimes been read in a very flexible way to accommodate certain changes that, were it not for that reluctance, would normally have triggered the process of constitutional amendment. The Constitution, for example, refers to 'compulsory military service' in article 30.2. In 1999, however, a statute passed by Parliament eliminated this service. In order to avoid constitutional problems, the statute established that the military service was 'suspended indefinitely'. There is no doubt, however, that the effect is exactly the same as if it had been formally extinguished. Since there was a broad majority in Parliament in favour of this legislative change, it would not have been hard to amend the Constitution. Yet, that move was out of the question. Similarly, the Constitution recognizes in article 32 the right of 'a man and a woman' to get married. A law was enacted in 2005 to allow same-sex marriages. The law can persuasively be defended on equality grounds: if we really believe that individuals have a right not to be discriminated against on grounds of sexual orientation, it follows that homosexuals should not be excluded from the institution of marriage. Yet, there is a textual dissonance between the 2005 statute and the way the constitutional clause is written. If political parties were more prepared to reform the Constitution, a bill would have been tabled to change article 32. (The Constitutional Court has recently upheld the statute, however: STC 198/2012).

In reality the existence of a political taboo when it comes to revising the Spanish Constitution has put the Constitutional Court in a delicate position. It knows that none of its rulings will be overridden through a constitutional amendment. In other European countries, such as France and Italy, for example, some changes in the Constitution have been introduced as a response to a jurisprudential position of the Court.[6] This healthy counter-weight to the Court's power is totally absent in Spain.

The unwillingness to change the Constitution has, of course, made it impossible to consider certain proposals to reform the institutions of government. As soon as a reasonable solution to overcome the short-comings of particular arrangements is discovered to require a constitutional amendment, it is immediately put off the political agenda. As we will see throughout the book, there are some changes to consider, in order to improve the current institutional set-up, that would necessitate the modification of the constitutional text.

The Problems with Procedural Dualism

The existence of two different avenues to produce a constitutional reform (an easier one regulated in article 167, and a harder one regulated in article 168) can give rise to some problems. How to decide, for exam-ple, when a 'total' revision of the Constitution is being entertained, so

---

[6] For references, see V Ferreres Comella, *Constitutional Courts and Democratic Values. A European Perspective* (New Haven, Yale University Press, 2009) 104–07.

that the complicated procedure of article 168 needs to be followed? Is it a question of numbers – how many provisions are to be modified? Is it a question of the qualitative importance of the matters under consideration? The claim has been advanced, for example, that eliminating the Constitutional Court would be a total revision – even if article 168 does not explicitly mention Title IX (where that Court is regulated).[7]

And how should one determine whether a partial revision of the Constitution 'affects' the set of clauses that are covered by article 168? The very first time the Constitution was reformed illustrated the complexity of the issue. The Maastricht Treaty that Spain wanted to ratify as part of the ongoing process of European integration provided that every European Union citizen would be entitled to vote and to stand as a candidate at the municipal elections in the Member State where he or she resides. The Spanish Constitution, however, provided in article 13.2 that only Spaniards enjoyed the rights of political participation mentioned in article 23, except that a Treaty or a law could extend to foreigners the right to vote (*sufragio activo*) in municipal elections, if this was done in accordance with the principle of reciprocity. Only the right to vote was covered by the exception, not the right to stand as a candidate (*sufragio pasivo*). In order for Spain to validly ratify the Maastricht Treaty, therefore, it was rather clear that article 13.2 had to be amended, to expand the scope of the exception.

The problem was this: article 13.2 is not included in the group of clauses that are covered by the more burdensome amendment procedure of article 168, but article 23 is. Given the connection between the two articles, does the amendment of article 13.2 'affect' article 23? There was doctrinal controversy about this, and the Constitutional Court was required by the Government to address the matter. The Court (in its Declaration 1/1992) held that article 23 had to be conceptually separated from article 13: one defines the substantive right, while the other says who is entitled to enjoy the right. It concluded that the easy procedure was to be followed. And so it was – which meant, among other things, that Parliament was not dissolved and no referendum was held. It is not obvious that the Court was right. Its prudential approach is understandable, however, given the political stakes involved.

---

[7]   Pérez Royo (n 4) 196–97.

Unamendable Constitutional Clauses?

An interesting question concerns the protection to be given to the most basic principles the Constitution embodies, such as democracy and human dignity. Is an amendment valid, even if passed through the pertinent procedures, if it infringes those values?[8] Some scholars argue that, since a 'total revision' of the Spanish Constitution is explicitly permitted, the answer is yes. Any change is possible. The only limitation the Constitution imposes is of a temporal nature: article 169 says that no constitutional reform can be initiated in the event of a war or when a state of emergency (alarm, siege or exception) has been declared.

Other voices counter that the Constitution is best interpreted as implicitly protecting certain core values against repeal. To reinforce this point, it is possible to appeal to Spain's membership in both the European Union and the Council of Europe. External limits in the name of democracy and rights are clearly applicable. A constitutional transformation against liberal democracy would be illegal under European supranational norms. The Constitution, which makes reference to supranational law, should thus be taken to make an irreversible commitment to democracy and rights.

A different question is whether the articles regulating constitutional amendments may themselves be amended. There seems to be no a priori reason to deny the possibility of changing the existing rules on amendment. There is no logical problem in using a procedure to change the rules that regulate that procedure. The real question is which procedure needs to be followed to modify articles 167 and 168: the easy one (regulated in article 167), or the more demanding one (regulated in article 168)? Since the Constitution has established a general rule (article 167) and an exception (article 168), the argument has sometimes been made that it is possible to use the easy procedure of article 167 to change both article 167 and article 168. The argument is based on the observation that neither article 167 nor article 168 is included in the exceptional list of matters that trigger the application of article 168. This textual argument leads to an outcome that sounds plausible when it comes to changing article 167. It seems correct, indeed, to use the easy

---

[8] On this issue, see BAláez Corral, *Los límites materiales a la reforma de la Constitución española de 1978* (Madrid, Centro de Estudios Políticos y Constitucionales, 2000).

procedure to modify the easy procedure. But it is not correct to use the easy procedure to change the difficult procedure of article 168. It is ultimately a constitutional fraud for a super-majority in Parliament to overcome the constraints that article 168 imposes, through the convenient strategy of using the easy procedure of article 167 to eliminate those constraints.[9]

THE CONSTITUTION AND SPACE: INTERNATIONAL AND
SUPRANATIONAL SOURCES OF LAW

We have so far analyzed the extent to which the Constitution opens itself to the future. We must now turn to the manner in which it opens itself to international and supranational sources of law.

The Status of International Treaties

According to the Constitution, the international Treaties validly ratified by Spain are automatically part of the domestic legal system, once they have been officially published (article 96.1). There is no need for a national statute to incorporate the Treaty into domestic law. The Treaty as such becomes part of the system, once it is officially published in Spain.

The Constitution establishes different procedures that need to be observed, depending on the kind of Treaty that is involved. Article 94 requires the previous authorization of the Cortes Generales for the State to be able to ratify Treaties that have a political or military nature; or that affect the territorial integrity of the State, or the fundamental rights and duties of Title I; or that entail financial obligations for the public treasury; or that imply a modification or repeal of any statute, or require legislative measures for their implementation. No statute is passed in such cases. What Parliament does is to 'authorize' the Treaty.[10] No amendments can be introduced to it, for the text has already been fixed during the negotiations with the other States. The Government, however, can be asked to include unilateral reservations to the Treaty (if they are possible under it), as well as declarations. The Government,

---

[9] On this problem, see de Otto (n 3) 66–67.

[10] The two chambers must agree on the authorization. Failing that, Congress decides by absolute majority. See art 74.2 of the Constitution.

moreover, is not required to conclude the Treaty that has obtained the legislative green light. In practice, however, only those Treaties that the executive branch wishes to subscribe are sent to Parliament to get the pertinent authorization. So it is not surprising that Treaties are normally concluded, once the permission has been given.[11]

For the rest of Treaties, in contrast, the Government merely needs to inform both chambers of Parliament immediately.

The Constitution, however, does not confine itself to establishing the procedures that must be followed to ratify international Treaties. It also imposes substantive limits. Treaties can only be validly entered into if their content is in keeping with the Constitution. Article 95.1 explicitly says that an international Treaty containing unconstitutional provisions can only be consented to if the Constitution is first amended.[12] Precisely in order to make sure that a Treaty is consistent with the Constitution, a special procedure exists to have the Constitutional Court address the matter. Article 95.2 allows the executive branch or a chamber of Parliament to request the Court to declare whether there is a contradiction between the two norms. This judicial check on Treaties is a priori: it takes place before the Treaty has been ratified and introduced into the Spanish legal system. It is also possible, however, for a Treaty to be subjected to scrutiny a posteriori, after it has entered into effect, by way of constitutional challenges brought in the abstract by certain public institutions, or through constitutional questions raised by ordinary judges. Declaring a Treaty unconstitutional, and thus non-enforceable, once it has been ratified may engage Spain's responsibility as a subject of public international law. But this is a separate question from the domestic legal force of the Treaty.

It is important to emphasize that the Constitution protects Treaties quite powerfully against national laws that are not in accord with them. Article 96 establishes that Treaty provisions can only be repealed, modified or suspended in the manner specified in the Treaties, or in accord-

---

[11] A Remiro Brotons, *La acción exterior del Estado* (Madrid, Tecnos, 1984) 154–56.

[12] Interestingly, a first version of the constitutional text adopted in January 1978 established that it was possible for Spain to conclude an unconstitutional Treaty, provided the parliamentary authorization was given through the same procedure that is employed to amend the Constitution. This is a different idea, of course, than requiring a constitutional amendment before a Treaty that collides with the Constitution can be validly concluded. The final draft eliminated that provision. See Remiro Brotons (n 11) 99.

ance with general rules of international law. This has been interpreted to mean that a Treaty, once ratified by Spain (in the manner provided in article 94) 'resists' any contrary statute that Parliament enacts later. The question then arises as to which courts have jurisdiction to declare a statute to run against a Treaty. The Constitutional Court has held that ordinary judges are in charge. Whether or not a statute contradicts a Treaty is a question of 'ordinary legality' for ordinary judges to settle. The Constitutional Court has the power to rule on the validity of statutes, but only to the extent that the Constitution – not a Treaty – is alleged to have been breached (STC 28/1991).

This general doctrine has thus made it possible for Spain to easily embrace the position taken by the European Court of Justice in the *Simmenthal case* to the effect that ordinary courts are empowered to set aside any national statute that contravenes European Union (EU) law.[13] In Spain, this sort of judicial review is not confined to EU law. Any Treaty ratified by Spain (through the procedure of article 94) can be employed by ordinary judges as a basis for a decision to set aside a statutory provision that is at odds with it.

In addition to the general regime that the Constitution establishes concerning international Treaties, there is a specific clause that gives some extra normative weight to human rights instruments. Article 10.2, as has been already pointed out, provides that the provisions in the Spanish Constitution concerning fundamental rights and liberties shall be interpreted in accordance with the Universal Declaration of Human Rights, as well as the international Treaties or Conventions ratified by Spain on such matters.[14] The most important document that courts have used to shed interpretive light on the Spanish Bill of Rights is the European Convention on Human Rights. The fact that the European Court of Human Rights in Strasbourg has produced a rich case law in many areas has transformed the Convention into a very important part of constitutional practice in Spain. Between 1999 and 2007, for example, the Spanish Constitutional Court has referred expressly to the Convention and the relevant case law in 17.5 per cent of its decisions.[15]

[13] Case 106/77 *Amministrazione delle Finanze dello Stato v Simmenthal SpA* [1978] ECR 629, [1978] 3 CMLR 263.

[14] On the role and impact of this clause, see A Saiz Arnaiz, *La apertura constitucional al Derecho internacional y europeo de los derechos humanos. El artículo 10.2 de la Constitución española* (Madrid, Consejo General del Poder Judicial, 1999).

[15] See A Torres Pérez, 'The Judicial Impact of European Law in Spain: ECHR and EU Law Compared' (2011) 30 *Yearbook of European Law* 161.

Unfortunately, however, Spain has adopted no law regulating the enforcement of judgments rendered by the European Court of Human Rights. In particular, there is no provision in Spain allowing for reopening judicial proceedings once the Strasbourg Court has found a breach of the Convention. The Constitutional Court once held that it was a violation of the Spanish Constitution for someone to be retained in prison after Strasbourg had declared a violation of the right to a fair trial.[16] But this is a very exceptional remedy. A legislative reform should be considered.[17] It is regrettable that the Constitution's openness to international human rights instruments has not been accompanied by a serious effort by the ordinary legislature to facilitate domestic compliance with Strasbourg's judgments. Paying a monetary compensation to the victim is not always a sufficient way to preserve the fundamental right that has been infringed.

The Constitution and European Integration

The Constitution includes a special provision, article 93, dealing with Treaties that create international or supranational organizations to which governmental powers derived from the Constitution are granted. What the framers had in mind was Spain's future membership in the European Communities.[18] The provision was thus used in 1985 to authorize the Treaty of Accession. But it has also been used in another case: to ratify the 1998 Rome Statute of the International Criminal Court.

Some scholars have criticized article 93, however, on the grounds that it does not require a sufficiently large parliamentary majority. An organic statute needs to be passed, which means that an absolute majority of members of Congress must vote in favour. (That is, more than 50 per cent of the total number of deputies must approve of it). This is not, in practice, a larger majority than that needed to authorize ordinary Treaties.[19] Because a nation takes an almost irreversible decision when it

---

[16] See STC 245/1991.
[17] Torres Pérez (n 15) 163–64.
[18] P Pérez Tremps, *Constitución española y Comunidad Europea* (Madrid, Fundación Universidad Empresa, 1994).
[19] See art 74.2 of the Constitution.

joins a supranational organization, a super-majority should be necessary, these critics claim.[20]

There is no doubt that joining the European Communities has brought significant changes from a legal point of view.[21] Spanish judges have had to assume responsibility for the correct application of European Community law (now EU law) in the course of ordinary adjudication. The doctrines of direct effect and supremacy, as constructed by the Luxembourg Court, are to be duly implemented by them.[22] It has taken a long while, however, for lawyers and judges to be aware of the impact of EU law on the domestic legal system. Many of them have been reluctant to engage the issues posed by a new branch of the law they are not familiar with. Those who were not taught EU law at law school are usually at a loss. They are unprepared to certify preliminary references to the Luxembourg Court, for example. Younger judges, in contrast, are more prone to be active in this field. (Between 1986 and 2010, Spanish courts submitted 244 references, 35 of which came from the Supreme Court).[23]

The Constitutional Court has also been slow to recognize the repercussions of EU law. In the last years, however, it has been paying increasing attention to them. In the area of rights, in particular, it has taken into account ordinary legislation enacted by the Union (such as Directives protecting equality in the workplace, for example), as well as the principles and rights enshrined in the Treaties or other foundational documents. In 2006, for example, the Court cited the Charter of Fundamental Rights of the European Union to support its conclusion that discrimination on the basis of sexual orientation was constitutionally prohibited, even if the Spanish Constitution does not explicitly mention this factor among the discriminatory grounds listed in article 14.[24]

---

[20]   Remiro Brotons (n 11) 27 and 114. Actually, the first draft of the Constitution approved by the congressional Ponencia in August 1977 required a three-fifths super-majority, which is identical to the super-majority that is needed to amend the Constitution through the ordinary procedure of art 167.

[21]   S Muñoz Machado, *La Unión Europea y las mutaciones del Estado* (Madrid, Alianza Editorial, 1993).

[22]   For a careful discussion of the way judges in Spain have dealt with the interaction between EU law and the domestic legal system, see R Alonso García, *El Juez español y el Derecho comunitario* (Madrid, Consejo General del Poder Judicial, 2003).

[23]   Torres Pérez (n 15) 171–72.

[24]   See STC 41/2006.

A hard problem concerns the relationship between the Constitution and EU Treaties. As was noted before, Treaties in general can only be validly ratified if they are consistent with the constitutional text. The Constitution can therefore maintain its supremacy over EU law at an early stage. To the extent that the consent of all Member States is required to give legal force to a new Treaty, Spain can insist on its own Constitution and refuse to ratify it. (Most probably, however, the Constitution will be amended, which is another way to preserve its supremacy. This is what happened in 1992, for example, with the Maastricht Treaty, as has already been explained). But things get more complicated when laws or acts adopted by the EU institutions seem to contradict the Spanish Constitution. Should courts be allowed to check those acts and laws in light of the Constitution? There are good reasons for the European Court of Justice to have rejected this kind of control by national judges, as it did in the *Internationale Handelsgesellschaft* case.[25] EU law can only be applied uniformly if national judges abstain from using their domestic Constitutions as grounds to block the enforcement of EU law.

The Spanish Constitutional Court was forced to say something about this problem when the failed Treaty Establishing a Constitution for Europe was sent to it for its review. The question arose whether the provision establishing the principle of primacy of EU law over national law was consistent with the principle that holds that the Spanish Constitution is the supreme law of the land. In its Declaration 1/2004, the Court saw no inconsistency. It argued, quite powerfully, that a systematic reading of the Spanish Constitution is to be entertained. The Constitution is the supreme norm, but Spain is constitutionally authorized by article 93 to become a member of an organization whose decisions and norms are binding. A balance needs to be struck, therefore. The Court held that, to the extent that the EU respects the same basic principles that the Spanish Constitution embodies (such as democracy, the rule of law, fundamental rights), and to the extent that the level of protection afforded those principles by the European institutions is similar, Spain can accept the principle of primacy of EU law. The Court marred its otherwise well-constructed argument with an additional point, drawing a formalistic distinction between supremacy and

---

[25] Case 11/70 *Internationale Handelsgesellschaft mbH v Einfuhr- und Vorratsstelle fur Getreide und Futtermittel* [1970] ECR 1125, [1972] CMLR 255.

primacy. It reasoned that the Spanish Constitution is 'supreme', though EU law enjoys 'primacy'. As many commentators have maintained, this additional argument offered no attractive way to harmonize the Spanish Constitution with EU law. It seemed to minimize the importance of the transformations that were going on.[26]

Recently, the Constitutional Court has confronted a very interesting question, concerning the potential conflict between the European arrest warrant and the Spanish Constitution (ATC 86/2011).[27] For many years the Court has interpreted the Spanish Constitution to impose very strict limits on the possibility of extraditing someone to another country, when the person concerned was not physically present at the trial that led to his criminal conviction. Under the laws regulating the European arrest warrant, however, the warrant has to be served, even if the person was not physically present at trial, provided the absence was voluntary and a lawyer was present. The Constitutional Court has decided to raise a preliminary reference to the Luxembourg Court – the first time it has ever done so. The question basically has two parts: are the applicable provisions regulating the European arrest warrant in conformity with the Charter of Fundamental Rights of the European Union? If so, may Spanish judges apply a more generous understanding of the fundamental rights at stake, so that the arrest warrant is subjected to stricter judicial review in Spain? Depending on the Luxembourg Court's answer, a potential conflict may emerge between EU law and the Spanish Constitution.

A special case of normative collision would appear if a constitutional amendment were enacted that were at odds with pre-existing EU law. If the Constitution is the supreme law of the land, such an amendment would have to prevail as far as Spain's legal system goes, it would seem. On the other hand, Spain's constitutionally-warranted membership in the European Union imposes obligations that need to be honoured by all law-making institutions, including those with the authority to amend the Constitution. There is no doctrinal consensus on how this tension should be resolved. The suggestion has been made for a mechanism of a priori review to be established, to permit the Constitutional Court to

---

[26] See A López Castillo, A Saiz Arnaiz and V Ferreres Comella, *Constitución española y Constitución europea* (Madrid, Centro de Estudios Políticos y Constitucionales, 2005).

[27] For a comment on this resolution, see A Torres Pérez, 'Constitutional Dialogue on the European Arrest Warrant: The Spanish Constitutional Court Knocking on Luxembourg's Door' (2012) 8 *European Constitutional Law Review* 105.

speak to the validity of constitutional amendments before they are enacted.[28] When deciding this question, the Court should raise a preliminary reference to the European Court of Justice, to get the latter's view as to the compatibility of the proposed amendment with EU law.

CONCLUSION

We have examined in this chapter the role the Spanish Constitution plays within the legal system. Because it is part of that system, the Constitution must be interpreted and applied by judges when adjudicating controversies. It has direct effect on the cases they have to decide. But the Constitution is a special kind of law. It is supreme over the rest of the norms that make up the legal system. In addition, it establishes and regulates the other sources of law.

The Spanish Constitution is technically rigid, in the sense that it cannot be amended through the ordinary legislative procedure. There is not a single avenue to change the Constitution, however, but two different avenues, depending on the subject matter that is involved. This dualism has given rise to some intricate problems, as we have seen.

What is most idiosyncratic to the Spanish constitutional practices is the reluctance with which political parties entertain the possibility of introducing changes to the constitutional document. Amending the Constitution has become a sort of taboo. To a large extent, this cautious attitude is understandable, given the difficulty with which a *consenso* was built among political parties at the constitutional stage in 1977–78. But it has had negative consequences. Some relatively minor reforms that require a modification of the text are not even considered, in spite of the improvements that they might bring about. And the interpretation of the text is sometimes too flexible, in order to accommodate certain legislative changes. Interestingly, the only two cases where the Constitution has been modified are linked to European supranational developments. The need to comply with European Union norms has pressed Spanish political forces to amend the Constitution.

---

[28] P Cruz Villalón, *La Constitución inédita* (Madrid, Trotta, 2004) 77–78.

FURTHER READING

Aguiló Regla, J, *Teoría general de las fuentes del Derecho* (Barcelona, Ariel, 2000).

Alonso García, R, *El Juez español y el Derecho comunitario* (Madrid, Consejo General del Poder Judicial, 2003).

de Otto, I, *Derecho constitucional. Sistema de fuentes* (Barcelona, Ariel, 1988).

de Vega, P, *La reforma constitucional y la problemática del poder constituyente* (Madrid, Tecnos, 1985).

García de Entería, E, *La Constitución como norma y el Tribunal Constitucional*, 4th edn (Madrid, Civitas, 2006).

López Castillo, A, Saiz Arnaiz, A and Ferreres Comella, V, *Constitución española y Constitución europea* (Madrid, Centro de Estudios Políticos y Constitucionales, 2005).

Muñoz Machado, S, *La Unión Europea y las mutaciones del Estado* (Madrid, Alianza Editorial, 1993).

Pérez Royo, J, *La Reforma de la Constitución* (Madrid, Publicaciones del Congreso de los Diputados, 1987).

——, *Las fuentes del Derecho* (Madrid, Tecnos, 2007).

Pérez Tremps, P, *Constitución española y Comunidad Europea* (Madrid, Fundación Universidad Empresa, 1994).

Remiro Brotons, A, *La acción exterior del Estado* (Madrid, Tecnos, 1984).

Saiz Arnaiz, A, *La apertura constitucional al Derecho internacional y europeo de los derechos humanos. El artículo 10.2 de la Constitución española* (Madrid, Consejo General del Poder Judicial, 1999)

Torres Pérez, A, 'The Judicial Impact of European Law in Spain: ECHR and EU Law Compared' (2011) 30 *Yearbook of European Law* 159–79.

4

The Crown

————————◆◆◆————————

The Legitimacy of the Monarchy – The King's Symbolic Function – The Countersignature Requirement – The Role of the King in Selecting the Government – The King's Authority to Sanction the Laws – The King's Political Neutrality – The King's Immunity – Regency, Guardianship, Marriage and Succession – Conclusion

W E MUST NOW proceed to study the different pieces that make up the Spanish political system, against the background of the general picture offered in chapter two. We need to examine with some detail the different institutions of that system. In this chapter, we start with the Crown. After that, in chapters five and six, we will fix our attention on Parliament and the executive branch.

As we will discuss in this chapter, the existence of the Crown poses a problem from a democratic point of view. What is the justification for the Head of State to be a King that is not elected by the people? And what constraints should the monarch observe to make that office compatible with democratic principles?

The Constitution enumerates the acts it is the King's responsibility to adopt. In general, the monarch is not supposed to make any decisions of political significance. His role is largely symbolic. There is some controversy, however, regarding the role he may play when it comes to promulgating legislation, as we will see.

The stability of the monarchy in Spain depends on its capacity to retain the support of the people as circumstances evolve. An important moment in the future will be the replacement of King Juan Carlos by his son, Prince Felipe. Juan Carlos acquired moral capital through his contribution to the process of transition to democracy, which was described in chapter one. His role in averting the *coup d'état* of 23 February 1981 has also loomed large in the public's mind. His son, however, will have to rely on new sources to draw moral capital from. Things have actually become harder for the monarchy in the last months, as a result of several scandalous events. One of the King's son-in-laws, Iñaki Urdangarín, is being investigated by the judiciary in connection with several crimes, involving corruption and tax fraud, among others. The King himself was under political fire in March 2012 when he suffered an accident while hunting in Botswana. The image of the King spending his time in Africa killing elephants, while Spain was facing a terrible economic moment, caused anger among many people. There was even open talk about the possibility that he would be asked to abdicate. The King, after leaving hospital, addressed himself to the media and said: 'I am sorry. I made a mistake. This will not happen again'. In the last months, he has resumed an intense agenda of activities, especially at the international level, to try to restore his prestige. Only time will tell whether the blow the institution has suffered is really fatal. What seems to be certain is that the Prince will have to work his way towards a new deal with the people. The monarchy needs some fresh air, as the memory over the successful transition to democracy fades away.

THE LEGITIMACY OF THE MONARCHY

As was already noted, one of the decisions the constitutional framers had to make in 1977–78 concerned the future of the monarchy. As the different leaders were discussing the constitutional text, the Crown was already there: Juan Carlos had been proclaimed King on 22 November 1975, two days after Franco's death. The monarch enjoyed all the powers that the Head of State was granted under the fundamental laws of Franco's regime. He became King because Franco had so decided in 1969, preferring him over Juan Carlos' father (Don Juan de Borbón Battenberg), who had been too distant from the dictatorship to make him a reliable successor to Franco. There would be no democracy, of course, until this part of Franco's legacy was dismantled. The parties on the left, moreover, had traditionally been republican, especially since the reign of Alfonso XIII.

The decision that was finally reached is a good example of the spirit of *consenso* that animated the constitutional debates, as was explained in chapter one. The form of government that was chosen was a monarchy, but one where the King would have no real power, but only moral authority.

The left's willingness to accept the monarchy had a lot to do with the attitude that Juan Carlos had exhibited during the process of transition. The King made it clear that he would not perform the function that Franco had entrusted him with. He would not be the guardian of the old fundamental laws, but would instead encourage the establishment of a democratic system. His very first speech as a monarch suggested that something new was to be expected. He explicitly said that a new historical era had started, and that he wanted to be the King of all Spaniards. Many citizens who would otherwise have opposed the monarchy started to view Juan Carlos with sympathy and respect. As has often been pointed out by commentators, there are in Spain many more *juancarlistas* than monarchists.

The Constitution explicitly mentions Juan Carlos. Article 57.1 says that the Crown shall be inherited by the successors of 'Your Majesty Don Juan Carlos I de Borbón, the legitimate heir of the historical dynasty'. This provision points to a pre-existing institutional reality: Juan Carlos, the 'legitimate heir' of the dynasty, is already King. Does this mean that his legitimacy does not derive from the Constitution, then? Not really, since a more important article in the Constitution (article 1.2) proclaims that sovereignty lies with the Spanish people, and that public institutions derive from them. The Crown cannot be an exception to this general proposition. As was already noted, it is perfectly possible to amend the Constitution and eliminate the monarchy. The Constitution establishes no limit to this possibility, provided the burdensome procedure of article 168 is followed. The Constitution is the only valid legal title, therefore, that currently supports Juan Carlos' authority.[1] It is important to recall, in this connection, that the Constitution expressly repeals Franco's fundamental laws, including those under which Juan Carlos was appointed King.[2]

Interestingly, the King 'promulgated' the Constitution in a ceremony held at the Cortes Generales on 28 December 1978, but he did not 'sanction' it. The message that was being sent by this gesture was that

---

[1] On this point, M Aragón Reyes, *Dos estudios sobre la monarquía parlamentaria en la Constitución española* (Madrid, Civitas, 1990).

[2] See Constitution, *Disposición Derogatoria* number 1.

the monarch had no authority – not even a merely symbolic authority – to decide whether to veto a Constitution that was the highest expression of popular will. The Constitution was directly promulgated and published, without being submitted to formal royal assent. On the other hand, Juan Carlos did not take an oath of allegiance to the new Constitution, since he had already been proclaimed King in 1975. In his speech, however, he expressed his commitment to observe and serve the new Magna Charter. (His son, Prince Felipe, did swear allegiance to the Constitution some years later, when he reached the age of 18, as provided by article 61.2 of the Constitution, and will have to do so again when he is proclaimed King in the future, as provided in article 61.1).

Hence Juan Carlos is acknowledged by the Constitution as the legitimate heir of the dynasty. Indeed, his father, Don Juan de Borbón, had waived his hereditary rights in favour of Juan Carlos on 14 May 1977, before the Constitution was enacted. He realized that Franco's decision to prefer Juan Carlos was now a *fait accompli*. It made no sense to try to reverse things. The discreet ceremony where the waiver of rights took place, however, had a certain 'revolutionary' character from a legal point of view. Because Franco had never restored the monarchy, he was free, as a dictator, to appoint anybody he wanted to become his successor. The waiver ceremony suggested otherwise – that Franco's legality was insufficient to determine the heir to the throne.

It is sometimes objected that the democratic sources of the monarchy are insufficient: in the 1978 referendum, people were asked to express their opinion about the Constitution as a whole, and not specifically about the maintenance of the monarchy. By way of reply, it can be argued that citizens were fully aware that the Crown was a crucial piece in the package that emerged from the conciliatory politics the framers had engaged in. It is true that a more focused referendum, like the one that was held in Italy after the Second World War, where citizens were specifically asked whether they approved of the monarchy, would have provided a stronger democratic warrant. But this does not necessarily mean that the democratic credentials are insufficient. For many decades, the polls have revealed that the Crown is widely supported by public opinion. In a survey in November 2006 undertaken by the Centro de Investigaciones Sociológicas, for example, the monarchy came out as the institution with the highest score. In a scale from 0–10, it received 5.19. In another survey conducted by Metroscopia on October 2007, 69 per cent of citizens supported the monarchy, while only 22 per cent preferred a republican form of government.[3] As we saw in chapter one, moreover, the left was able to reduce the role of the monarchy by including that issue in a larger constitutional pact. Paradoxically, a separate referendum on the Crown might have led to a different type of monarchy, one that would have been subject to fewer parliamentary constraints.

Things have started to change in recent times, however. As was noted in the introduction, the recent scandals concerning the business activities of Iñaki Urdangarín, the King's son-in-law, have eroded the prestige of the Crown. And the behaviour of the King himself, taking a hunting trip to Botswana, has deeply harmed the institution. The public media, moreover, now discuss with total frankness issues that were regarded as 'taboo' some years ago. That the King's marriage is in crisis, for example, is an open secret. Freedom of speech is more robust now than it was some decades ago. In 1982, for example, a journalist was convicted of a crime of *injurias al Jefe del Estado*, for having published an article criticizing Juan Carlos for his past involvement with Franco. The Constitutional Court finally quashed the decision, on freedom of speech grounds.[4] It would now be unthinkable for anyone to be punished for saying such things. This is ultimately healthy for the institution. The King should be aware of what different sections of society opine about him.

THE KING'S SYMBOLIC FUNCTION

The Constitution assigns an important symbolic role to the King, but no real governmental powers are bestowed upon him. According to article 56, the monarch is the Head of State, the symbol of its unity and permanence; he arbitrates and moderates the well-functioning of the institutions; he assumes the highest representation of Spain in international relations and he exercises the functions that are expressly attributed to him by the Constitution and the laws. The Constitution then specifies, in articles 62 and 63, a list of acts that it is for the King to formally adopt. As a matter of fact, the content of these acts is decided by other political institutions. The King does not even take the initiative, except in a

---

[3] JM Magone, *Contemporary Spanish Politics* (London and New York, Routledge, 2009) 91.

[4] STC 20/1990.

few cases (such as when the King wishes to award honours and distinctions, for example).

The symbolic role of the King as the expression of the unity and permanence of the State is particularly notable. Such unity can be understood to include two dimensions. One is political: all citizens are equal members of the community, no matter what political party they vote for. The different Governments implement distinct programmes, in light of diverse ideological conceptions. But the King symbolically represents all citizens, no matter their political sympathies, since he is above politics. The other dimension is territorial.[5] The rich diversity of languages and cultures that characterizes Spain is reduced to unity through some common institutions. The King is one of them. The Crown does not belong to the national as opposed to the regional level. It symbolizes the State as a whole, including all its parts. In this connection, it is interesting that the Constitution establishes that the King, on being proclaimed before the Cortes Generales, shall take an oath to guard the Constitution and the laws, and to respect the rights of citizens 'and of the Autonomous Communities' (article 61.1).

THE COUNTERSIGNATURE REQUIREMENT

In order to make sure that the King exercises no real power, the Constitution categorically provides in article 56.3 that the King's acts 'shall always be countersigned' by the President of the Government, the Ministers, or the President of Congress, as the case may be, having no 'validity' whatsoever if they are not. The general rule is that the countersignature (*refrendo*) is provided either by the President of the Government or by a Minister. There are only two instances where the countersignature must be supplied by a different office-holder, the President of Congress. This is so when a President of the Government is proposed or appointed, and when the parliamentary chambers are dissolved as a result of the impossibility of selecting a President of the Government.[6]

Incidentally, it should be noted that the Constitutional Court has held that an ordinary law cannot extend the list of officers entitled to ratify

---

[5] M Herrero y Rodríguez de Miñón, 'La posición constitucional de la Corona' in *Estudios sobre la Constitución española (Homenaje al Profesor E García de Enterría)* (Madrid, Civitas, 1991) Tomo III, 1930–33.

[6] See art 64.1 of the Constitution.

the King's acts. Even if a different officer from those mentioned in the Constitution is actually closer to the institution that has made the underlying decision that the King has to sign, that officer cannot be given the authority to countersign. So, for example, when a regional legislative assembly elects the President of the Autonomous Community, the formal appointment is made by the King.[7] The countersignature must be supplied by the President of the national Government, not by the President of the regional assembly, even if the latter is closer to the institution that made the substantive decision. An ordinary statute cannot alter the rules the Constitution establishes in this connection (STC 5/1987 and STC 8/1987).

The Constitution, however, sets out some minor exceptions to the countersignature requirement. First, the King can freely appoint and remove the civil and military members of his household (article 65.2). Second, he can freely distribute the amount of money fixed in the budget to sustain his family and household (article 65.1). In addition, of course, he can make his own decisions in the sphere of his personal life – such as choosing a spouse, for example. It is debatable whether other acts need to be countersigned, such as his decision to appoint in his will a tutor for the future King (article 60.1), or his decision to abdicate (article 57.5).

It should be noted, parenthetically, that the amount that is assigned to the King's household (*Casa de Su Majestad el Rey*) is fixed by the Government on the basis of a proposal sent by the royal house. It figures as the first section of the State's general budget, and needs to be approved by Parliament on an annual basis. These funds are meant to cover the regular expenses of the King's household and the royal family. Some of the expenses are taken care of directly by various ministerial departments, however. Thus, the trips to foreign countries are covered by the Ministry of Foreign Affairs; security is paid by the Ministry of the Interior; some civil servants are directly paid by the Ministry of the Presidency; and the royal palaces are part of the National Patrimony, so that the expenses to maintain the buildings in good shape are the responsibility of the entity that is in charge of the National Patrimony. The amount fixed in the general budget for the King's household in 2011, for example, was €8,434,280. This was 5.2 per cent lower than the budget that was drawn up the previous year, a reduction that was decided

---

[7] See art 152.1 of the Constitution.

as part of the overall restrictive policies to confront Spain's fiscal crisis. In 2012, the budget was further reduced by 2.02 per cent.

Because the monarchy that the Constitution establishes is of a 'parliamentary' sort, as article 1.3 of the Constitution proclaims, the general pattern is for the King to merely give form to decisions made elsewhere in the political system. Not only is the countersignature required for his acts to be valid. He is actually under the duty to sign the acts that formalize the underlying decisions made by the democratically-accountable political branches. A few examples will clarify this.

According to the Constitution, for instance, the King is in charge of 'appointing and removing the members of the Government, as proposed by its President' (article 62). The decision to appoint or remove someone is actually taken by the President. The King merely issues the act that formalizes that decision. It is obvious that the King cannot adopt that act alone, for it would be invalid without the countersignature stamped by the President of the Government. But the King is even more constrained: if the President decides to appoint or remove a member of his Cabinet, the King must sign the pertinent act. It is true that, literally interpreted, the Constitution simply says that the King's acts are not valid without the proper countersignature. It does not say that the King must sign whatever is sent to his table by the other political institutions. But it would be inconsistent with the very notion of a parliamentary monarchy to draw a distinction between actions and omissions in this context. It would make no sense to hold that nothing the King does is valid without the countersignature, but that the King is nevertheless free to refuse any formal act that requires his signature.

Similarly, the Constitution establishes that the King appoints the justices of the Constitutional Court, on the proposals made by Congress, the Senate, the Government and the General Council of the Judiciary (article 159.1). The appointments are formally made by the King, but it is these other institutions that make the pertinent decisions. The monarch must be understood to be required to accept their proposals.

THE ROLE OF THE KING IN SELECTING THE GOVERNMENT

The King takes a part in the procedure to appoint the President of the Government. According to the Constitution, Congress cannot unilaterally vote someone to become President. It is the King's function to make a proposal. The candidate then goes to Congress to explain his or her governmental programme and seek the vote of a majority of deputies. (Absolute majority is required in a first vote; failing that, simple majority is sufficient 48 hours later). If the candidate gets the necessary votes, the King must appoint that person President. The Constitution is uncontroversial when it says that the King 'shall' appoint him or her. The potential controversy arises at the initial stage. How much margin of manoeuvre does the King enjoy when he proposes a candidate?

The Constitution establishes two clear limits on the King's authority on this front. It provides, first, that the King shall hear the leaders of the political groups that are represented in Parliament. Second, the King's proposal must be countersigned by the President of Congress. Without that countersignature, the proposal is invalid. These two constraints should push the King to present a candidate that the political parties have told him will enjoy the required parliamentary support. Consequently, when a political party has obtained an absolute majority of seats in Congress, there is no doubt that the King will nominate the person that figured in the electoral process as the candidate to the Prime Ministership. When no party has garnered an absolute majority of seats, but it is clear that only the victorious party has any possibility to govern, the King has no discretion at all either. Up to now, these are the two scenarios that have emerged after the general elections. If a third scenario arose in the future, under which more than one Government were possible, given the electoral results and the various coalition agreements, the expectation is that the King would wait for the political parties to negotiate and publicize a coalition agreement. He would then act accordingly. It would be embarrassing for him to propose someone who would lose the parliamentary vote, when a different candidate was known by the public and the political parties to have the necessary support.

Similarly, the King is not likely to interfere with party politics when the governing party or coalition gets into a crisis. In 1980, for example, Adolfo Suárez resigned as President of the Government, once he realized that he no longer had the support of his own party, UCD. Even in the extremely difficult situation that Spain confronted at that time (due to terrorism, rumours of military rebellions, and a serious economic crisis, among other things), the King waited for the governing political party to hold its congress. Once the party decided to select Leopoldo Calvo-Sotelo to replace Suárez, the King proceeded to appoint him as candidate. (As was already noted, it was during the parliamentary session on 23 February 1981 to vote on Calvo-Sotelo's investiture that Antonio Tejero's failed military *coup d'état* took place).

THE KING'S AUTHORITY TO SANCTION THE LAWS

A controversial issue concerns the King's role in 'sanctioning and promulgating the laws' enacted by Parliament (article 62). One of the traditional attributes of kings in ancient times was to decide whether or not to assent to the laws. The kings were empowered to veto legislation passed by the popular assembly. Under a parliamentary monarchy, however, the king loses this veto power. Even though the royal sanction may still be formally necessary, the assumption is that the king cannot refuse to sign the laws. Article 91 of the Spanish Constitution seems quite categorical when it provides that the monarch 'shall sanction' the laws passed by the Cortes Generales, and 'shall promulgate them and order their immediate publication'. The article establishes a time-limit of 15 days, moreover, for these purposes. This clear language does not seem to admit of any possible exception. It bears emphasis that one of the deals that were struck at the constitutional stage in 1977–78 was that the Crown would be reduced to a symbolic institution. If the King refused to sign particular laws, the constitutional equilibrium that was then achieved between the monarchical and the republican political forces would be disrupted.[8]

The King himself seems to be aware of this. When the first abortion law was passed by a socialist majority in 1985, for example, some conservative circles published articles pressing the King to reject the law. The Bishop of Cuenca said that the King should object on conscientious grounds. But Juan Carlos was impervious to these pressures. It is now taken for granted that he will always sign. Indeed, when a new law was passed in 2005 allowing same-sex marriage, the King was asked by some journalists whether he would sign it. He responded that he was not King Baudouin of Belgium – who some years earlier, in 1990, had generated a big constitutional crisis in his country when he asked the Government to suspend his powers for some hours, so that he would

---

[8] See JJ Solozábal Echavarría, *La sanción y promulgación de la ley en la monarquía parlamentaria* (Madrid, Tecnos, 1987).

not have to stamp his signature on an abortion statute that he disagreed with on Catholic moral grounds. We should bear in mind that Juan Carlos was born in Rome, in 1938, into a royal family that was in exile. The fact that his grandfather, Alfonso XIII, had to abandon Spain when the Second Republic was established is a good reminder of the risks for a king to stand in opposition to the parliamentary majority.

It is sometimes suggested that the King should be empowered to veto laws in very exceptional cases, however, either because the King thinks the law is clearly unconstitutional, or because he finds it extremely objectionable on moral or other grounds. The problem with this thesis is that, once a small exception is permitted, the integrity of the Crown is quickly eroded. The minute the King breaks the taboo and refuses to sanction a law in a particular case, not only does the King show his opposition to the majority that has passed that law, but the expectation starts to develop that the King will have something to say about future laws. If, on future occasions, the King sanctions controversial statutes, comparisons will be made. The King will reveal what his preferences and priorities are. The advantage of the King being expected to sanction all the laws without exception is that nobody takes his signature to entail any kind of endorsement. It is a mechanical act, which is not to be interpreted to mean that he agrees with the law in question.

Even if the grounds for refusing to sign a law were based on constitutional principles, the path taken by the King would be dangerous. For many citizens, the distinction between a law being unconstitutional and a law being wrong is not so clear. The King would be entering political debates if he acted as a constitutional guardian. It is true that the Constitution establishes in article 61.1 that the King must swear in his proclamation that he will guard the Constitution (*guardar y hacer guardar la Constitución*). But this commitment has to be understood in the context of the parliamentary monarchy that article 1.3 announces. The King cannot become the guardian of the Constitution through the exercise of powers that are inconsistent with the parliamentary nature of the regime. It should be noted, in addition, that, strictly speaking, article 61.1 cannot be relied upon to justify King Juan Carlos' alleged authority to veto laws, for he never took that oath, as was noted earlier.

The fact, moreover, that the Constitutional Court has the monopoly to declare that a law is unconstitutional is obviously in tension with the idea that the King is also to serve as a check. One of the advantages of the Court, in addition to its legal expertise, is that it can focus its review on the particular provisions that are deemed to be unconstitutional. The King, in contrast, would have to veto the whole statute, and not only the specific provision that was found to be objectionable.

THE KING'S POLITICAL NEUTRALITY

There are, in sum, good arguments to justify the conclusion that the King cannot refuse to adopt the formal acts that express the decisions that are made by the pertinent democratic institutions. This is in keeping with the political neutrality that the Crown should observe. Only that neutrality ensures that the King will be a 'symbol of the unity of the State'.

In this regard, the law regulating the elections establishes that all the members of the Royal Family, as well as their spouses, cannot stand as political candidates.[9] This is in order to preserve the Crown's neutrality. They are not denied, however, the right to vote. As a matter of fact, the King has never exercised this right, except when referenda have been held. He participated in the referenda to ratify the 1976 Law on Political Reform, to ratify the Constitution of 1978 and, most controversially, to decide on Spain's continued membership in NATO.

The King's general attitude of neutrality does not mean, of course, that he should be indifferent to the values of the constitutional system. In his messages to the nation, for example, he is expected to endorse those values. Nor does neutrality mean that the King should be uninterested in politics. The Constitution explicitly establishes in article 62 that the King must be informed of State affairs. The law authorizes him to request any report from the various ministerial departments. The Constitution also permits the monarch to preside over the sessions of the Council of Ministers, if he deems it appropriate, but only if the President of the Government so requests (article 62). The meetings between the monarch and the President of the Government are quite frequent, and so are his meetings with Ministers (especially that of Foreign Affairs). The King may express his own opinion and advice during these encounters – but they are kept confidential.

The King, in particular, has developed a prominent role in foreign affairs. In the past, for example, he made frequent visits to Latin

---

[9]   See art 6, LOREG, *Ley Orgánica 5/1985 del Régimen Electoral General.*

American countries that were facing transitions to democracy, and he exploited his moral capital as the engine of the Spanish transition to give advice, and to press the existing Governments in the region to move towards a democratic regime. Nowadays, he has a significant presence in the summits of the Comunidad Iberoamericana. It must be mentioned that he is the first King of Spain ever to have visited Spanish America. Also, his close connections to royal families in other countries have given Juan Carlos some leverage that the Spanish Government has taken advantage of on various occasions. The King's personal links with monarchies in the Arab world (such as Morocco and Jordan) have been particularly salient.

In addition, the King is familiar with military matters. He can attend the meetings of the Consejo de Defensa Nacional, for example. The Constitution provides that he is the 'supreme commander of the armed forces' (article 62). It is the Government, however, that defines and implements military policies, in accordance with the laws passed by Parliament. The Constitution clearly establishes that the Government directs the military administration and the defence of the State (article 97).[10] It is true that in the extraordinary circumstances of the *coup d'état* of 23 February 1981, Juan Carlos played a crucial role to convince the rebels to stop the uprising. The latter had taken Congress, and the Government was held hostage. The King exercised an important de facto power, as a unifying figure in the country, and as someone who had pursued a military education that had allowed him to establish close relationships with the highest officials. But it is not his role to lead the army, not even under the exceptional situations of alarm, exception and siege regulated in article 116 of the Constitution. What happened in the February crisis of 1981 was that the exceptional measures regulated in article 116 could not be taken, for the relevant office-holders were under the control of the rebels.[11]

THE KING'S IMMUNITY

The Constitution proclaims that the King is 'inviolable' and is not subject to responsibility (article 56.3). This makes sense, to the extent that

[10] See, also, art 5, *Ley Orgánica 5/2005 de la Defensa Nacional.*
[11] For an engaging literary exercise on the protagonists of the *coup d'état*, see J Cercas, *The Anatomy of a Moment* (Bloomsbury Publishing, 2011).

his acts need to be countersigned. The Constitution establishes that responsibility for the King's acts is to be placed on the persons who countersign them (article 64.2).

This rule operates quite smoothly at the political level. The King cannot be accountable for any of the acts that are formally attributed to him. Since he takes no real part in the decision-making process, there is nothing he should be made to answer for.

As far as criminal liability is concerned, however, we may need to draw some distinctions. If the crime has been committed through any of the acts that are formally ascribed to the monarch, it is clear that he is exempt. Only the office-holders who countersign the acts (or who made the underlying decisions) are criminally liable. Arguably, therefore, there was no constitutional problem for Spain to ratify the Rome Statute of the International Criminal Court. Article 27 of this Treaty provides that official capacity as a Head of State 'shall in no case exempt a person from criminal responsibility' under the Statute. To the extent that criminal responsibility is triggered by an act that is formally adopted by the King, the burden must be placed on the shoulders of the persons who took the underlying decision or ratified it.[12]

Things get more complicated, however, when the criminal action is not tied to the King's official capacity. Suppose he murders someone. Is he protected against the enforcement of criminal law? There has been debate about this issue.[13] There is no provision in the Criminal Code that supplies an answer. The discussion develops on the constitutional plane. Some scholars maintain that he is immune even in that case. The King is 'inviolable', after all. Others think this outcome runs against the principle of equal treatment under the law, and is not very helpful to maintain the prestige of the Crown. They suggest that the King can be declared 'incapacitated' (*inhabilitado*) to exercise his authority. They rely on article 59.2, which provides that the Cortes Generales may establish that the King is incapacitated. A regent is then to be appointed. The King having lost his office, he no longer enjoys inviolability, and he can thus be prosecuted, convicted and punished. It is controversial, however, whether

---

[12] On this issue, the Council of State published a report on 22 July 1999, concluding that there was no contradiction between the Rome Statute and the Spanish Constitution. The report is available at www.consejo-estado.es.

[13] See L Rodríguez Ramos, 'La inviolabilidad del Rey' in M Cobo del Rosal, *Comentarios a la legislación penal, Tomo I (Derecho penal y Constitución)* (Madrid, EDERSA, 1982) 281–87.

this is a fair reading of article 59.2. It is not obvious that the monarch is deprived of the immunity privilege when he is incapacitated.

With respect to civil liability, the King is also personally protected. The Casa de Su Majestad el Rey is the institution that has legal personality to contract, and can thus engage in liability and ultimately be sued.[14]

REGENCY, GUARDIANSHIP, MARRIAGE AND SUCCESSION

The Constitution includes clauses dealing with various specific issues. It establishes a system to appoint a regent, when the King is a minor or is incapacitated (article 59). It also provides for the appointment of a guardian, to take care of the King during his minority (article 60). A specific limitation is also established, concerning the persons with a right of succession to the throne: if they form a particular marriage against the express prohibition of the King and the Cortes Generales, those persons are excluded from the line of succession, and so are their descendants (article 57.4). The Constitution also stipulates that the King's spouse (called Queen) and the Queen's spouse (not called King) cannot assume any constitutional functions, except those of the regency (article 58).

The Constitution, in addition, lays down the rules to pick the King's successor. It incorporates the traditional criteria that have been applied in Spain for these purposes, and which can ultimately be traced to the medieval *Ley de Partidas* of King Alfonso X. In the event that all the lines of succession were extinguished, the Cortes Generales would then select the successor most appropriate to Spain's interests (article 57.3).

We need not delve into the details of all these rules, except to highlight a feature that has given rise to some controversy: article 57.1 of the Constitution gives preference to men over women, within the same line and degree of succession. Although women can be crowned, they suffer discrimination, since men have priority. Thus, Juan Carlos and his wife, Queen Sofia, have three children. The first two children are female (Elena and Cristina); the third is a male (Felipe). By virtue of the discriminatory rule, Felipe is the Prince entitled to become King. Prince Felipe, in his turn, has had two children with his wife (Princess Letizia), both of whom are girls (Leonor and Sofía). If no more children are

---

[14] The Casa de Su Majestad el Rey is regulated in *Real Decreto 434/1988*.

born in the future, the eldest daughter, Leonor, will be the future Princess, and no discriminatory rule will be applied. But if a son were born, he would be first in line.

Obviously this discriminatory treatment of women is not in keeping with the basic convictions of most citizens. Political parties are in agreement that this deviation from the principle of sex equality is no longer acceptable. In 2005, under José Luis Rodríguez Zapatero's Government, a proposal was discussed to reform the Constitution in this regard. The plan was to eliminate the effects of the rule in the future, while preserving the rights of Prince Felipe. The proposal was part of a larger reform that also affected other sections of the Constitution (concerning the European Union, the Autonomous Communities, and the Senate). The Consejo de Estado issued an important report on the proposed reform.[15] The main party then in the opposition, the PP (Partido Popular) was not supportive of the overall reform, however, and the effort was abandoned. This party did not defend the discriminatory rule of article 57.1, but disagreed with other aspects of the larger project.

One of the problems is that for article 57.1 to be amended the extraordinary procedure of article 168 (not the normal procedure of article 167) needs to be followed. As was explained in chapter three, any reform that 'affects' Title II of the Constitution is covered by the special procedure of article 168, and it just happens that the discriminatory rule under examination is included in Title II. This entails that a super-majority of two-thirds of both parliamentary chambers must initiate the process, general elections need to be held immediately, a new Parliament must approve the reform by a two-thirds super-majority, and the people must ratify the decision in a referendum. There is fear in some quarters that such a referendum might be used as a plebiscite on the monarchy. But quite apart from this sort of fear, many people have the impression that it makes no sense to have to follow all these steps to eliminate this ridiculous discriminatory rule. The framers appear to have been a little clumsy: they established article 168, not only to protect the monarchy as a general institution, but also to freeze all the more detailed rules on the Crown that are of lesser importance. Is there a way around this problem?

---

[15] See the report of 16 February 2006, available at www.consejo-estado.es. For scholarly comments on this document, see *El Informe del Consejo de Estado sobre la reforma constitucional. Texto del informe y debates académicos* (Madrid, Consejo de Estado y Centro de Estudios Políticos y Constitucionales, 2006).

One way, of course, would be to change the amendment rules them-selves. If article 168 is deemed to be too rigid, it is possible to modify it. The discriminatory rule of article 57.1, in particular, could be excluded from the list of clauses that are protected by article 168, so that any future amendment of article 57.1 could be passed through the less oner-ous procedure regulated in article 167. The problem, however, is that such a change can only be introduced through the demanding proce-dure of article 168. This means, among other things, that a referendum must be held. Now, it would be quite remarkable to ask citizens whether they agree to change article 168 to transfer certain matters (such as the discriminatory rule of article 57.1) to the normal procedure of article 167. This seems too technical a question to ask people in a referendum. It would be better, therefore, to make that question part of a more ambitious constitutional reform that deals with other matters citizens are more familiar with.

The rigidity of the Spanish Constitution in this regard appears to be so intolerable that imaginative solutions have been advanced. Miquel Roca, for example, one of the seven *padres de la Constitución* (that is, one of the seven members of the Ponencia that drafted the Constitution), has argued in several public speeches as follows: there is a clear tension between the discriminatory rule of article 57.1 and the sex equality principle enshrined in article 14. In some jurisdictions, it is possible to assert that a constitu-tional clause (whether included in the original Constitution, or introduced later by way of an amendment) is contrary to a deep constitutional princi-ple and is thus invalid. In Germany, most notably, the Constitution has been read by the Constitutional Court to embody a system of values that makes it possible for the Court to conclude that a particular constitutional clause is invalid. In Spain, there is scholarly debate on this issue. This means that there is a 'legal doubt' as to what to do when confronting a contradiction between the rules on succession, on the one hand, and the principle of equality, on the other. Now, the Constitution includes a provi-sion (article 57.5) to the effect that 'any factual or legal doubt with respect to the order of succession' shall be resolved by an organic law passed by Parliament. In so far as there is a legal doubt about the applicability of article 57.1, given its tension with the principle of equality enshrined in article 14, Parliament should be deemed to be authorized to enact an organic statute clarifying that men are not to be given priority over women. That statute should be taken to 'resolve' the doubt about the succession, and would arguably be immune against constitutional attack.

One wonders whether this reading offered by Miquel Roca is still a fair interpretation of the Constitution, or is instead a well-intentioned effort to repair one of its defects under an interpretive guise. The fact that the thesis has been advanced by one of the constitutional framers raises many interesting issues on the theory of interpretation. (Should the interpretive opinions of the framers have special weight? Should we distinguish between those framers who have left politics, and those who have not?). In any case, this controversy illustrates the troubles that may result from the fact that the Constitution is so hard to amend in some fields. As the monarchy adapts itself to the new times, and as Prince Felipe gets prepared for his future role as King of Spain, the need to eliminate the discriminatory rule is more strongly felt, not only by society at large, but by the royal family too. Quite likely, only by including the removal of this discriminatory rule into a larger package of constitutional reforms will it ever be eliminated.

CONCLUSION

The preservation of the monarchy under the Constitution is an example of the conciliatory politics that the framers practiced in 1977–78. The institution was maintained, but many qualifications were introduced to make it consistent with democratic principles. The basic technique to ensure that the King merely reigns, but does not govern, is the countersignature requirement. No act by the King is valid unless it is ratified by the President of the Government or the pertinent Minister. But consistency with democracy is not enough to justify the existence of the monarchy. It is necessary for it to perform a role that most citizens believe serves an important public purpose. The King can be a symbolic expression of the unity of the country, for example, and he is in a position to help the Government at the international level in informal ways. These and other responsibilities may bring public opinion to endorse the Crown, thus renewing the support that was indirectly expressed in the 1978 referendum to ratify the Constitution. But popular acceptance of the Crown requires, in addition, a certain measure of respect for the King and his royal family, whose private and public behaviour should be exemplary. It is in this connection that the prestige of the Crown has seriously suffered in recent times. The succession of King Juan Carlos by his son Prince Felipe will be the great test in the coming years.

FURTHER READING

Aragón Reyes, M, *Dos estudios sobre la monarquía parlamentaria en la Constitución española* (Madrid, Civitas, 1990).

García Canales, M, *La monarquía parlamentaria española* (Madrid, Tecnos, 1991).

Porras Ramírez, JM, *Principio democrático y función regia en la Constitución normativa* (Madrid, Tecnos, 1995).

Powell, C, *Juan Carlos of Spain. Self-made Monarch* (St Anthony's/Macmillan, 1995).

Solozábal Echavarría, JJ, *La sanción y promulgación de la ley en la monarquía parlamentaria* (Madrid, Tecnos, 1987).

5

Parliament

Introduction – The Electoral System – The Status of Members of Parliament – Parliament's Regulatory Autonomy: The Role of By-laws or Standing Orders – Parliament's Internal Organization – Parliament's Role in Selecting and Checking the Government – Parliament as a Legislative Body – The Future of the Senate – Conclusion

INTRODUCTION

The national Parliament, the Cortes Generales, is a key institution in Spanish democracy. The Constitution conceives it as the organ that 'represents the Spanish people' (article 66.1). Since Members of Parliament are the only representatives that are directly elected by citizens at the national level, this proposition is well-grounded. Other institutions in the governmental scheme, in contrast, derive their democratic legitimacy, at least in part, from their connections to the Cortes Generales. The President of the Government, for example, as well as other office-holders, such as the Ombudsman, the members of the General Council of the Judiciary, and most judges of the Constitutional Court, are selected by Parliament. The regional legislative assemblies, in turn, are also directly elected by citizens, but they do not represent the Spanish people as a whole, but only a fragment of it.

In what follows, we will first study the electoral rules that govern the selection of the deputies and senators. We will then examine their status and some of the privileges that are linked to it. We will then proceed to study Parliament's internal organization, and will finally focus on the most relevant functions that are entrusted to it. As we will see, even if the Government has a dominant position in parliamentary life, there is some space for parties in the opposition to influence the contents of legislation, and to control the executive branch.

THE ELECTORAL SYSTEM

The Constitution includes several provisions concerning the electoral system. This is exceptional in Spanish history, since earlier Constitutions (except for that of 1812) basically delegated the regulation of the elections to the ordinary legislature. This resulted in a very unstable normative framework. The current Constitution, in contrast, addresses the matter. Its norms, moreover, have been developed and specified through an organic law that has been very stable: the *Ley Orgánica 5/1985, del Régimen Electoral General* (hereinafter: LOREG). This law preserves many of the features of the 1977 law under which the first democratic elections were held after the fall of the dictatorship.[1]

One of the main worries of the constitutional framers was to avoid the high level of parliamentary fragmentation that had occurred during the Second Republic. They wanted to make sure that the number of political parties that captured congressional and senatorial seats under the new system would be relatively low, so that governmental stability would be facilitated.[2] As we will see, the electoral system has been effective in this regard.

The elections to both Congress and the Senate take place periodically. The Constitution establishes that the term of both houses is four years (articles 68.4 and 69.6). When the term expires, new elections are automatically called. It is possible, however, for Parliament to be dissolved before the four-year period has elapsed. The President of the Government, in particular, has the authority to dissolve the legislative assembly and call early elections (article 115).[3] This is a powerful weapon in his hands, as we will see. The Constitution also establishes two instances where early dissolution is required as a matter of law:

[1] See *Real Decreto-ley 20/1977.*

[2] R Gunther, JR Montero and J Botella, *Democracy in Modern Spain* (New Haven, Yale University Press, 2004) 88–89.

[3] The Constitution gives the President discretion to decide whether to dissolve both chambers of Parliament, or only one of them. In practice, however, the dissolution has always affected both. As a result, the congressional and the senatorial elections have always been held simultaneously.

when the special procedure of constitutional amendment is initiated (article 168) and when Congress has been unable to invest a President of the Government after a certain period of time has elapsed (article 99.5).

The elections extend to the totality of deputies or senators. There are no partial elections. There is only one exception to this principle of complete renewal. As we will see, a small group of senators is appointed by the regional parliaments. The pertinent regional laws regulate the term of such senators, and may choose to make it dependent on the term of the regional parliament (STC 40/1981).

Political parties are the key players during the elections, as was already noted in chapter two. They propose the lists of candidates for citizens to vote for. In the case of Congress, the lists are 'closed' (citizens cannot choose candidates from different lists) and 'blocked' (the order of the names cannot be altered). In the case of the Senate, in contrast, the lists are open: citizens can freely choose the candidates, drawn from all the different lists. In practice, however, citizens very rarely exercise this freedom. Normally, they do not alter the lists made up by the political parties of their choice.

In general, the participation of citizens in the general elections to Congress and the Senate is relatively high, especially when the elections lead to a parliamentary majority of a different political colour. Since the first democratic elections of 1977, the level of participation has been this: 78.83 per cent (1977), 68.04 per cent (1979), 79.97 per cent (1982), 70.94 per cent (1986), 69.74 per cent (1989), 76.44 per cent (1993), 77.38 per cent (1996), 68.71 per cent (2000), 75.66 per cent (2004), 73.85 per cent (2008) and 68.94 per cent (2011).[4]

The electoral rules that apply to Congress differ from those of the Senate, as will be explained next.

Congress

Congress consists of 350 deputies. The Constitution merely says that the number must be at least 300 and no more than 400. The LOREG enacted in 1985 chose the number to be 350 (which was

---

[4] These results refer to Congress. The figures for the Senate are roughly the same. The information is available at www.infoelectoral.mir.es/min.

already the number under the 1977 law). The deputies are not elected in a single, nation-wide district, but in different districts. For these purposes, each of the 50 provinces in Spain is a district. In addition, the two Spanish cities in Africa (Ceuta and Melilla) elect a deputy each.

The Constitution requires the system to be based on the principle of proportional representation, but it introduces and allows for qualifications. First, the number of deputies that are allotted to each district depends on its population. A minimal representation is guaranteed to each district, however. Under current law, two seats are automatically assigned. As a result, rural areas are over-represented in comparison to urban areas. Second, the distribution of seats among the different political parties depends on the number of votes each party has obtained in the pertinent district. The Constitution does not require the system to be purely proportional, however. It permits the use of formulas that reduce proportionality to a certain extent. The LOREG has chosen the so-called 'D'Hondt formula', which does not generate pure proportionality. The law, moreover, imposes certain requirements before the votes of a political party can be counted at all for purposes of the distribution of seats. A minimum threshold of 3 per cent of the votes in the district must be satisfied. If no such percentage is achieved, the votes obtained in that district are therefore 'lost': they cannot be taken into account for purposes of getting representation in a different district. The threshold was once challenged, but it was upheld by the Constitutional Court (STC 75/1985). Actually, because voters are aware of the fact that the system penalizes smaller parties, they tend to cast 'useful votes' (*voto útil*), in favour of less preferred (but still acceptable) parties with a greater probability of securing seats in the district.[5]

The system is not in practice very proportional, however, since too few seats are at stake in most districts. Experts say that seven is the minimum number of representatives per district that guarantees some measure of proportionality. Since many provinces in Spain get less than seven deputies, the result cannot be very proportional. To correct this feature of the electoral system, larger electoral units would be necessary (regions instead of provinces, for example). Whether this would be a desirable reform, however, is an open question. Some argue that it is good for the largest parties to be advantaged by the electoral system, as

---

[5] Gunther, Montero and Botella (n 2) 255–57.

they currently are, so that Parliament is not too fragmented, and so that governability is facilitated.[6]

To illustrate the degree to which the application of the current rules does not fully realize the principle of proportionality, here is the relevant information about the most recent general elections, which were held on 20 November 2011:

PP: 186 seats; 44.62% of the popular vote
PSOE: 110 seats; 28.73% of the popular vote
CiU: 16 seats; 4.17% of the popular vote
IU: 11 seats; 6.92% of the popular vote
AMAIUR: 7 seats; 1.37% of the popular vote
UPyD: 5 seats; 4.69% of the popular vote
EAJ-PNV: 5 seats; 1.33% of the popular vote
ERC: 3 seats; 1.05% of the popular vote
BNG: 2 seats; 0.75% of the popular vote
CC-NC-PNC: 2 seats; 0.59% of the popular vote
COMPROMÍS-Q: 1 seat; 0.51% of the popular vote
FAC: 1 seat; 0.4% of the popular vote
GBAI: 1 seat; 0.17% of the popular vote

As can be observed, a large number of parties obtained parliamentary representation. The distribution of seats is not purely proportional, however. The two largest parties (PP and PSOE) get some more seats than pure proportionality would allow. PP, with 44.62 per cent of the popular vote, obtained 186 seats, which is 53.14 per cent of the total number of seats. And PSOE, with 28.73 per cent of the popular vote, obtained 110 seats, which is 31.42 per cent of the total number. There is rough proportionality between these two parties, but both are advantaged by the system. It is also noteworthy that some of the smaller parties were attributed more seats than others that had obtained a larger amount of votes. This is true of the nationalist groups that run candidates in a single region. Both CiU (a Catalan party) and AMAIUR (a party from the Basque Country) obtained more seats than IU and UPyD did, in spite of the fact that the latter garnered more votes. This is a

---

[6] The Consejo de Estado issued an interesting report on these matters in February 2009, available at www.consejo-estado.es. For some doctrinal commentary, see *Informe del Consejo de Estado sobre la reforma electoral. Texto del informe y debates académicos* (Madrid, Consejo de Estado y Centro de Estudios Políticos y Constitucionales, 2009).

consequence of the fact that the electoral unit is the province, and most provinces are too small to guarantee proportionality. Many of the votes that IU and UPyD received were 'lost' – since they could not be translated into seats. CiU and AMAIUR, in contrast, concentrate their efforts in a few provinces – those of the region whose interests they wish to represent.

The Senate

The rules that apply to the Senate are different, and they deviate from proportionality more radically. Each province counts as an electoral district, entitled to appoint four senators each. In addition, Ceuta and Melilla get to elect two senators each. Special rules apply to the islands.[7] The total number of senators that are elected in accordance with these rules is 208. Since the difference between the most populous and the less populous provinces is very high, this rule generates a distribution of seats that is far from being proportional.

The Constitution says nothing about the system that needs to be followed to distribute the senatorial seats in each district. The LOREG establishes a majoritarian system, but of a moderate sort. According to that law, each citizen selects three candidates. The four candidates with the highest number of votes get appointed. The minority gets some representation, therefore, since each citizen is only entitled to pick three senators. (Special rules apply to the cities of Ceuta and Melilla, and to the islands). In the last elections, held on 20 November 2011, the results were these: PP: 136 seats; PSOE: 48 seats; CiU: 9 seats; PSC-ICV-EUA: 7 seats; EAJ-PNV: 4 seats; AMAIUR: 3 seats; CC-NC-PNC: 1 seat.

Since the voters formally pick senators individually, there is no official data about how many votes the different political parties received. But it is clear that the system deviates from proportionality more seriously than in the case of Congress. The victorious party (PP) has a much larger percentage of seats than the percentage of popular votes their senators obtained.

In addition to these so-called 'provincial' senators elected by the people, the Constitution establishes that the regional parliaments can

---

[7] Three senators are assigned to Gran Canaria, to Mallorca and to Tenerife. One senator is assigned to each of the following: Ibiza-Formentera, Menorca, Fuerteventura, Gomera, Hierro, Lanzarote and La Palma.

appoint some senators. Each Autonomous Community is entitled to at least one. Another senatorial seat is assigned for every million people that live in that territory. The regional parliament must select these so-called 'autonomic' senators through a system that ensures proportional representation (article 69.5 of the Constitution). Given the size and the distribution of the population in Spain, these rules do not lead to the appointment of many autonomic senators. The number is currently 58, which is relatively low when compared to the 208 provincial senators. Those seats are allocated among the Autonomous Communities in the following way: Andalucía (nine), Aragón (two), Asturias (two), Baleares (two), Canarias (three), Cantabria (one), Castilla-La Mancha (three), Castilla y León (three), Catalonia (eight), Comunitat Valenciana (six), Extremadura (two), Galicia (three), Madrid (seven), Murcia (two), Navarra (one), Basque Country (three), La Rioja (one).

This mixture of provincial and regional senators has attracted criticism. Many scholars have pointed out that, if the Senate is to become 'the chamber of territorial representation' where the voices of the regions can be heard (as article 69.1 of the Constitution proclaims), all its members (or at least a large majority of them) should be selected by the Autonomous Communities. In chapter seven, we will discuss the reforms the Senate might undergo, in light of some deeper transformations of Spanish regionalism.

THE STATUS OF MEMBERS OF PARLIAMENT

Conditions to Become Deputy or Senator

Once elected, the deputies and senators become Members of Parliament. Certain conditions have to be met, however. The Constitution, for example, establishes that being a Member of Parliament is incompatible with other positions, such as judge, member of the military and police forces, certain high governmental officials, the Ombudsman, and other positions established by the law (article 70.1). If there is an incompatibility, the deputy or senator has to choose which of the two offices in conflict to occupy.

The parliamentary standing orders, moreover, require deputies and senators to swear or promise that they will observe the Constitution.[8]

---

[8] See art 20.1.3, *Reglamento del Congreso de los Diputados* and art 11, *Reglamento del Senado*.

This condition was introduced in 1982, in the context of a difficult moment in Spanish democracy. The failed *coup d'état* of February 1981 led to a general feeling that it was important to strengthen the political parties' commitment to the Constitution. An oath of allegiance was thought to reinforce that commitment. In addition, Herri Batasuna, a Basque nationalist party, was posing a problem. This party had refused to participate in Parliament, on the grounds that it objected to the Constitution. Their deputies failed to show up in the legislative assembly, but they were counted as members of it, thus enjoying all the applicable rights and privileges. To respond to the situation created, the new standing orders introduced in 1982 conditioned the full enjoyment of the parliamentary status to the taking of the oath.[9]

The change proved controversial. The Constitutional Court was asked to rule on the meaning and effects of such an oath (SSTC 101/1983, 122/1983, 119/1990). It emphasized, first, that the oath is not a condition that needs to be fulfilled to become a Member of Parliament. The elections establish the only relevant title for these purposes. What the law can do is to condition the full enjoyment of the parliamentary status to the taking of the oath. This condition can be fulfilled, therefore, any time. Until this happens, the elected representative is not replaced by anyone else. Second, and more importantly, the Court held that the oath of allegiance should not be interpreted to express an endorsement of all the provisions that figure in the Constitution. It is perfectly possible to change the Constitution following the established procedures of amendment. The oath entails the commitment to respect those procedures, not an acceptance of the substantive content of the current norms. The Court thus concluded that it was acceptable for the parliamentary by-laws to require deputies and senators to promise their allegiance to the constitutional charter.

Interestingly, this 'procedural' reading of the oath is roughly the same that Torcuato Fernández-Miranda had advocated during the transition, with respect to the old laws of the dictatorship. Juan Carlos had asked this influential professor and politician about the fundamental laws of Franco's regime, which Juan Carlos had twice sworn to observe (in 1969, when he became Prince under Franco, and in 1975, when he became King after Franco's death). Since the King had some qualms

---

[9] On the origins of this rule, see F Caamaño Domínguez, *El mandato parlamentario* (Madrid, Congreso de los Diputados, 1991) 112–13.

about having sworn to guard a set of fundamental laws that he later helped to dismantle, Fernández-Miranda explained to him that what really mattered was the procedure, not the substance. Since the new Constitution of 1978 was enacted following the steps defined in the old laws, the King had committed no perjury.

The Constitutional Court also ruled that if the deputy or senator, when taking the oath, says that he does so 'by legal imperative', the act is still valid (STC 119/1990). Such a statement, the Court reasoned, does not vitiate the promise to observe the Constitution. It is perfectly possible for a Member of Parliament to take the oath, and later explain that he did so because the law so requires. It is also possible for a candidate to say that he will take the oath if he is elected, but only because the law imposes this requirement. If so, the Court concluded, we should not interpret that the oath becomes invalid if the expression 'by legal imperative' is immediately attached to it. The Court was quite generous, one must say. Arguably, there is a tension between this holding and the Court's procedural reading of the oath of allegiance. If, indeed, when a deputy or senator promises to observe the Constitution, he is not necessarily saying that he agrees with the substance of the document, but is merely expressing his commitment to abide by the procedures of constitutional amendment, there seems to be no justification for the promise to be qualified through any kind of formula. The sincerity of the commitment should be clear.

The Dominance of Political Parties and Parliamentary Groups

An interesting question concerns the power of political parties over Members of Parliament. The deputy or senator is technically free to act according to his or her own beliefs. As a matter of fact, though, the laws assume that political parties will play a large role in parliamentary life. Thus, all deputies and senators must necessarily belong to a 'parliamentary group'. (This is not established by the Constitution, however, but by the parliamentary by-laws).[10] Such groups, in practice, mirror the diverse political parties that run in the elections. Thus, it is not possible for a political party, or a coalition of parties that present the same lists at the

---

[10] On the legal status and functions of parliamentary groups, see A Saiz Arnaiz, *Los grupos parlamentarios* (Madrid, Congreso de los Diputados, 1989).

electoral stage, to create two different groups. A minimum number of deputies (15) or senators (10) is required to form a parliamentary group.[11] This means that the smallest parties at the national level will be unable to create one. In that case, their members will be ascribed to the so-called 'mixed group', which will inevitably be very heterogeneous.

The existence of parliamentary groups, which receive facilities and funds, is justified by the need to simplify the workings of the legislative assembly. When debates take place, for example, the participants are not individual deputies or senators, but the spokespeople of the different parliamentary groups. There is strong discipline within the groups, moreover. Members of Parliament can be fined by the groups they belong to if they fail to attend the meetings without justification, or if they do not vote according to the party line. In the Parliamentary Commissions, moreover, deputies and senators can be replaced by others at any point in time, according to party wishes.

Individual deputies and senators are also weak, as a result of their not having their own staff to help them with their parliamentary activities. They have to rely on the services provided by the groups they belong to, in order to get the information and the advice they need to deal with the complex issues that are discussed in a modern Parliament. It is important to note, in this connection, that there is a high level of rotation from legislature to legislature, sometimes reaching levels between 45 and 60 per cent.[12] This lack of continuity is not conducive, of course, to the professionalization of the Spanish Parliament.

Even the rights that are granted to individual Members of Parliament are sometimes subject to the requirement that the spokesperson of the parliamentary group be informed. The deputies and senators, for example, are entitled to request information from the executive branch. This request is transmitted by the parliamentary organs. The standing orders establish that the applicant must first inform his own group about the initiative.[13] The practice has been to ask for the signature of the spokesperson of the group. The problem is that the spokesperson may simply refuse to stamp the pertinent signature. The Constitutional Court has had to intervene to protect individual members in this regard. In 2007,

---

[11] Special rules apply in Congress to those parties that have not presented lists in all provinces. See art 23.1, *Reglamento del Congreso de los Diputados*.

[12] JM Magone, *Contemporary Spanish Politics* (London and New York, Routledge, 2009) 112.

[13] See art 7, *Reglamento del Congreso de los Diputados* and art 20.2, *Reglamento del Senado*.

for example, a deputy sought to obtain from the executive branch certain reports on the environmental impact of a particular dam in Seville. He sent a fax to his parliamentary group (the Socialist Group), explaining the terms of his request. Even if there was no doubt that the group had received the fax and was thus properly informed about the request, the application was rejected by the pertinent legislative bodies, for the spokesperson's signature was absent. The deputy filed a complaint before the Constitutional Court. The latter held that the deputy's fundamental rights had indeed been violated. The parliamentary practices, it reasoned, were in tension with the right to obtain information. If the only legal requirement was for the group to be notified, there was no reason to reject the request in this case. The deputy had complained, actually, that his group had been systematically obstructing his parliamentary work.[14]

So parliamentary groups (and the parties they stand for) are of great significance in practice. Now, what happens if a Member of Parliament is expelled from his party? Should he abandon his seat – which he obtained, after all, because he was included in the electoral list of that party? Or should he keep it? There has been great controversy over this problem. The Constitution explicitly says that the members of the Cortes Generales are not subject to *mandato imperativo* (article 67.2). The parliamentary mandate is 'free'. The historical meaning of this rule is clear: the Members of Parliament represent the interests of the nation in its entirety, and they meet in the general assembly in order to deliberate and negotiate. They cannot, therefore, be subjected to instructions issued by their local electors. The question, however, is whether Members of Parliament can also be immune from the decisions of the political parties, which the Constitution conceives as the main instruments of political participation (article 6). The Portuguese Constitution explicitly provides that deputies will lose their seats if they register as a member of a party other than that for which they stood for election (article 160). The Spanish Constitutional Court, in contrast, has ruled that the representative is entitled to keep the seat (STC 5/1983, STC 10/1983).[15] The Court's holding rests on the view that when citizens cast their votes in the elections, they express their support for individual

---

[14] The Court's decision is STC 57/2011.

[15] The Court's decision concerned a law that regulated municipal elections, but its holding is clearly applicable to members of the Cortes Generales.

representatives, and not for a political party. The Court is aware, of course, that (with the exception of the Senate) political parties present electoral lists that are closed (citizens cannot combine candidates from different parties) and blocked (citizens cannot alter the order of the candidates within a particular list). Yet, the Court insists that the individual representative is directly connected to the voters, so that it violates the latter's fundamental rights to political participation (as guaranteed in article 23 of the Constitution) for a law to provide that representatives must relinquish their seats if they are expelled from the party. Some judges in the Court filed dissenting opinions, however, and scholars disagree among themselves.

It is important to note that the Court has held that representatives retain their parliamentary posts when they are *expelled* from the party. It has not ruled on the different question that arises when representatives freely abandon their parties.[16] Some scholars are of the view that in this latter case it would be constitutional for the laws to provide that the deputies lose their seats.[17]

Parliamentary Privileges

Deputies and senators enjoy certain privileges that were historically necessary to protect Parliament against interferences from the executive branch. Because of the instrumental nature of these privileges, they cannot be waived by the individuals concerned. Whether their maintenance is justified nowadays is a debatable proposition, however. The Constitution establishes, first, that Members of Parliament shall enjoy 'inviolability' for the opinions they express in the course of their functions (article 71.1). No liability of any kind –whether civil, administrative or criminal – can be attached to those opinions. The votes are also protected, as part of the opinions. The privilege extends to the future, moreover: when the deputy or senator ceases to be a Member of Parliament, he cannot be sued for what he said or voted.

The Constitutional Court has given a restrictive interpretation of the scope of this privilege, however (STC 51/1985). It has held that only

---

[16] The Court, in its STC 28/1984 decision, made it clear that this was an open question.
[17] See, eg Caamaño Domínguez (n 9) 275.

the opinions that are expressed in Parliament (or that merely reproduce what was said in Parliament) are covered by the privilege. So what deputies and senators say in a press conference, for example, or in an electoral meeting, is speech that has to comply with whatever restrictions flow from the general free speech regime. Such statements are not absolutely privileged as opinions proffered in Parliament are. The Court has thus tried to reduce the ambit of the inviolability rule, to make it consistent with the principle of equality before the law.

The second privilege (mentioned in article 71.2 of the Constitution) is that deputies and senators cannot be arrested, save in the event of a flagrant crime. Moreover, they cannot be prosecuted without the authorization of their own parliamentary chamber. This privilege is called 'immunity', and seeks to protect the assembly against attempts to alter its composition or functioning through a politically-biased abuse of the criminal justice system. It does not matter whether the alleged facts took place before or after the person involved became a Member of Parliament.

Again, the Constitutional Court has read this privilege in a restrictive manner, to ensure equality before the law. It has insisted, first, that only criminal procedures are covered. It thus declared unconstitutional a law that tried to extend this privilege to civil cases (STC 9/1990). Second, the Court has held that Parliament must justify why it does not authorize the criminal prosecution against one of its members. If the justification is not persuasive, the Court can invalidate the parliamentary decision, as it once did (STC 206/1992).

The third privilege that the Constitution stipulates is that criminal charges against deputies and senators can only be decided by the Supreme Court (article 71.3). The justification for this prerogative is not obvious. It is sometimes said that Members of Parliament should be judged by the most qualified tribunal. This rationale does not sound very attractive – for it implies that ordinary citizens get a less qualified kind of justice when their cases are decided by the rest of courts. A different argument goes in the opposite direction: criminal cases against deputies and senators must be sent to the Supreme Court, in order to ensure that the judges will be courageous enough. Lower judges might be too timid, or not strong enough to resist pressures.

Whatever the rationale, the truth is that this privilege has posed a problem: if the Supreme Court convicts a deputy or senator of a crime, the decision cannot then be challenged, for there is no appeal to a higher court. (The Constitutional Court can only step in to correct errors in constitutional judgment, not to review the application of ordinary criminal law). This is in clear tension with the fundamental right to have a criminal conviction reviewed by a higher tribunal, a right that is included in the International Covenant on Civil and Political Rights (in article 14.5), and in Protocol 7 to the European Convention on Human Rights.[18]

PARLIAMENT'S REGULATORY AUTONOMY: THE ROLE OF BY-LAWS OR STANDING ORDERS

To protect Parliament's capacity to regulate its own internal life without governmental interference, the Constitution grants a special treatment to parliamentary by-laws or standing orders (*reglamentos parlamentarios*). Each chamber of the Cortes Generales freely passes its own by-laws.[19] No other law (besides the Constitution) can regulate the internal life of a legislative chamber. Only internal actors, moreover, can initiate the procedure to enact or amend parliamentary by-laws. The executive branch, in particular, cannot submit any proposal. And, once approved, such norms are not sent to the King for their sanction and promulgation. Instead, they are automatically published in the *Boletín Oficial de las Cortes Generales* and in the *Boletín Oficial del Estado*.

These norms are very important to guarantee the well-functioning of the parliamentary procedures and the rights of minority groups. An absolute majority of votes is required for their passage (article 72.1 of the Constitution). One of the crucial things these by-laws do is to regulate in a detailed manner the different procedures that can be employed to pass legislation. For a statute to be passed in the right way, the steps defined in the by-laws need to be followed. Only the most important flaws, however, those that violate principles of democratic pluralism, are relevant for purposes of declaring the unconstitutionality of a piece of legislation. (See STC 99/1987).

---

[18] The Protocol, however, explicitly authorizes the States to introduce an exception when the person concerned was tried in the first instance by the highest tribunal. See art 2.2.

[19] In addition, the two chambers can adopt a regulation to deal with questions that jointly affect them (art 72.2 of the Constitution). No such regulation has yet been adopted, however.

Finally, it is important to note that, although parliamentary by-laws are not 'statutes', they are awarded the same treatment as statutes. Ordinary courts, therefore, have no authority to declare their unconstitutionality. Only the Constitutional Court can do so.[20]

PARLIAMENT'S INTERNAL ORGANIZATION

Each House of Parliament has a complex internal structure. We should not delve into all the details here, but a few words are necessary to offer a picture of what the main organs are.

First, three organs are in charge of the internal governance of parliamentary affairs: the President, the Mesa, and the Junta de Portavoces. The President is the highest authority in the chamber, and acts as its external representative. He presides over the debates in the Pleno (the general meeting of the assembly), and issues resolutions to interpret the relevant by-laws. In the very first session, the chamber has to elect its President. The Mesa, in turn, is a collective body, which includes the President and representatives of the various political groups. This is the organ that organizes the parliamentary affairs from an administrative point of view. Finally, the Junta de Portavoces consists of the spokespeople of all the parliamentary groups (each group has one spokesperson), together with the representatives of the Government. It is a political organ, which organizes the contacts between the legislative assembly and the executive branch, and fixes the parliamentary agenda. It is presided over by the President of the chamber, and its decisions are taken through weighted votes: each spokesperson has as many votes as the number of deputies or senators that belong to his or her group.

To carry out its functions, each parliamentary house can operate both through the Pleno (the whole assembly) or through Commissions. The most important debates take place in the Pleno, where members of the Government are entitled to participate – they are seated on the so-called 'blue bench'. The Commissions, in turn, are in charge of the more technical work. They are especially important for the legislative process, since the legal texts that are finally approved by the Pleno are very close to the texts that have been negotiated at the pertinent Commission. The Commissions are like small parliaments, where the different political

[20] See art 27.2, *Ley Orgánica 2/1979 del Tribunal Constitucional*.

groups are represented in proportion to the number of deputies or senators that form part of the Pleno. The legislative Commissions are organized according to different fields that roughly correspond with the ministerial departments of the executive branch. Actually, the parliamentary by-laws are often modified, to adjust the Commissions to the changes introduced by the Government to its own ministerial organization. In January 2012, for example, they were amended to replicate the names of the ministerial departments that were restructured after a new Government was installed under President Mariano Rajoy, in the wake of the November 2011 general election. The legislative Commissions in Congress are currently the following: Constitutional Matters; Foreign Affairs; Justice; Home Affairs; Defence; Economy and Competitiveness; Treasury and Public Administration; Budget; Public Works; Education and Sports; Labour and Social Security; Industry, Energy and Tourism; Agriculture, Food and Environmental Protection; Public Health and Social Services; International Cooperation to Development; Culture and Equality. In the Senate, there is an additional Commission, which deals with matters involving Local Entities.[21]

Some Commissions deal with non-legislative matters. Some of them are permanent, as is the case, for example, of the Commission on the Status of Members of Parliament. Others are active for a limited period of time, such as Investigative Commissions.

The chambers are in session from September to December, and from February to June. When they are not in session, meetings can nevertheless take place in 'extraordinary' sessions. An important institution in this connection is the Diputación Permanente, which the Constitution regulates in article 78. It is a small assembly called to act when Parliament is not in session or when it has been dissolved or its term has expired. Congress and the Senate each select a Diputación Permanente. Their members are appointed by the parliamentary groups, in proportion to the number of deputies or senators of each group. The Diputación Permanente can decide to call all the members of the respective parliamentary chamber to hold an extraordinary session, and it performs certain functions when the term of the assembly has come to an end. That of Congress, for example, is in charge of validating the *decretos-ley* enacted by the executive in the event of an extraordinary necessity, and

---

[21] Art 46, *Reglamento del Congreso de los Diputados* and art 49, *Reglamento del Senado*.

of taking the pertinent decisions when the executive declares or wants to declare a state of emergency.

Through all these organs, each House of Parliament does its work and makes its decisions. According to the Constitution, the general rule that applies in the decision-making process is simple majority (article 79.2). Simple majority means that the votes in favour outnumber the votes against. Larger majorities may be required, however, by other clauses in the Constitution, or by organic laws. The parliamentary by-laws, in addition, may also impose qualified majorities to make particular appointments. Sometimes an absolute majority is required, which means that the votes in favour are more than 50 per cent of the total number of deputies or senators. Other times, super-majorities of two-thirds or three-fifths are established.

To protect its autonomy, each house is entitled by the Constitution to approve its own budget, which is automatically made part of the general budget of the State (article 72.1). Parliament also enjoys great leeway when it comes to making decisions. Its acts are not immune from judicial review, however. Both the Supreme Court and the Constitutional Court have jurisdiction to check their validity. Although the judiciary has exhibited considerable deference to Parliament in many areas, it has held that parliamentary decisions can be nullified if they entail a breach of fundamental rights – particularly the right to political participation (STC 118/1988). Apart from this, of course, the Constitutional Court can review the validity of the laws and other norms that are produced by Parliament, as we will study in chapter eight.

PARLIAMENT'S ROLE IN SELECTING AND CHECKING THE GOVERNMENT

We should now proceed to study the various tasks that are assigned to the Cortes Generales. A first function we must focus on concerns the selection and control of the Government.[22]

Because Spain has adopted a parliamentary system, there needs to be a tight relationship between the majority in the legislative assembly and

---

[22] M Revenga Sánchez, *La formación del gobierno en la Constitución española de 1978* (Madrid, Centro de Estudios Constitucionales, 1988); J García Morillo, *El control parlamentario del Gobierno en el ordenamiento español* (Madrid, Congreso de los Diputados, 1985).

the executive branch. The system works on the assumption that there is a majority in Congress that endorses the political programme and the specific policies that the President of the Government and his cabinet are pursuing. Should that parliamentary support cease to exist, several mechanisms are available to overcome the *impasse*, which may lead to the appointment of another President, or to the calling of an early general election. The crucial figure here is the President: since the rest of the cabinet is freely appointed by him and will have to step down if he is removed, it is the President that needs to obtain and retain the parliamentary confidence.

Selecting the Government

The investiture of the President requires an explicit decision by Congress. Normally, the decision is made when general elections have been held and a new Parliament has been formed. But the same procedure has to be followed in the more extraordinary cases where the President dies, resigns, or is removed as a result of loss of parliamentary confidence.

As was already explained in chapter four, the candidate to the presidency is formally proposed by the King, with the countersignature of the President of Congress. The monarch, however, has to act in light of the electoral outcome and the agreements reached by the political parties. The candidate proposed by the King must then proceed to explain his governmental programme to Congress. A debate takes place, where the different political groups express their points of view, and votes are taken. Deputies are called one by one, and are asked to express their vote orally. If an absolute majority of deputies vote in favour, the candidate is appointed President by the King. Otherwise, a second vote is cast 48 hours later, and a simple majority of deputies is then sufficient. If the candidate does not obtain a simple majority, the King has to make new proposals (which does not necessarily mean new candidates), and the same procedure is followed. If no candidate gets the required majority within two months after the first vote is taken, the Constitution provides that both Houses of Parliament must be dissolved and general elections called (article 99). This has never happened, however, although at some point during the difficult negotiations between PP and CiU to install a new Government after the 1996 elections, the possibility that new elections would have to be held was not excluded.

Under the Constitution of 1978, six presidents have been invested by Congress so far, following the procedure just described: Adolfo Suárez (1979–81), Leopoldo Calvo-Sotelo (1981–82), Felipe González (1982–96), José María Aznar (1996–2004), José Luis Rodríguez Zapatero (2004–11) and Mariano Rajoy (since 2011).

Loss of Parliamentary Confidence: Motion of Censure, Question of Confidence

Because a strong connection must exist between the parliamentary majority and the President of the Government, the Constitution provides that the latter can be removed, if the confidence he initially obtained disappears at a later stage. The Constitution, however, seeks to protect governmental stability by limiting the circumstances under which the President of the Government is obliged to step down. The mere fact, for example, that the executive has lost a vote on an important bill does not mean that the Government comes to an end. Only specific mechanisms can force a governmental change, according to the Constitution. It is worthy of note, in this connection, that the constitutional framers believed that minority governments would be frequent. Actually, it was a minority Government in the hands of UCD that ruled the country when the Constitution was being written in 1977–78. The framers thought that it would be extremely rare for a single party to obtain an absolute majority of congressional seats in the following years. Among other things, they had the memory of the very fragmented parliaments that were formed during the Second Republic.[23] Events developed differently than predicted, however: both PSOE (in 1982–86; 1986–89 and 1989–93) and PP (2000–04 and 2011 to the present time) obtained absolute majorities. The periods of minority governments were only those of 1993–96 and 2004–08 (under PSOE) and 1996–2000 (under PP). Hence, as it turned out, the framers were too worried about the risks of governmental instability.

A first mechanism to force the Government down is the so-called *moción de censura* (articles 113 and 114.2 of the Constitution). The motion can be brought by at least one-tenth of the deputies. Following the

---

[23] LM Maurer, *El poder del Parlamento: Congreso y políticas públicas en España* (Madrid, Centro de Estudios Políticos y Constitucionales, 2008) 125.

German model, the Constitution requires a 'constructive' motion: the challenging deputies must present their own candidate to the presidency. It is thus not sufficient for the assembly to agree that the current President should step down. It is also necessary to reach an agreement as to who should replace him. The debate in the assembly focuses on the candidate to the presidency. For the motion to be approved, moreover, an absolute majority is required. Note the asymmetry, in favour of governmental stability: to be invested President, a simple majority is ultimately sufficient; for someone to be appointed later, through a 'motion of censure', a larger majority is required. If the motion is successful, the King automatically appoints the alternative candidate to the presidency.

In practice, no motion of censure has succeeded so far. The two motions that were filed in the past sought to show public opinion that the leader in the opposition had an attractive programme to offer the nation. Such was the goal of the motion submitted by Felipe González against President Adolfo Suárez in May 1980, and that of Antonio Hernández Mancha against President Felipe González in March 1987. In both cases it was clear from the very beginning that the motion would not be approved. In the first case, the political goal the motion sought was fully achieved: Felipe González was able to convince large sections of public opinion that he was a mature leader ready to rule the country. In the second case, in contrast, the motion was a complete failure. Antonio Hernández Mancha proved to be a bad candidate, and his party had to look for a new leader.

The other mechanism that can lead to the removal of the President is initiated by the President himself, after having listened to his Ministers. The Constitution provides that he can submit a so-called *cuestión de confianza* to Congress, concerning his governmental programme or a general policy statement (articles 112 and 114.1 of the Constitution). The idea is to test the waters in the assembly and press the majority to express clearly whether the Government still enjoys parliamentary confidence. The President cannot submit a specific legal proposal and condition his continuance in office to the parliamentary approval of that proposal. A more general political statement or programme is to be debated. The President survives the motion if a simple majority of the votes in Congress are favourable. Otherwise, the President is removed, and a new President needs to be proposed by the King, following the ordinary procedure that was explained before.

In practice, governments have very rarely used this mechanism. President Adolfo Suárez resorted to it once (in September 1980) as did President Felipe González a decade later (in April 1990). If the President is confronting a difficult situation, the normal reaction is for him to dissolve Parliament and call early elections. This is a powerful weapon that the Constitution places in his hands. The mere threat that elections will be held earlier than expected may push the majority in the legislative assembly to be more disciplined. The coalition of parties that support the Government, in particular, may reinforce their ties to prevent the dissolution of Parliament. In addition, the dissolution prerogative allows the President to choose the best moment to hold elections, in light of the general interests of the country or, more likely, for partisan reasons. The Constitution, however, places some limitations, in order to prevent abuses. The President cannot dissolve Parliament when a motion of censure has been presented (article 115.2). Also, when a state of emergency (alarm, siege or exception) has been declared, no early elections can be called (article 116.5). In addition, no dissolution can be decreed when less than one year has elapsed since the previous dissolution (article 115.3).[24] A crucial guarantee is also established in the Constitution: the decree dissolving Parliament must specify the date of the new elections (article 115.1), which must take place no later than 60 days after the expiration of Parliament (article 68.6).

Controlling the Government

In the two procedures we have described (*moción de censura, cuestión de confianza*), the Senate plays no role at all. But there is another way for Parliament to check the Government, through techniques that do not seek to remove the President and his Government, but merely to criticize and control their actions. Here the Senate, as well as Congress, plays a part. In practice, of course, it is the political parties in the opposition that monitor and censure the activities of the executive branch. The

---

[24] Art 115.3 makes it clear that this rule does not apply, of course, when the parliamentary dissolution is not discretional, but required by the law. This is the case when Congress has not succeeded in investing a President of the Government (art 99.5). The article says nothing, however, about the automatic dissolution that takes place when a constitutional amendment is proposed following the procedure stipulated in art 168.

parliamentary majority will instead be supportive of the Government – and uncritically so.[25]

The Constitution, for example, allows both chambers to request from the Government any information they need (article 109). The parliamentary bodies must send the Government the requests submitted by individual members. The Constitutional Court has been active in protecting this right against the legislative bodies. In contrast, it has been extremely deferential to the Government, even when the latter has refused without justification to bring forth the pertinent information or documents. The Court has argued that political conflicts of this sort should not be judicialized.[26]

The Constitution also empowers Congress and the Senate to require the presence of members of the Government (article 110). This check on the executive branch is rather weak, however, since it is the parliamentary majority – not the opposition – that decides whether to call them.

Conversely, the Government can have access to Parliament to inform and be heard. One of the most important instances of this is the 'debate on the state of the nation' that usually takes place every year in Congress, where the executive explains its plans, after which the various parliamentary groups enter a debate.

Questions of various sorts can also be asked of the Government (article 111). The Tuesday evenings in the Senate and the Wednesday evenings in Congress are devoted to question time.

In addition, it is possible for 'Investigative Commissions' to be set up by Congress, by the Senate, or jointly by the two chambers, to enquire into a particular problem (article 76). Citizens and public servants are under a duty to appear before such Commissions, if they are summoned. The conclusions the Commissions reach – which are submitted to a vote in the Pleno – are not binding on courts, but they are sent to the Office of the Public Prosecutor. Unfortunately, the decision to create a Commission is in the hands of the parliamentary majority, which is usually reluctant to vote for it. In the middle of the current financial

---

[25] M Aragón Reyes, 'Gobierno y forma de gobierno: problemas actuales' in M Aragón and ÁJ Gómez Montoro (eds), *El Gobierno. Problemas constitucionales* (Madrid, Centro de Estudios Políticos y Constitucionales, 2005) 61.

[26] For a criticism of the Court's case law on this matter, see A Cidoncha Martín, 'El control del Gobierno desde la perspectiva del parlamentario individual' in Aragón and Gómez Montoro (n 25) 286.

crisis, for example, the Government has refused to establish a Commission to investigate the mismanagement of the banks that have been bailed out by the State. In the past, Commissions were set up to investigate various matters, involving, for example, the production and sale of adulterated oil that killed many people (in 1981), the expropriation by the Government of the shares of an important company, RUMASA (in 1983), the Government's involvement in the dirty war against ETA's terrorism (in 1995) and the terrorist massacre of 11 March 2004 (in 2004).

PARLIAMENT AS A LEGISLATIVE BODY

In addition to selecting and checking the Government, the Cortes Generales have the key responsibility to enact legislation. The Government, however, has pre-eminence in the legislative process: the vast majority of statutes that are passed by Parliament originate in a proposal drafted by the executive branch. This is consistent with the notion that, in a parliamentary democracy, the Government has a political programme that a majority in the legislative assembly endorses, and that needs to be translated into new laws that the Government is expected to initiate. There is some room, however, for Parliament to influence and qualify the governmental legislative proposals, as we will see.

Most legislation takes the form of 'ordinary statutes'. There are two special kinds of statutes, however, we should pay some special attention to: 'organic statutes' and the statutes that approve the general budget of the State. We will devote special sections to them.

The Legislative Process

The way the legislative process is initiated reveals some important features of the Spanish system. The process can get started through a 'project of statute' (*proyecto de ley*) sent by the Government to Congress. In practice, the vast majority of statutes passed by Parliament are based on such texts. A study found that the percentage of enacted statutes that had been initiated by the executive branch in the different parliamentary periods was as follows: 76.2 per cent (1979–82); 85.3 per cent (1982–

86); 88.4 per cent (1986–89); 73.7 per cent (1989–93); 80 per cent (1993–96) and 78.9 per cent (1996–2000).[27] It is important to note that the projects submitted by the executive have priority in the parliamentary agenda (article 89 of the Constitution). The Government, moreover, is always entitled to withdraw the legislative proposal it has sent Congress.[28]

Because of the Government's pre-eminence, the Constitution establishes certain requirements on the legislative proposals it drafts. Article 88, in particular, provides that the Government must attach to the bill the necessary documents and statements of purpose, so that Members of Parliament can know the grounds of the proposal. Ordinary law, in turn, regulates the internal procedure that the executive branch must follow before it sends a legislative proposal to the assembly. The Ministries involved, it provides, must obtain various reports, concerning the necessity of the new law, its gender impact, and its economic cost.[29]

Alternatively, the legislative process can begin when Congress or the Senate presents a 'proposition of statute' (*proposición de ley*). Here the special role of political parties – through the parliamentary groups – manifests itself: such propositions can only be submitted by 15 deputies, or by a parliamentary group with the sole signature of its spokesperson (in the case of Congress); or by 25 senators or a parliamentary group (in the case of the Senate).

The law and the actual practice take it for granted that parliamentary groups are the engines of the legislative process, together with the Government. Very marginally do other actors initiate the legislative proceedings, such as citizens or regional parliaments. Concerning citizens, we already saw in chapter two that the Constitution is very restrictive. Proposals must be signed by at least 500,000 citizens, and many matters are excluded.

With respect to the regional parliaments, the Constitution allows them to request the national Government to submit a 'project of statute'. More importantly, the Constitution also permits them to send a 'proposition of statute' directly to Congress, and to appoint a group of no more than three regional deputies to defend that proposition before Congress. The number of proposals submitted in this manner has

---

[27] Maurer (n 23) 59–60.

[28] See art 128, *Reglamento del Congreso de los Diputados*.

[29] See art 22, *Ley 50/1997 del Gobierno*.

increased throughout the years, but it is still relatively low. In the legislative period of 1993–96, for example, 18 proposals were tabled. The number rose to 42 in the legislative period of 2000–04. Some Communities are more active than others. Catalonia, for example, has submitted more than 20 proposals so far.

The laws are discussed in the pertinent Legislative Commissions, which appoint a smaller group of representatives to negotiate a text. The bills are finally voted by the assembly as a whole. The role of the Commissions is so important that it is even possible for the Pleno to delegate to them the final vote on the legislative text. The Constitution (article 75) explicitly allows for this possibility, though it excludes it in certain cases (involving constitutional amendments, international matters, organic statutes, laws that confer legislative powers on the executive, and the laws establishing the general budget of the State). The Pleno, moreover, can always withdraw the delegation.

As far as the Senate is concerned, it is important to emphasize that it plays a marginal role in the legislative process. The Constitution establishes (in article 90) that a statute passed by Congress can be vetoed by the Senate only if an absolute majority of senators are agreed – a simple majority is insufficient. Moreover, the veto can be immediately overcome by Congress if an absolute majority of deputies insists on the initial text. If no such absolute majority obtains, Congress need only wait for two months, and a simple majority is then sufficient to overcome the veto. If, instead of a veto, the Senate seeks to introduce amendments, it can do so by simple majority, but Congress may immediately decide whether to accept them or not, also by simple majority.

There are two ways to expedite the legislative process. One is for the Pleno to decide not to send a legislative proposal to a Commission, maintaining all stages in the process within the Pleno. This procedure of *lectura única* (single reading) can be chosen when the legislative proposal is simple enough, 'or when its nature recommends it', the law provides.[30] This is a very vague standard. Interestingly, the recent reform of the Spanish Constitution (enacted in September 2011) was approved in this manner. The Government and the main party in the opposition agreed that a very fast track should be followed to amend the Constitution, given the convulsions in the European financial markets. The smaller parties, as well as many commentators, criticized this procedural choice.

---

[30] See art 150, *Reglamento del Congreso de los Diputados*.

They argued that the constitutional charter should not be modified in a rush, with no sustained debate, given the complexity of the issues involved.

The other way to expedite the legislative process is to use an 'urgent procedure', which reduces the parliamentary deadlines. Both Congress and the Senate can freely decide to employ it. In addition, the Senate can be required to use it when either the Government or Congress declares that a particular legislative proposal is urgent. In such a case, the Senate has only 20 days to amend or veto the law (see article 90.3 of the Constitution).

Parliament's Capacity to Influence Legislation

As has already been pointed out, the Government is the key player throughout the legislative process. This does not mean, however, that the parliamentary groups have no capacity to influence the legislative outcomes. This influence has varied over time, as a result of several factors.[31]

Thus, during a certain period after the enactment of the Constitution, Parliament had an especially powerful role to play. The reason is that, until 1982, the Government was in the hands of UCD, a party that was very heterogeneous in its composition, and lacked internal discipline. The Government had to negotiate with the members of its own parliamentary group in Congress in order to secure the necessary votes. In addition, many important laws at that time were passed to organize the democratic regime and to adjust existing legislation to the new constitutional values. The UCD Government felt that those laws should be based on a broad parliamentary consensus, even if a simple majority was technically sufficient. The constitutional 'spirit of *consenso*' was still present at that time. Those years were rather exceptional, however. Things became normalized once UCD almost disappeared in the 1982 elections, and AP (afterwards PP) gradually replaced it as the main party on the right of the political spectrum. Ever since, the centre of gravity of the system is occupied by two large parties (PSOE and PP) which are internally cohesive.

The key factor then becomes whether the Government can simply rely on its own party, which has obtained a majority of the seats in

---

[31] For a systematic study of these different factors, see Maurer (n 23).

Congress, or instead needs the additional support of some other parties. As was already mentioned, there have been periods of majority governments (under PSOE: 1982–86; 1986–89; 1989–93; under PP: 2000–04; 2011 to the present time), as well as periods of minority governments (under PSOE: 1993–96, 2004–08, 2008–11; under PP: 1996–2000). Not surprisingly, the capacity of parliamentary groups to influence the legislative agenda is larger in the latter cases. Both the PSOE and the PP minority governments had to negotiate with regional and other smaller parties to have their legislative programmes enacted into law, though no coalition government was agreed upon. During 1993–96, PSOE relied on CiU, a Catalan nationalist party. The PP, in turn, during 1996–2000, had to obtain the support of CiU, as well as of PNV and CC. When PSOE came back to government during the period from 2004–11, it reached various agreements depending on the issues, normally with parties on the left, such as IU and ERC.

In the context of such minority governments, legislative proposals were discussed between the executive branch and the smaller parties. Sometimes the Government had already negotiated the contents of the text; other times, the bargaining process took place throughout the parliamentary stages. In any case, there was room for qualifications to be introduced to the governmental initiatives. It was even possible for a sufficient number of parties to agree to enact a law against the wishes of the executive. In 2000, for example, a statute on the rights of foreign citizens was passed by Parliament, against the objections of the Government, then in the hands of PP, which did not have a majority of seats. The law was later changed, when PP obtained an absolute majority in the 2000 general elections.

When governments are supported by a party that has captured an absolute majority of seats, they are less likely to reach to the other parties. But sometimes they do, for different reasons. During the 1989–93 period, for example, the Government under PSOE was open to negotiate with the Catalan and Basque regional parties, because it feared that it would lose the majority of seats in the next elections (as indeed it did in 1993). The Government wanted to create a good relationship with those parties, to secure their future support. Other times, the Government has considered it advisable for a particular law to be stable, and has sought the agreement of the main party in the opposition to ensure that the law will not be repealed in the future, if the Government changes hands. The Criminal Code of 1995, for example, was supported both by the

Government under PSOE and the main party in the opposition, PP, many of whose amendments to the original bill were accepted. (The PP abstained in the final vote, but it was fundamentally satisfied with the text). Still other times, the Government seeks the help of the main party in the opposition to legitimize a legislative choice that may be unpopular. In 1991, for instance, the Government under PSOE decided to maintain the compulsory military service, in spite of the many voices in society in favour of eliminating the service. The majority was interested in obtaining the support of the main party in the opposition (PP), against these critics. The law was thus based on a bipartisan consensus.

It should also be noted, finally, that when parliamentary groups submit propositions that are bound to be rejected by the majority, they may contribute to the legislative agenda in indirect ways. Sometimes, even if the proposition is rejected, the Government realizes that an important topic has been placed on the political agenda that needs to be addressed. It therefore decides to submit a proposal of its own, sometimes not very different from the initial proposition. And even if the Government does not react in this manner, the parliamentary group has made visible to the public part of the programme it may enact into law if it wins the next elections.

In sum, though it is undoubtedly true that the executive branch dominates the legislative process, there is some space for the parliamentary groups to have a say. This space is larger or smaller, depending on various political factors.

Extending Constitutional Consensus Over Time: Organic Statutes

Legislation normally takes the form of 'ordinary statutes'. The Constitution, however, establishes in article 81 that some matters must be regulated by an 'organic statute' (*ley orgánica*). An organic statute is a special kind of law that can only be passed and modified by an absolute majority of the members of Congress, in a final vote over the whole statute. Ordinary statutes, in contrast, can be enacted and amended by simple majority.

The constitutional framers drew inspiration from the French Constitution, article 46 of which provides for the existence of organic laws. The Spanish framers believed that certain matters that had not been regulated in detail in the Constitution, but which were important enough, should be governed in the future by a law that had broad parliamentary support. The idea, in part, was to continue the conciliatory efforts that had characterized the transition to democracy and the framing of the Constitution. Such matters include, among others, the development of fundamental rights, the establishment of the electoral system, and the design of certain institutions of government. The legislature that enacts 'organic statutes' – the 'organic legislature' – is somehow continuing the work of the constitutional framers.

There is a mismatch, however, between the goal that the framers sought when they introduced this special kind of statute in the Constitution, and the particular form they chose. If, indeed, they wanted to ensure that the spirit of *consenso* would preside over the future enactment of laws in certain fields, they should have required a parliamentary super-majority (of two-thirds, or three-fifths, say). Only such a super-majority would mirror an agreement reached by the major political parties from the right and from the left. Requiring an 'absolute' majority (of the lower house only) does not mean, in practice, that such an agreement is obtained. There is no need for the governing majority to negotiate with the main party in the opposition for it to get the necessary votes to pass an organic statute. If the governing party does not have an absolute majority of the seats, it can get the support of a minor party that is willing to help – there is no need to reach to the major party in the opposition. And if the ruling party does have an absolute majority, then it makes no political difference whether an organic law or an ordinary law needs to be approved. In both instances, the ruling majority has enough votes to impose its will.

Interestingly, the Constitutional Court has espoused a restrictive view of the matters that the Constitution reserves to organic statutes. The Court has reasoned that the general principle in a democracy is that Parliament should vote the laws by simple majority. Requiring 'absolute' majorities for the passage of laws is a deviation from this general principle. The scope of the exception should therefore be interpreted restrictively (SSTC 5/1981, 76/1983). The Court, for example, has held that when the Constitution says that the 'development of fundamental rights and public liberties' is to be channelled through an organic statute, this expression should not be understood to refer to all the rights and liberties that figure in Chapter 2 of Title I of the Constitution (a rather long list). Only a sub-set is meant to be covered: those comprised between articles 15 and 29. The Court, moreover, has held that only the regulation of the basic aspects of the right or liberty is ascribed to an organic statute. The other, more secondary, aspects of the right can be dealt with by ordinary statutes. This, of course, has produced an extremely complicated and casuistic jurisprudence that seeks to demarcate, for each right and liberty, which part of it must be covered by an organic statute, and which part is to be regulated by an ordinary statute.

The Court has also explained that there is no hierarchy between organic statutes and ordinary statutes, but a distribution of 'competences' between the two sources of law. If Parliament chooses to regulate organic matters together with ordinary matters in the same legislative piece, it must include a clause at the end of the piece clarifying which articles are to be regarded as organic, and which are to be treated as ordinary (STC 137/1986).

There is an asymmetry, however, that needs to be highlighted. Whereas the ordinary statute that should have been organic is to be declared constitutionally invalid by the Court, the organic statute that should have been ordinary is not. It is instead 'degraded' into an ordinary law (which a simple majority in Parliament will be able to amend or repeal in the future). This asymmetry makes sense. In the first case, a simple majority tried to do what only an absolute majority is entitled to do. In the second case, in contrast, the majority that endorsed the law was larger than required.

Given this asymmetry, it is understandable that Parliament usually prefers to err on the safe side. When it is not clear whether a particular matter should be regulated through an organic statutory provision, the governing majority prefers to assume that the answer is yes, and to proceed accordingly (if getting an absolute majority of the votes is politically feasible). In the event that the Constitutional Court says that the assumption is wrong, the organic legal provision will be converted into an ordinary one, but it will still be valid.

All things considered, it is doubtful that the introduction of organic statutes has been a good idea. If the goal was to preserve the 'spirit of *consenso*', larger super-majorities should have been imposed. Requiring an absolute majority does no real work in this direction. The cost for the legal system, moreover, has been quite high: the Court's case law has been unable to draw a sufficiently well-defined frontier to separate the matters that are reserved to each type of statute. This has led to a considerable level of complexity.

Approving the General Budget of the State

We should now say a few words about Parliament's responsibility with regard to a very special and extremely important law: the *Ley de Presupuestos Generales del Estado*. This is the law that gets passed every year to authorize governmental expenditures at the State level. While taxes are fixed by ordinary laws that have an indefinite legal life, until they are repealed or modified, public expenses, in contrast, need to be authorized on an annual basis. The Constitution establishes some rules in this connection (in articles 134 and 135).

First, only the Government can draft the budget.[32] It must do so, moreover, three months before the next budgetary period begins on 1 January. If the budget is not approved in time for it to be applicable on 1 January, the previous budget is extended for another year (until it is replaced by the new budget).

Second, the Cortes Generales have to decide whether to approve the budget submitted by the Government, and what amendments to introduce. There are limitations, however: the parliamentary by-laws establish that any amendment that implies more expenditure is only admissible if it includes a reduction of an equivalent amount of money in the same budgetary section. And any amendment that entails a reduction of resources needs the authorization of the Government. Consistent with Spain's obligation to honour its public debt, moreover, the Constitution establishes in article 135 that the authorization to pay interest and capital is always to be included in the budget, and no parliamentary amendment or modification to it is admissible, provided that the authorization is in conformity with the law that enabled the issuance of the public debt. The constitutional reform of September 2011 has reinforced this commitment to fiscal discipline through a rule that establishes that the payment of interest and capital shall have 'absolute priority'.

Third, the law approving the budget cannot establish taxes. The latter are regulated in separate ordinary statutes. The law approving the budget, however, can modify the existing taxes, if the pertinent tax statute so authorizes. So, for example, the law regulating the income tax can

---

[32] On the central role played by the Government throughout the budgetary process, see IM Giménez Sánchez, 'La intervención del Gobierno en el ejercicio de la función presupuestaria' in Aragón and Gómez Montoro (n 25) 287.

establish that certain modifications can be introduced in the future, by means of the law that fixes the budget. On the basis of that authorization, many changes are introduced every year, when the budget is approved.

Because of the limited scope of the law approving the budget, the Constitutional Court has held that such law cannot address matters that are not sufficiently tied to budgetary decisions (STC 63/1986). As a response to the Court's holding, the practice developed in 1993 for Parliament to enact a parallel law, normally called 'law on economic, fiscal, administrative and social measures', which introduces legislative changes in many different fields. Since this parallel law is detached from the law that fixes the budget, the Court's doctrine on the limits of the latter does not apply (see STC 136/2011).

It bears emphasizing that the approval of the budget is a crucial moment in political life. It is impossible for the Government to implement its legislative choices without getting the parliamentary authorization to spend money for the various programmes. If the Government lost that vote, it would be in serious trouble. Even if the previous budget could be extended, the Government would no longer enjoy sufficient legitimacy to continue. In 1995, for example, the minority Government in the hands of PSOE failed to secure the agreement of its key parliamentary ally (CiU) to pass the budget for the next year. As a result of this failure, early elections were called, and a new Government under PP was installed in 1996.

THE FUTURE OF THE SENATE

As the previous discussion has illustrated, Spain's bicameralism is strongly asymmetrical. Only Congress is involved in the procedures to select or remove the President of the Government. When a law (or the general budget of the State) is to be enacted, moreover, only Congress ultimately matters. Does it make sense to have a Senate with such a limited role?

It is true that in some instances the Senate is treated equally to Congress. This is so with regard to various appointments, for example.[33]

---

[33] Thus, each house selects 4 judges of the Constitutional Court, 10 members of the General Council of the Judiciary, and 6 members of the Court of Audit (Tribunal de Cuentas). Congress and the Senate need to agree, moreover, upon the appointment of the Ombudsman (Defensor del Pueblo).

When Parliament has to make decisions concerning the Crown, moreover, the two houses have to meet in a joint session (article 74.1 of the Constitution). But these are marginal responsibilities.

The Senate was originally planned to be the chamber of 'territorial representation' (article 69.1). Its tasks in the regional field, however, are very limited. As will be explained in chapter seven, the Senate's consent is required when the central Government decides to enact a law to 'harmonize' the regional laws, or to enact measures against an Autonomous Community that does not comply with its obligations, or that acts in a manner that is gravely detrimental to Spain's general interests. These are very extraordinary measures, however. In normal times, when ordinary politics is played, the Senate's consent is irrelevant. The Constitution provides, for example, that when certain agreements between Autonomous Communities need to be authorized by Parliament, or when resources from the Fondo de Compensación Interterritorial need to be distributed among the regions, the Senate initiates the pertinent procedure, but an absolute majority in Congress ultimately decides (article 74.2).

Many experts believe that the current form of weak bicameralism is not a reasonable arrangement. The Senate should be assigned larger tasks, they suggest, in order to channel the interests, and in order to protect the competences, of the Autonomous Communities. In 1994, a Commission was created in the Senate to deal with problems concerning the Autonomous Communities. The presidents of the different regions are entitled to intervene in the debates that are organized in that forum. The regional languages can be spoken in those sessions too.

In addition, 'territorial groups' can be created in the Senate, within the ordinary parliamentary groups. The former are composed of senators that represent a single Autonomous Community. The idea is that the specific interests of the different regions should be given institutional expression. When an issue is debated, for example, that concerns a particular Community, the territorial groups can participate in the discussion, in addition to the ordinary parliamentary groups.[34]

These are all small steps in the right path, experts say. But much more needs to be done to transform the Senate into an effective voice of the Communities. In March 2005, the Government asked the Council of State to issue a report about a proposal of constitutional reform that

---

[34] See art 32 and 33, *Reglamento del Senado*.

involved the Senate. The Council submitted its study in 2006,[35] but no political action was taken, given the resistance of PP to change the Constitution. As we will see in chapter seven, the direction in which the Senate must be redesigned depends on how the territorial organization of Spain is finally restructured.

CONCLUSION

The national Parliament (Cortes Generales) performs a key role in Spanish democracy. Because it is elected by the Spanish people as a whole, it can claim a special democratic legitimacy. The two main tasks it is asked to carry out is to select and control the Government, as is typical in parliamentary democracies, and to produce legislation. Because there is a strong link between the executive branch and the party (or coalition of parties) that has a majority of seats in Congress, there is no true system of checks and balances between the executive and legislative branches. The only checks come from the parliamentary opposition, which is expected to criticize the ruling majority and to offer the country its own alternative programme. There is some space for Parliament to influence the Government's policies, however, depending on a host of factors we have examined. The big question on the constitutional table when Parliament is considered is what to do with the Senate, which does not seem to be well designed as the chamber that represents the interests of the Autonomous Communities. Any serious reform of the Spanish Constitution in the future will have to confront that question, which can only be properly addressed in light of other reforms of the Spanish quasi-federal system, as we will study in chapter seven.

FURTHER READING

Caamaño Domínguez, F, *El mandato parlamentario* (Madrid, Congreso de los Diputados, 1991).

---

[35] See the report of 16 February 2006, available at www.consejo-estado.es. For scholarly comments on this document, see *El Informe del Consejo de Estado sobre la reforma constitucional. Texto del informe y debates académicos* (Madrid, Consejo de Estado y Centro de Estudios Políticos y Constitucionales, 2006).

García Morillo, J, *El control parlamentario del Gobierno en el ordenamiento español* (Madrid, Congreso de los Diputados, 1985).

Gunther, R, Montero, JR and Botella, J, *Democracy in Modern Spain* (New Haven, Yale University Press, 2004) ch 5.

Maurer, LM, *El poder del Parlamento: Congreso y políticas públicas en España* (Madrid, Centro de Estudios Políticos y Constitucionales, 2008).

Molas, I and Pitarch, I, *Las Cortes Generales en el sistema parlamentario de Gobierno* (Madrid, Tecnos, 1987).

Revenga Sánchez, M, *La formación del gobierno en la Constitución española de 1978* (Madrid, Centro de Estudios Constitucionales, 1988).

Saiz Arnaiz, A, *Los grupos parlamentarios* (Madrid, Congreso de los Diputados, 1989).

Solé Tura, J and Aparicio Pérez, MA, *Las Cortes Generales en el sistema constitucional* (Madrid, Tecnos, 1984).

6

The Government and Public Administration

———·◦·———

The Government – The Public Administration – Controlling the Government and the Administration – Conclusion

UNDER THE TRADITIONAL concept of separation of powers, a simple distinction is drawn between the legislative, the executive and the judicial branches. In any modern political system, however, the executive branch is very complex. In Spain, like in other countries, this department is composed of two levels, the 'Government' and the 'public administration', which carry out quite different tasks. The latter enforces the law, and supplies the many services and goods that are typical of a modern, social State. The Government, however, goes beyond this purely executive function.

As we will see in this chapter, it is for the Government to define public policy – to select the goals to be achieved in the name of public interests, and to look for the best strategies to satisfy them. The Constitution bestows upon it a 'directive function'. The Government, indeed, has a central role in making the different pieces of the State machinery reach the desired goals. As was explained in chapter five, the executive branch can usually rely on a stable parliamentary majority to enact its political programme into statutory law. The Government, moreover, is empowered to issue administrative regulations that work out the details of statutory law. In some cases, it is even authorized to issue norms that have the same rank as statutes, as we will see.

To attain the ends it defines in the exercise of its directive function, the Government has at its disposal the different organs that make up the public administration. The bureaucratic branch is thus the instrument the Government uses to implement its policies.

Because of the large powers that the executive branch accumulates, it is important to establish the appropriate mechanisms to curb its excesses. As we will study, several institutions have been created to serve this purpose, the most important of which are the Council of State, the Ombudsman, the administrative courts and the Court of Audit.

Our discussion in this chapter will start with the Government. We will then fix our attention on the administration. We will finally examine the various mechanisms to check their actions.

THE GOVERNMENT

Several constitutional clauses and a set of ordinary statutes regulate the structure and functions of the Government. The most important legislative piece in this connection is the *Ley 50/1997 del Gobierno* (Law on the Government). There was some academic controversy when a first draft of this Law was presented in 1995. Some scholars were of the view that it constrained the Government too much, in terms of the structures and decision-making procedures it laid down. Since the Government is a direct creature of the Constitution, it enjoys a certain level of autonomy that ordinary statutes passed by Parliament must respect. The statute that was finally adopted in 1997 was more flexible.[1] We cannot exclude the possibility of constitutional disputes arising in the future, however. The Law, for example, regulates the internal steps that the Government must follow before it sends a bill to Congress.[2] Suppose the internal procedure is not fully observed, but the legislative proposal that the Government submits to Congress is finally enacted into law. Is the law unconstitutional, as a result of the Government – not Parliament – having failed to respect the procedures laid down in the *Ley del Gobierno*? It would be a safe bet to predict that the Constitutional Court would uphold the statute. It might argue, either that the procedural flaw is not so grave as to impeach the constitutionality of the statute, or that the Government cannot be required to follow the internal steps defined in the *Ley del Gobierno* to begin with, given

---

[1] On this controversy, see JJ Solozábal Echavarría, 'El estatuto del Gobierno y su configuración efectiva como órgano del Estado' in M Aragón and ÁJ Gómez Montoro (eds), *El Gobierno. Problemas constitucionales* (Madrid, Centro de Estudios Políticos y Constitucionales, 2005) 76.

[2] See art 22, *Ley del Gobierno*.

the governmental autonomy that the Constitution should be read to guarantee.

The Structure of the Government

The Constitution establishes that the Government comprises the President and the Ministers. It can also include Vice-Presidents and any other members that the laws establish (article 98.1). In practice, the only members are the President, the Vice-presidents and the Ministers. No other position has been added. This means that the Government and the *Consejo de Ministros* ('Council of Ministers') are co-extensive. The Secretaries of State, in particular, are not part of the Government. The law provides that they can be asked to participate in the meetings of the Council of Ministers, but they are not formal members of this organ.[3]

The Government relies on certain auxiliary bodies, such as the Secretariado del Gobierno, and the Comisión General de Secretarios de Estado y Subsecretarios. It can also delegate some of its functions to the so-called Comisiones Delegadas del Gobierno, which include the Secretaries of State.

The President and the Vice-President(s)

Within the Government, the President enjoys clear pre-eminence. This is due to the fact that the link of support between Parliament and the Government runs through him. The President is invested by Congress, and can be removed by the latter through the two mechanisms we examined in the previous chapter (motion of censure and question of confidence). The Vice-Presidents and the Ministers, in contrast, get their positions from the President, who freely appoints and removes them.[4] Similarly, Congress may decide to express disapproval or censure of a particular Minister or Vice-President, but the President is free to decide what to do with him or her.

---

[3] See art 5.2, *Ley del Gobierno*.

[4] The candidate to the Presidency is not required to announce the composition of his future Government when his investiture is discussed and voted upon in Congress. The practice is for the President to divulge the name of his Ministers after being appointed. An exception occurred in 1982, when Felipe González gave the list of his future Ministers during the parliamentary debates leading to his investiture.

A feature consistent with the centrality of the President is the fact that the Constitution establishes that all the members of the Government lose their positions when the President leaves (article 101). This situation occurs when general elections are held, when the President loses parliamentary support in the manner specified in the Constitution, or when he dies or resigns. The Government then becomes a caretaker government (*gobierno en funciones*) that needs to be replaced by a new one. A new President will be chosen, who will then proceed to make the pertinent ministerial appointments. The caretaker Government can only administer ordinary matters, unless the general interest or an urgent situation justify taking special measures. It is not allowed to call general elections or a referendum, for example, or draft the general budget, or submit legislative proposals to Parliament.[5]

The President's formal powers are reinforced by the fact that he is the leader of the political party that won the general elections. Although his appointment depends on the votes of a majority of deputies, democratic legitimacy is also transferred to him in a more direct way. Because citizens have in mind the different candidates to the Presidency of the Government when they cast their votes in the parliamentary elections, the candidate that belongs to the victorious party can claim to have a mandate from the people. Because the King in Spain is merely a symbolic figure, with no actual power to exercise, the President of the Government concentrates all the democratic legitimacy that is transferred to the executive branch. His position is thus similar to that of the Prime Minister in the United Kingdom, for example.

The pre-eminence of the President of the Government would be reduced, however, if the Government were based on a coalition of parties. In that case, the President's popular legitimacy would be less direct, for it would depend on the deals struck by two or more parties. As a result, he would have less leeway to decide the composition of his team, since the different parties would have to negotiate this matter, at least in part. So far, however, there has never been a coalition government in Spain. Even when the victorious party in the general elections has needed the support of smaller parties to get the necessary votes for the investiture, the agreement has focused exclusively on the legislative programme to be developed – the smaller parties have not occupied ministerial positions. As was noted in chapter five, when neither the PSOE

---

[5] See art 21, *Ley del Gobierno*.

nor the PP obtained an absolute majority of the congressional seats in the periods of 1993–96, 1996–2000, 2004–08 and 2008–11, single-party minority governments were installed into office. The party with most seats reached more or less stable pacts with smaller parties (often with the Catalan and the Basque nationalist parties), to secure the necessary votes to get into the Government. At the regional and local levels, in contrast, coalition governments have sometimes been established. Experience reveals that the regional presidents and local mayors have seen their pre-eminence eroded in such cases. The same would happen if, in the future, a coalition government were formed at the national level.

Whatever the political scenario is, the Constitution assumes that the President will perform the key function of directing and coordinating the Government, even though Ministers are each directly responsible for the matters they administer (article 98.2). The *Ley del Gobierno* specifies, in this regard, that the President is empowered to issue 'instructions' to the members of his Government.[6] A number of scholars have expressed constitutional doubts about the binding character of such instructions. They argue that Ministers are free not to follow them. In practice, however, they comply with the instructions, for the simple reason that the President has the power to remove any member of his Cabinet.[7] The law also provides that the President can settle the controversies that arise between different ministerial departments. And he is in charge of calling and presiding over the meetings of the Council of Ministers.[8]

The Constitution, moreover, entrusts the President with some specific decisions of great political import, such as deciding whether to submit a parliamentary question of confidence (article 112), calling a referendum (article 92), calling general elections (article 115) or attacking a law through an abstract challenge brought to the Constitutional Court (article 162). These attributes help reinforce the President's prominence within the executive branch.

To carry out his tasks, the President is supported by the Secretaría General de la Presidencia and the Gabinete de la Presidencia. The latter is a network of persons freely appointed by the Government who offer advice on political and technical matters. They cannot adopt any

---

[6] See art 2, *Ley del Gobierno*.
[7] On this problem, see JM Bilbao Ubillos, 'La dirección de la Administración civil y militar por el Gobierno de la Nación' in Aragón and Gómez Montoro (n 1) 166.
[8] See arts 2 and 18, *Ley del Gobierno*.

decision, however, that is formally attributed to the regular organs of the public administration.[9] This staff occupies offices that surround the Palacio de la Moncloa where the President lives. There are sometimes frictions between the higher officers of the ministerial departments and the advisory staff that directly works with the President.

The President is also helped by the Vice-President (or Vice-Presidents), whose responsibilities are not defined in the Constitution, but in the *Ley del Gobierno*. The practice has been for them to replace the President in various circumstances (such as absence and illness), and to coordinate the governmental activity.[10] It is important to note, however, that the Vice-President does not replace the President permanently in the event that the latter resigns or dies. In such cases, a new President has to be invested by Congress, following the ordinary procedure that was explained in chapter five. So far, no President has died while in office. And only once has a President resigned: Adolfo Suárez did so in January 1981. Leopoldo Calvo-Sotelo was then installed by Congress as the new President.

Ministers

As far as Ministers are concerned, they have a dual function. On the one hand, they are members of the Government, and thus participate in the decision-making process that leads to the policies and strategies that the Government defines. On the other hand, they are the heads of the ministerial departments into which the public administration is divided. They are therefore the highest administrative authority within each Ministry. In a way, the Ministers are the bridge between the sphere of politics (expressed in the Council of Ministers) and the administrative sphere (expressed in the ministerial department). It is possible, however, for someone to be appointed Minister without being in charge of any department (*ministros sin cartera*), but this has not been done for many decades.

In order to introduce the necessary flexibility, the number of Ministries and their competences are not fixed in any statute: they can be defined by the President through a decree.[11] Thus, as a result of the need to reduce public expenses in the middle of the current economic

---

[9] See art 10, *Ley del Gobierno*.

[10] See arts 3, 8.2 and 13.1, *Ley del Gobierno*.

[11] See art 2.2j, *Ley del Gobierno*.

crisis, President Mariano Rajoy (who took office in December 2011) has decreased the number of Ministries from 15 to 12.

Because no coalition governments have ever been installed, the decisions within the Council of Ministers are made rather informally. Internal disagreements are to be expected, but the law is explicit in not imposing on the Government a majoritarian decision-making process.[12] The Government is expected to reach a consensus as to what courses of action to pursue. The centrality of the President, who can freely replace the Ministers, helps bring cohesion to the group. The discussions, moreover, must be kept confidential.

The Status of the Members of the Government

Finally, a few words are in order concerning the status of the members of the Government. The Constitution provides, first, that a position in the Government is incompatible with the exercise of any commercial or professional activity, or with any other public function that is not connected to the office. The only exception is being a parliamentarian – indeed, the actual practice is for the President of the Government (and most Ministers) to be a deputy in Congress. The Constitution remits to a law the detailed regulation of this matter (article 98).

The Constitution also provides that criminal charges against members of the Government can only be brought before the Supreme Court (article 102). This is the same jurisdictional privilege that deputies and senators enjoy. Two special rules are established, however: first, no pardon can be issued for any of these crimes. In a way, the privilege of having been tried by the Supreme Court is compensated by the rule that excludes the conviction from the benefit of a possible pardon. Second, if the charges involve treason or any other crime committed by members of the Government against the security of the State, the accusation needs to be triggered by one-quarter of the deputies in Congress, and it requires the approval of an absolute majority of the deputies. It is important to note that the criminal charges are not brought by Congress, but by the pertinent public prosecutors or private parties. What Congress does is to authorize the criminal process to get started, similarly to what happens when Parliament lifts the criminal immunity of one of its members.

---

[12] See *Disposición Adicional Primera, Ley 30/1992 de Régimen Jurídico de las Administraciones Públicas y del Procedimiento Administrativo Común.*

The Government's 'Directive Function'

We must now turn to an examination of the main tasks the Government is charged with. The Constitution provides that the Government 'directs domestic and foreign policy, the civil and military administration and the defense of the state'. In addition to this directive function, the Constitution empowers the Government to issue regulations and to exercise the 'executive function' (article 97). It is quite clear, therefore, that the Government plays a leadership role. Its powers are certainly not confined to the execution of the laws.

Actually, the executive function the Government performs is rather marginal. It is largely for the public administration, not the Government, to execute the laws on a daily basis: giving a license for an activity; fining an infraction of the law; taxing and taking private property; providing services and goods people are entitled to, and so on. Only in some cases of special significance does the law provide that the decision is for the Council of Ministers to make. Contracts for public works, for example, can only be authorized by the Government, if the costs involved exceed a certain amount of money.

So the Government's main function is to define the national policy, a responsibility that needs to be placed in the context of a parliamentary democracy. Parliament is a key institution, as we saw in the previous chapter, insofar as it has the responsibility for selecting and then check-ing the Government, and for enacting statutes, which are the most important rules of the legal system (apart from the Constitution). But the impulse to define new goals, to choose the means to satisfy them, and to coordinate the different branches of the State for these purposes, lies with the Government. The President, we should recall, is invested by Congress on the basis of a political programme that needs to be translated into a set of laws. The Government is expected to rely on a sufficient majority in Parliament for such purposes. As was already noted, the Government is the main source of legislation: most statutes in Spain are based on bills that the Council of Ministers sends Congress. Some initiatives, moreover, can only be taken by the Government, such as drafting the general budget of the State (article 134) or calling a refer-endum (article 92). Consistent with this, the Government is given the weapon of dissolving Parliament and calling elections when it feels it necessary to renew the public's support to its general programme.

The Government's directive function is even more salient in the field of foreign affairs. The need for States to deal and negotiate with other States has often led constitutional systems to grant the executive branch more leeway when engaging in foreign policy. The way international Treaties are agreed upon, for example, is revealing. Negotiations to enter a Treaty can only be entertained by the executive. Parliament intervenes later, sometimes to be informed about the Treaty, other times to give its consent, as we saw in chapter three. Similarly, it is for the Government to declare war or peace, though it needs Parliament's approval (article 63.3 of the Constitution). And the Government has the power to commit the participation of the armed forces in missions that take place outside the Spanish territory, with the previous authorization of Congress.[13]

The directive function that the Government is charged with can only be exercised if the public administration is also directed by the Government, as the Constitution provides (article 97). The bureaucratic branch is a neutral instrument that must serve the policies defined by the Government. The Ministers are the highest organs within each ministerial department, and they bring to bear the strategies and priorities that the Government defines. For these purposes, the Government has the authority to appoint and remove key officials at the highest echelons of the administration (just below the Minister). Depending on the cases, the appointment may be totally free, or certain legal requirements may instead have to be met (such as choosing from among certain types of public servants).

The Government, moreover, is entitled to issue instructions and guidelines for the administration to follow. But these instructions must comply with the law. Article 103 of the Constitution explicitly says that the administration must 'serve with objectivity the general interests', and must act in accordance with 'statutes and the law'. There is a potential tension here, of course, between the political direction by the Government and the bureaucratic objectivity of the administration. The mediating function of the law is crucial in this area. The statutes and regulations enacted by the

---

[13] See arts 4.2 and 5, *Ley Orgánica 5/2005 de la Defensa Nacional.* The prominence of the President within the Government gets reinforced in this field. The direction of defence policies is attributed to him, whereas the Ministry of Defence is in charge of developing and executing those policies. The Consejo de Defensa Nacional is an organ that serves the President directly when dealing with these matters. See arts 6, 7 and 8, *Ley de la Defensa Nacional.*

democratically accountable branches define the 'general interests' that the administration must pursue in its activity. The latter must apply the body of relevant law in an impartial manner. The Government cannot derogate from the general rules in a particular case, to benefit or harm the interests of a particular person.[14] If the Government issues instructions that deviate from the existing laws, judicial checks can be put in motion. It bears emphasizing that the fact that the Government can normally rely on a parliamentary majority to easily change any statute it does not like makes it less necessary for the Government to disrupt the law through internal administrative instructions.

The Government's Authority to Enact Regulations

In addition to the directive function, the Constitution explicitly provides that the Government is authorized to issue regulations (*reglamentos*). These norms have a lower rank than statutes passed by Parliament. They must therefore be consistent with the latter.

The *Ley del Gobierno* establishes the procedure that needs to be followed for regulations to be enacted.[15] Basically, an initial proposal has to be drafted by the pertinent administrative unit. Various reports have to be submitted, on the necessity of the new regulation, and on its impact on economic matters and gender equality. If the norms being considered affect the rights and legitimate interests of citizens, the latter have a right to be heard, either directly or through the associations recognized by the law to represent their interests in the relevant field. If appropriate, the proposed regulation can also be subject to public information.

An important distinction applies with respect to the organ that is authorized to finally approve a regulation. If the regulation develops or executes a pre-existing statute, only the Council of Ministers can approve it, through a decree. Otherwise, the regulation can be issued by the relevant Minister, through a Ministerial Order.[16] This distinction would be very important in practice if a coalition government were ever established: the Government as a whole would have to negotiate the terms of a regulation that implemented a statute.[17]

[14] See art 52.2, *Ley 30/1992.*

[15] See art 24, *Ley del Gobierno.*

[16] See art 5, *Ley del Gobierno.*

[17] In Austria, eg the distribution of regulatory labour between the Government and the Ministers is of great importance when coalition governments are formed.

It is uncontroversial that statutes are superior to regulations, but there is debate as to the foundations of this hierarchy. In the past, a democratic case could easily be made: while statutes came from a popularly elected assembly, administrative regulations were the product of an unelected King and his Government. The historical fight for democracy in Europe was the fight to curtail the power of the executive, to make it subordinate to the laws passed by Parliament. Today, however, both Parliament and the Cabinet are democratic institutions. As we have already noted, the President of the Government enjoys a strong democratic legitimacy, given the way he or she is appointed. It is not obvious that the distinction between statutes and regulations mirrors the distinction between a more democratic institution and a less democratic one. A better view is that the distinction still makes sense, but it is not based on the character of the law-making institution, but on the public visibility of the procedure through which the norms are approved. Whereas statutes are the outcome of a parliamentary procedure that attracts public attention – given, to a large extent, the role of the opposition as a dialectical check on the ruling majority – regulations are instead adopted through a procedure that is more hidden from public view.

A further complication, of a more technical sort, relates to the so-called 'statutory reserves' (*reservas de ley*). The Spanish Constitution does not merely rank statutes over regulations. It does something else: it establishes that certain matters can only be regulated by statute. The Constitution 'reserves' those matters to statutes, thus making it impossible for executive regulations to intervene in the absence of statutes. The Constitutional Court has read these reserves in a flexible manner: it has held that regulations can still be issued, provided they serve as mere technical auxiliaries to implement or specify the legal provisions contained in the pertinent statute. The statute, however, has to contain the heart of the normative discipline in the field. The legislature cannot enact an almost empty statute that actually transfers the law-making task to the executive branch (STC 83/1984). As the expression goes, the regulation must have an 'executive' character, not merely an 'authorized' character.

There has been controversy, however, about the scope of such 'statutory reserves'. Throughout the Constitution we find many clauses

See M Stelzer, *The Constitution of the Republic of Austria. A Contextual Analysis* (Oxford, Hart Publishing, 2011) 92.

specifying that a particular subject matter is reserved to statutory law. Article 53.1, for example, provides that the fundamental rights and liberties enumerated in Chapter II of Title I can only be regulated by statute. Matters that have to do with the organization of the State are also reserved to statutes in many instances. Article 103.3, for example, provides that the norms regulating the civil service must be established by statute, and article 117.2 states that the reasons to suspend or remove judges must be enumerated in a statute. There are actually many examples of statutory reserves throughout the Constitution. The question that has sparked the debate is this: is there a 'general reserve' in favour of liberty? More precisely: apart from the many specific reserves mentioned in the Constitution, is there an implicit rule to the effect that any norm that affects the negative liberty of individuals (to act as they wish) must be based on a statute? Note that the Constitution protects many liberty rights of a fundamental nature (religious liberty, freedom of speech, freedom of association, the right to strike, etc). The question that is being asked is whether any provision that constrains the behaviour of individuals, even if it does not affect a constitutionally protected fundamental right, should be based on a statutory enactment. Scholars disagree on this matter, and courts have not settled the issue.[18]

The Government's Authority to Enact Norms that have the Same Rank as Statutes

In addition to enacting regulations, the Government is empowered by the Constitution to produce two types of norms that have the same rank as statutes. Because they have the same rank, such norms are capable of repealing or amending any previous statutory provision.

Decretos-ley

The first possibility is for the executive branch to issue a special type of decree that is called *decreto-ley*.[19] Article 86 authorizes the Government to

---

[18] For divergent views, see, eg I de Otto, *Derecho constitucional. Sistema de fuentes* (Barcelona, Ariel, 1988) 214–42 and E García de Enterría and T-R Fernández, *Curso de Derecho administrativo* (Madrid, Cizur Menor, 2011).

[19] For a systematic examination of this type of norm, see A Carmona Contreras, *La configuración constitucional del Decreto-ley* (Madrid, Centro de Estudios Políticos y Constitucionales, 1997).

do so in the event of 'an extraordinary and urgent necessity'. The *decreto-ley* produces effects since its promulgation, but it is necessary for Congress to ratify it within 30 days. (The Senate does not take part in this procedure). If the decree is validated by Congress, it continues to operate for the indefinite future. If, instead, it is not validated, it is 'repealed', as the Constitution states. The decree thus stops producing legal effects.

At a first stage, Congress is asked to either ratify or repeal the decree. It cannot introduce any amendments. It is possible, however, for Parliament to decide to transform the decree that has been validated into a *proyecto de ley*, a statutory project proposed by the executive. In that case, the decree is used as the starting point of a regular legislative procedure, which may end up with the passage of an ordinary statute, which may include all kinds of amendments to the original text. Once passed, the statute will replace the decree that was originally ratified. (The Constitution establishes an urgent legislative procedure to transform the decree into a statute).

The Constitutional Court has had to review the constitutionality of various *decretos-ley*. The question arose what interpretation should be given to the expression 'extraordinary and urgent necessity'. The Court distinguished this situation from the more extreme states of emergency that the Constitution regulates in article 116. The kind of necessity that allows the Government to issue a *decreto-ley* is less stringent than the necessity that arises under such emergency situations. It is not an 'absolute necessity', but a 'relative' one (STC 6/1983). The idea is that sometimes measures need to be adopted to deal with a particular situation, and the ordinary legislative procedure (even the urgent one) is too slow to get them enacted in time. The Government must expressly indicate which situation amounts to a state of 'necessity', and the measures it adopts must be linked to that situation. The Court, however, has been very deferential in its review of the governmental judgment that an extraordinary or urgent need exists.

The Constitution places some substantive limits, however. Article 86.1 provides that a *decreto-ley* cannot affect certain matters: the regulation of the basic institutions of the State; the rights, duties and liberties enumerated in Title I; the legal regime of Autonomous Communities and general electoral law. The Constitutional Court has had to specify the scope of these limits. It has tried to interpret them in ways that do not end up making it almost impossible for the Government to resort to this type of legal measure. The Court, in particular, has chosen to interpret the limitation that is connected to rights, duties and liberties, in a restrictive manner. It has held that a *decreto-ley* cannot have an impact on the general regime of those rights, duties and liberties, but it can affect them incidentally. Applying this distinction in practice is not easy, of course. The Court, for example, was deeply divided in one of the most controversial decisions it has ever rendered, concerning a *decreto-ley* that expropriated the shares of a set of banks that were in trouble and risked undermining the whole financial system. The decree was attacked on the grounds that it affected private property. The Court upheld it, over the dissent of half of the judges. The President cast the decisive vote. (See STC 111/1983).

The Government has used this legal instrument quite often. Many important changes in the economic sphere, for example, have been introduced by *decreto-ley*. The fact that the Court has been very deferential towards the Government has encouraged the latter to make an active use of this source of law.[20] The current Government under President Mariano Rajoy, in particular, has employed the *decreto-ley* to enact the vast majority of measures that European institutions have imposed or recommended as a way for Spain to solve its financial problems. From December 2011 to the end of May 2012, in particular, 19 such decrees have been adopted, introducing drastic changes in social and economic matters. All of them have been ratified by Congress without any problems, since the Government's political party (PP) has an absolute majority of the parliamentary seats. Of those 19 decrees, only 4 have been converted into ordinary laws. This means that only in four cases has it been possible for Parliament to introduce amendments to the Government's initiative.

Finally, it is important to point out that, because *decretos-ley* are awarded the same rank as statutes, the Constitutional Court gets jurisdiction to pass on their constitutional validity.

Decretos legislativos

The other manner in which the executive branch can enact norms that have the same rank as statutes is for it to obtain a 'delegation' of legisla-

---

[20] The Court, however, has struck down *decretos-ley* in a few cases. See, eg STC 68/2007 and STC 137/2011.

tive authority from Parliament.[21] Articles 82–85 of the Constitution regulate this possibility.

The first step is for the Cortes Generales to enact a statute that allows the executive branch to enact regulations that have the same force as statutes. Only the Government as a whole (not the President or the Ministers, or inferior administrative authorities) can be authorized to do so. Parliament must expressly define the matters for which legislative power is being transferred, and it must establish a deadline for the delegated power to be exercised. The Government is authorized to veto any legislative proposal that runs contrary to the existing delegation. Parliament, however, can choose to repeal the enabling statute (totally or partially).

The second step is for the Government to issue the regulations, which are called *decretos legislativos*. Once the Government has issued the pertinent *decreto legislativo*, the delegation is over (even if the deadline has not expired).

The Constitution distinguishes two kinds of possibilities. The enabling statute may be a *Ley de bases*, or a *Ley ordinaria*. In the first case, the delegation is more substantial: the Government is asked to issue a new articulated text. The enabling law must therefore fix the basic principles the Government must follow when making use of the delegated power. It cannot authorize the Government to change the enabling law, or to issue norms with retroactive effects. In the second case, the Government is merely entitled to put together a set of already existing legal texts, sometimes harmonizing the possible inconsistencies.

There is an important limitation that the Constitution establishes: no delegation of legislative power is valid if the matter to be regulated is one of those matters that the Constitution reserves to organic statutes.

The *decreto legislativo* is a useful technique to produce more coherent legislative pieces, and to introduce clarity in areas that are governed by scattered texts. Important laws such as the Civil Code, and the laws regulating civil and criminal procedures, for example, were historically introduced in Spain through this mechanism, which the Constitution of 1978 preserves. The Council of State, as we will see, has actually recommended the Government to use this type of norm more often, to better codify the existing law.

---

[21] On this legal technique, see I Gutiérrez Gutiérrez, *Los controles de la legislación delegada* (Madrid, Centro de Estudios Constitucionales, 1995).

There has been some debate concerning the mechanisms to review the constitutionality of *decretos legislativos*. What happens, in particular, when the allegation is made that a *decreto legislativo* is ultra vires, in that it goes beyond the scope of matters (or does not comply with the substantive constraints) defined in the underlying statute? Some scholars have argued that the ultra vires *decreto legislativo* is still a norm with a statutory rank, and is therefore under the exclusive jurisdiction of the Constitutional Court. Others have countered that the *decreto legislativo*, if and to the extent that it is ultra vires, loses its statutory rank, and must therefore be treated as an ordinary administrative regulation that can therefore be set aside by any court. Both the Constitutional Court and ordinary judges have embraced this latter theory.[22]

Confronting a Crisis: States of Emergency (Alarm, Exception and Siege)

When carrying out all the functions we have examined so far, the Government is expected to abide by the laws and constitutional constraints that apply in normal times. The Constitution, however, allows the Government to enter a special legal regime, under which more power is attributed to the executive branch, and various fundamental rights can be restricted or suspended in a manner that would be unlawful under ordinary circumstances.[23] The state of emergency can come in three different forms: 'alarm', 'exception' and 'siege'. They may affect all Spanish territory, or specific parts of it. They are all temporally limited legal regimes, their ultimate goal being the restoration of constitutional normalcy.[24]

The *state of alarm* is the least serious of the three. It is the only one that has ever been declared by the Government so far. It involves public catastrophes, health crisis, paralysis of essential public services, or short-

---

[22] The practice has textual support in art 82.6 of the Constitution, which refers to the control to be exercised by 'courts'. See, also, art 1.1, *Ley 29/1998, reguladora de la Jurisdicción Contencioso-Administrativa*.

[23] See arts 116 and 55.1 of the Constitution. The details of this exceptional regime to deal with an emergency are specified in an organic statute: *Ley Orgánica 4/1981, de los estados de alarma, excepción y sitio*.

[24] See P Cruz Villalón, *Estados excepcionales y suspensión de garantías* (Madrid, Tecnos, 1984).

age of first necessity goods. It is decreed by the Council of Ministers, for a maximum period of 15 days. Congress must be informed immediately. Any extension of the period requires congressional authorization. During a state of alarm, all civil authorities and their staff are placed under the command of the Government, which can issue orders that impose extraordinary services. The measures to be enacted depend on the nature of the circumstances. They include restricting the free movement of people, taking property temporarily, imposing personal services, occupying industries, limiting consumption of first necessity goods or services, among others. Thus, on 4 December 2010, the Government declared a state of alarm and militarized the airports to ensure the normal functioning of transport, as a response to a wild strike by air traffic controllers.

The *state of exception* entails a graver situation: a serious alteration of public order. It is also decreed by the Council of Ministers, but it needs the previous authorization of Congress. The maximum period allowed is 30 days, but it can be extended in the same manner. Under the state of exception, certain fundamental rights can be 'suspended': a person can be arrested for a maximum period of 10 days (though courts must be informed in 24 hours); houses and papers can be registered without judicial warrant, and communications can be intercepted (but courts must be informed immediately); free movement can be restricted in several ways; publications and broadcasts in the media can be suspended; public meetings and demonstrations can be prohibited (but not, interestingly, the organic meetings of political parties, trade unions and business associations) and strikes and measures of collective conflict can be banned. Other measures that do not technically entail a 'suspension' of fundamental rights are also allowed (such as occupying industries, for example). The measures that are designed for a state of alarm, moreover, can also be used, if necessary.

Finally, the *state of siege*, which is the most extraordinary of the three types of emergencies, can only be declared by an absolute majority of Congress. The situation being confronted in such a state is an insurrection or threat of insurrection, or any other act by force against the sovereignty or independence of Spain, its territorial integrity, or its constitutional system. In addition to the measures that can be taken under a state of alarm or exception, the rights of the arrested person (the right to be informed, the right to silence, the right to a lawyer) can be suspended. The Government appoints the military authority that, under its direction, will execute the appropriate extraordinary measures. The crimes committed under a state of siege can be transferred to the jurisdiction of military tribunals.

The Constitution explicitly says that the life of Parliament and the other constitutional institutions cannot be interrupted during any of these emergency situations. Congress, in particular, cannot be dissolved. If it had already been dissolved or its mandate had expired, the Diputación Permanente would then be in charge.

The Constitution also provides that the declaration of any of these states does not alter the general principles and rules of state liability. Individuals who are harmed by the measures adopted are thus entitled to recover damages, on the basis of general legal doctrines. The legal validity of the extraordinary measures, moreover, can be attacked through the judicial procedures. So far, however, this legal regime has not proven to be very effective in protecting individuals. Thus, the traffic controllers who were subjected to the militarization measures that the Government decreed in December 2010 tried to challenge them. They initiated proceedings before the Supreme Court, which refused to hear their case on the grounds that, because the executive decree had been ratified by Parliament, it could not be controlled by ordinary courts. The traffic controllers had also filed a complaint before the Constitutional Court, which also refused to take the case, on the grounds that for a parliamentary action of that kind to be reviewed, a constitutional complaint was not the right procedure. Instead, it was for ordinary courts to raise a question to the Constitutional Court in the context of ordinary litigation![25] This was a rather disappointing response. Three judges on the Court published a powerful dissent, arguing that the complaint should have been admitted.

THE PUBLIC ADMINISTRATION

The Government can only exercise its directive function in an effective manner if it can use the public administration (Administración Pública) to implement its policies. The administrative apparatus in a 'social State' (as the Constitution proclaims Spain to be) is bound to be large. Beyond exercising traditional police powers, the administration provides many

---

[25] See ATC 7/2012.

important services and goods to citizens, who are entitled to certain levels of social and economic well-being. The administration is basically staffed by permanent civil servants, who must be recruited on the basis of criteria that relate to their 'merit and ability', as the Constitution specifies.

The different administrative bodies in Spain can be classified in various ways. First of all, we need to draw a distinction between the 'central' organs of the administration and the 'peripheral' organs. The latter exercise their functions in the Autonomous Communities and in the provinces that Spain is territorially divided into. Thus, a *delegado del gobierno* directs the state administration in the Autonomous Community, and a *subdelegado del gobierno* does so in the province. These peripheral organs should not be confused with the administrative bodies that belong to the various regional and local governments, which we will study in the next chapter. The peripheral organs we are here referring to are part of the 'State administration' at the national level (Administración General del Estado).

In addition, the administration also includes other entities that have no territorial basis. Some are 'public corporations', which are based on associations of people. Professional associations, which are assigned some public missions, are an example of such corporations. Other entities are the so-called 'public organisms', which are created to pursue a particular public goal. The Social Security Institute, the National Health Institute, and public undertakings have adopted this institutional form. Some administrative entities enjoy a large degree of autonomy vis-à-vis the territorial administrations. The existence of these 'independent administrative authorities or agencies', as they are usually called, raises some constitutional problems, as we will see later.

The Constitution lists some principles that govern the structure and performance of the administration. Article 103 mentions the principles of hierarchy, decentralization, coordination, objectivity and efficacy. It also includes some rules concerning civil servants: they must be recruited through a system based on merits and ability, and their right to union membership can be subjected to a special regime.[26] One of the traditional defects of the Spanish public administration is that a significant

---

[26] Within the administration, the military are subject to an even more restrictive regime: the Constitution explicitly prohibits them to petition the government collectively (art 29), and authorizes the law to prohibit or limit the right to union membership (art 28).

number of the highest officers that are appointed by the Government are not the best from a technical point of view. As many critics have pointed out, it is perfectly understandable for Ministers to choose persons they consider to be politically reliable. It is not acceptable, however, for so many of the appointees to lack the professional qualifications that are necessary to perform their jobs. The Government should be free to recruit the experts from among the best public servants, or from outside the administration. But it should make sure their appointees are really qualified for the tasks they are being charged with. Political connections and friendships should not have the weight they tend to have in practice.[27]

In this regard, some scholars have proposed that the law should require the Government to inform Congress of the appointments being considered. Parliament would then be in a position to scrutinize the technical credentials of the candidates. Even if no veto power were granted to Congress, at least there would be some kind of check.[28] It bears mentioning that, in general, the Constitutional Court has been very deferential to the executive branch when it comes to reviewing the legality of promotions within the administration. The Court has held that standards of 'merit and ability' that apply to promotions are less strict than those that apply to selections at the entrance level (see, for instance, STC 293/1993).

Given the politicization of the highest levels of the administrative apparatus, it is not surprising that the reaction, in part, has been to establish independent agencies or authorities in some fields. The need has been felt to create institutions that are detached from the Government, in order to depoliticize certain decision-making processes.

The first such agency was the Council of Nuclear Security.[29] The law drew inspiration from the American and British models. A more important example is the Bank of Spain, which was given an independent status in order to comply with European Union norms, as laid down in the Maastricht Treaty.[30] Other examples are the National Stock Exchange Commission, the Market of Communications Commission, the

---

[27] For a critical view, see R Jiménez Asensio, *Altos cargos y directivos públicos (Un estudio sobre las relaciones entre política y administración en España)* (Oñati, IVAP, 1996).

[28] For a proposal along these lines, see R Blanco Valdés, *Las conexiones políticas* (Madrid, Alianza Editorial, 2001) 156–64.

[29] It was established by *Ley 15/1980*.

[30] See *Ley 13/1994, de Autonomía del Banco de España.*

National Competition Commission, the Data Protection Agency, and the State Council of Audiovisual Media.[31]

Some features tend to be common among these different agencies. First, the Government often appoints their members, but it cannot freely remove them. They hold their positions for a limited period of time (though it is often possible to renew the appointment once). This job security ensures a certain level of independence. Sometimes, the Government is expected, or is even required, to fill the vacancies with people that represent different political groups. Other times, Parliament has a say in the appointment process. Second, the Government cannot issue instructions to the agencies as to how they should perform their tasks. Third, the agencies are often partially funded out of the fees they charge for their services. This ensures a certain measure of economic independence. Fourth, many of the decisions made by the agencies cannot be challenged before the Government. Instead, they are directly reviewed for their validity by the courts. These and other features secure the autonomy of the agencies, but it is a limited autonomy. The Government, after all, does appoint the members of many of these administrative entities. And it is sometimes possible for the Government to influence their strategies in informal ways. The Minister of Economy and Finance, for example, can attend the meetings of the Bank of Spain.

The existence of these independent administrative agencies has raised some doubts from a constitutional perspective. Thus, one of the crucial principles the Constitution embodies is the principle of administrative legality (article 103). This principle serves rule of law values, of course, but it is also connected to democratic considerations. The administration is a bureaucratic branch whose legitimacy is largely based on expertise and instrumental capacity. This legitimacy, however, needs to be reinforced from a democratic perspective. All the organs of the State must have some links, whether direct or indirect, to the will of the people. In the case of the administration, this link is established, first, through its connection to a Government that is accountable to Parliament and public opinion. Secondly, and very importantly, the administration is subject to the laws – to the statutes and regulations that have been enacted by democratically accountable bodies. Judicial review of administrative decisions under the laws thus serves democratic principles.

---

[31] See *Ley 24/1988*, *Ley 32/2003*, *Ley 15/2007*, *Ley 15/1999* and *Ley 7/2010*, respectively.

This general picture blurs when independent agencies are considered. As was already indicated, the Government has a much more limited capacity to direct their activities – no instructions can be issued, for example, nor is it possible for the Government to freely remove those who run such agencies. It is true that the agencies must observe the law, but the law that is to be applied or developed is often very open-ended. It is precisely because of the technical expertise of such administrative entities that the law to be implemented by them tends to be less detailed. So the democratic legitimacy that the statutes can confer on the agencies is rather marginal.

As a result of all this, there has been some scholarly debate about the constitutionality of such entities.[32] We should bear in mind that there was no independent agency when the Constitution was enacted in 1978. The first one was set up in 1980. It is thus not surprising that the Constitution grants the Government an unqualified directive function over the administration as a whole. Independent agencies were not part of the legal landscape when the Constitution was written. In general, scholars have emphasized the advantages of independent agencies, in terms of technical expertise. Those agencies can be used, moreover, to curb the excesses of a potentially partisan Government. But some commentators have suggested the need to amend the Constitution and introduce a clause that expressly allows for administrative independence. A more secure legal foundation is necessary, they argue. The only possible exception, it is sometimes said, concerns the Bank of Spain, whose autonomy is imposed by EU law. Since EU law can override national law, there may be a sufficient title here for the Bank to be shielded from the directive function that the Government can ordinarily exercise.

CONTROLLING THE GOVERNMENT AND THE ADMINISTRATION

After having examined the structure and functions of the two levels that make up the executive branch (the Government and the administration), we should now focus on various mechanisms to control their

---

[32] On this debate, see M Magide Herrero, *Límites constitucionales de las Administraciones independientes* (Madrid, INAP, 2000) and A Rallo Lombarte, *La constitucionalidad de las administraciones independientes* (Madrid, Tecnos, 2002).

actions. This topic is particularly important, since the capacity of the Government and the administration to abuse their powers and to harm individual rights and interests is high, given the powerful machinery of the modern State.

There are, first, 'political controls'. Parliament, as we know, is expected to control how the Government and the administration go about their business. The parliamentary opposition is the key check here. Public opinion too is supposed to be attentive to whatever abuses are perpetrated. Citizens, moreover, can check the executive branch through participation in the administrative decision-making process. The Constitution guarantees the right of citizens to be heard, directly or through organizations or associations recognized by the law, when general regulations are issued (article 105). It also protects the right of interested parties to be heard when specific administrative acts are adopted. The Constitution, moreover, facilitates citizen participation through the right of access to administrative registers and files (unless the matter involves the security and defence of the State, criminal investigations or individual privacy).

In addition, specific institutions have been created to make sure that the Government and the administration comply with the law. In what follows, we will first examine two non-judicial bodies: the Council of State and the Ombudsman. We will then study the role of courts as checks. We will refer, in particular, to administrative tribunals and to a special court: the Court of Audit (Tribunal de Cuentas).

The Council of State (Consejo de Estado)

The Council of State is a key institution to press the executive branch towards compliance with the law before decisions are made. According to the Constitution, the Council of State is the Government's 'supreme advisory body' (article 107). The structure and competences of this institution are regulated in a specific organic statute.[33]

The Council consists of a President, who is freely appointed and dismissed by the Government, and three types of members. 'Permanent' counsellors are appointed by the Government, and they serve for life. They must hold or have held certain positions, such as Minister, civil

---

[33] See *Ley Orgánica 3/1980, del Consejo de Estado.*

servant, member of a royal academy, university professor, and others. 'Elective' counsellors are also appointed by the Government, but their term is limited to four years. They must have pertained to certain categories specified in the law. The third group includes the so-called *consejeros natos*, which derive their membership from some other office they occupy. They comprise, for example, the Presidents of Royal Academies, the State Public Prosecutor, the President of the Spanish Bar Association, and the Bank of Spain's Chairperson. Former Presidents of the Government are also part of the Council.

The Council's basic mission is to issue reports on legal and constitutional questions that affect the Government. It must act in an independent and objective manner. It can also speak to the opportunity of decisions, beyond their conformity with the law. The Government, moreover, can request the Council to draft a legislative proposal, or a proposal for constitutional reform, in light of particular criteria.

The Council has thus issued thousands of reports on very specific decisions to be taken by the executive branch, as well as more general reports on broader issues. The reports submitted from 1987 onwards (more than 50,000) are available electronically on the Council's website.[34] Recent general reports have dealt with issues as different as the amendment of the Constitution (report of 16 February 2006), the mechanisms to guarantee the observance of European Union law by Spanish authorities (report of 15 December 2010), and measures that may be adopted to restrict advertisements on sex and prostitution in the public media (report of 9 March 2011).

Normally, the Council acts on the request of the Government, but it can also act on its own initiative, making proposals for the Government to consider. Each year, for example, the Council must submit a general report on its activities (*memoria*), which can include ideas about possible changes. In the 2010 report, for example, the Council emphasized that, as a general principle, citizens should be given the possibility to interact with the administration through electronic means, but should not be required to do so. The Council also suggested that the Government should consider clarifying and harmonizing the existing laws in different fields, through a more intense use of *Decretos legislativos*. The report included many other recommendations.

---

[34] The Council's website is: www.consejo-estado.es.

The law permits affected individuals to be heard by the Council before it renders its opinions. The regional governments can also ask to be heard, if their interests are at stake. Experts, moreover, can be invited to express their judgments on the issues being considered. The reports by the Council are to be agreed upon by the majority of councillors that participate in the case. Dissenting opinions are allowed.

The general rule is that the Government – that is, the Council of Ministers or a Minister – is free to request reports from the Council. The presidents of the regional governments can also obtain advice from the Council. Sometimes, however, the law makes it legally necessary for the Council to issue a report. This is so, for example, when a regulation implementing a statute is to be enacted; or when a decision by an Autonomous Community is to be challenged by the Government before the Constitutional Court; or when certain problems concerning an administrative contract or public concession arise; or when liability for damages has been requested by a citizen.[35]

Similarly, the general rule is that the reports are not binding: the Government is free not to follow the Council's legal advice. Sometimes, however, the opinions are binding. When the executive branch wants to declare that an administrative act or a regulation is null and void, for instance, it needs to obtain a 'favourable report' from the Council of State.[36] Even when the reports are not binding, the Government pays attention to them, given the Council's professional prestige. To reinforce the Council's influence, the law establishes that when a Minister disagrees with a report that the Council has rendered, the matter must be addressed by the Council of Ministers (in those cases when the legal advice is necessary). So a matter that would normally be decided by a single member of the Government is transferred to the whole Government. Similarly, the decisions by the Government must indicate whether or not they are made in accordance with the Council's reports. The formula 'in accordance with the Council of State' can only be employed when the governmental act follows the conclusions reached in the report. If the conclusions are not followed, the formula to be used is 'having heard the Council of State'. The Government, of course, will be an easier target for legal and political criticism if it refuses to respect the positions held by its supreme advisory body.

[35] These and other cases are listed in arts 21 and 22, *Ley Orgánica del Consejo de Estado*.

[36] See art 102, *Ley 30/1992*.

The Ombudsman (Defensor del Pueblo)

Another relevant institution to control the actions of the administration is the Ombudsman.[37] He or she is appointed by the Cortes Generales to supervise the administration, for purposes of guarding the fundamental rights protected in Title I of the Constitution.

Because the administration is the target of the Ombudsman's checking activities, the Constitution establishes that he must be appointed by Parliament. The Congress and the Senate have to agree on the appointment.[38] The term of office is five years, though reappointment is allowed.

The Ombudsman's authority extends to all bodies within the public administration, including those at the regional and local levels. The Autonomous Communities can create similar organs to supervise their own administrations, but such organs do not replace the national Ombudsman.[39] All authorities and public servants, including the Ministers, can be subject to the Ombudsman's inquiries. Private persons who serve the administration are also covered, and so is the military administration. The most important exclusion concerns the judiciary: any complaint about the courts has to be remitted to the Office of the Public Prosecutor, which may decide to submit the matter to the General Council of the Judiciary.

The role of the Ombudsman is to investigate the workings of the administration, to make sure that fundamental rights are observed, and that public authority is exercised in an objective, efficient and legal fashion. He can initiate his enquiries on the request of interested individuals. The complaints cannot be anonymous (they must be signed), but no lawyers are required, and no fees are charged. The complaints can be filed online.[40] In 2011, about two-thirds of them were sent electronically. In addition, the deputies and senators (or the pertinent Parliamentary

[37] This institution is established in art 54 of the Constitution, and is further regulated in an organic statute: *Ley Orgánica 3/1981, del Defensor del Pueblo.*

[38] A super-majority of three-fifths is required in each chamber. Failing that, a second vote of three-fifths in the Congress and absolute majority in the Senate is then sufficient.

[39] A law was enacted to coordinate the activity of the Ombudsman with that of similar officers established at the regional level: *Ley 36/1985.*

[40] The Ombudsman's website, where complaints can be submitted, is www.defensordelpueblo.es.

Commissions) can ask the Ombudsman to investigate a particular matter. And he may start an enquiry on his own motion.

In 2011, for example, 24,381 cases were initiated (506 of which were started by the Ombudsman on his own motion). A significant part of the complaints (7,522) were not filed individually, but by groups of people. At the end of the year, 4,800 were pending.[41]

A particular field the Ombudsman is required to investigate concerns torture. Spain ratified in 2006 the Optional Protocol to the Convention against Torture and Other Cruel, Inhuman or Degrading Treatment or Punishment. The law establishes that the Ombudsman will serve as the 'independent national preventive mechanism' for purposes of that Protocol.

Public authorities must offer their cooperation to the Ombudsman. The latter is entitled to read administrative documents and files, and to interview the pertinent staff. It is actually a criminal offence for someone to refuse the cooperation requested. Even documents that are classified as secret can be accessed, unless the Council of Ministers decides otherwise. If a judicial decision is pending in a particular case, however, the Ombudsman must abstain from investigating.

When the Ombudsman finishes his investigation concerning a particular affair, he can make proposals. The administration is free to follow them or not. The Ombudsman can also make suggestions of a more general character, concerning the norms and practices that need to be changed. In general, the administration tends to agree with the Ombudsman when it answers its suggestions and recommendations. In 2011, for example, the administration's response was positive in around 70 per cent of the cases.

The Ombudsman is in institutional touch with Parliament, through a Congress–Senate Joint Commission. He must submit an annual report, indicating the complaints received and the decisions made with respect to them. No personal data are included in the report, but it is possible to mention the identity of the public officers who exhibited a hostile or obstructionist attitude during the investigations. The Ombudsman must present a summary of his report in both Congress and the Senate, where the different parliamentary groups can participate in a discussion and express their opinions.

---

[41] All this information is included in the 2011 general report of the Ombudsman's activities, which can be accessed on its website.

The Constitution gives the Ombudsman a powerful weapon, beyond the general supervisory attributions we have just examined. He can bring complaints before the Constitutional Court, for violation of fundamental rights, and he can also file constitutional challenges against statutes. The Ombudsman has made a moderate use of this power, however, in spite of the fact that the Court has interpreted it broadly. (The Court has held that the Ombudsman can challenge statutes, even if the grounds of attack are not related to fundamental rights: STC 150/1990).

Administrative Courts

In addition to the non-judicial bodies we have studied so far, courts are relied upon to verify the conformity of the actions of the executive branch with the Constitution and the laws.

A set of courts are specialized in this task: the 'administrative courts', which exercise the so-called *jurisdicción contencioso-administrativa*. At their summit sits the third chamber of the Supreme Court. In spite of their specialization, these are not separate tribunals. They belong to the ordinary judicial branch, and are granted the same guarantees of independence that apply to courts in general (which we will examine in chapter eight).

Administrative courts handle many cases every year. This is not surprising, given the many instances in which citizens interact with the public administration in a modern State. The third chamber of the Supreme Court, in particular, receives a large case load. In 2010, for example, 8,757 cases were brought to it. Even if the Court decided 9,455 cases, there were still 14,377 pending cases at the end of that year. The Ministry of Justice and the Supreme Court have signed several agreements to ensure that more resources are assigned to the third chamber, in order to increase the legal staff that can help judges cope with the situation.[42]

The Constitution is quite categorical when it provides that the administration is 'fully subject to the statutes and the law' (article 103.1). This is an important statement, in that it clarifies that the norms to be observed cannot be reduced to statutes (or regulations). There are, in

---

[42] See 'Memoria del Tribunal Supremo' (2010), available at www.poderjudicial.es.

addition, constitutional principles to be taken into account, as well as 'general principles of law', which have traditionally provided courts with a powerful instrument to curb the excesses of the executive branch.

The full subjection to the law also means that there are no areas of activity that are exempt from the law.[43] Sometimes the content of the decision to be rendered by the executive branch is clearly predetermined in the relevant legal provision. Other times, in contrast, the executive branch has discretion to decide (*discrecionalidad*): the law merely lays down a framework, within which there is ample room for manoeuver. But even in these cases, legal limits apply. The Government, for example, is authorized to appoint the State Public Prosecutor, but the appointment must respect the requirements and conditions defined in the law. The Supreme Court once invalidated such an appointment, on the grounds that it failed to comply with the legal requirement that the person have at least 15 years of legal professional experience.[44]

In this connection, the principle of proportionality is increasingly used by courts, to test the reasonableness of administrative decisions that affect private interests. Those decisions, courts have held, must attain public goals with the least restrictive means, and must be based on a reasonable balance of the costs and benefits involved.[45] So judges may be more or less deferential when reviewing governmental and administrative acts, but they cannot hold a category of acts to be exempt from judicial review.[46]

There is some uncertainty as to which courts must review decisions made by the Government. According to the law, the administrative courts can only control the legality of the Government's decisions when the latter are 'subject to administrative law'.[47] What does this mean in practice? A distinction is sometimes made in this connection between

---

[43] Art 26 of the *Ley del Gobierno* is very explicit too when it provides that the Government is subject to the Constitution and the rest of the law 'in all its actions'.

[44] See decision of 28 June 1994, of the third chamber of the Supreme Court.

[45] For a very complete analysis of the application of the principle of proportionality by Spanish courts, see D Sarmiento Ramírez-Escudero, *El control de proporcionalidad de la actividad administrativa* (Valencia, Tirant lo Blanch, 2004).

[46] There has been debate on how deferentially courts should review the discretionary decisions made by the executive branch. For a complete picture of the debate, which was especially passionate in the 1990s, see M Bacigalupo Sagesse, *La discrecionalidad administrativa (Estructura normativa, control judicial y límites constitucionales de su atribución)* (Madrid, Marcial Pons, 1997).

[47] See art 1 of the *Ley 29/1998 reguladora de la Jurisdicción Contencioso-administrativa*.

governmental decisions that belong to the 'executive' and 'regulatory' functions, on the one hand, and those that pertain to the 'directive' function, on the other. The former are subject to administrative law, and can be reviewed by administrative courts. The latter, in contrast, cannot: they are only subject to control by the Constitutional Court, on the grounds, for example, that they have breached fundamental rights. (See, for example, STC 45/1990). But this distinction has been criticized as untenable in practice. Some scholars think that administrative courts should be empowered to intervene in all cases, even if the Constitutional Court can have the last say.[48]

The judiciary has been eager in some remarkable cases to craft doctrines that usefully constrain the actions of the executive branch. An important decision in this regard was rendered by the Supreme Court on 4 April 1997, when it required the Government to deliver certain documents that had been classified as secret. A criminal court had started investigations against public servants that had been involved in the dirty war against ETA's terrorism. The law regulating official secrets (*Ley 9/1968 de Secretos Oficiales*) did not establish any form of judicial review of governmental decisions in this field. The Court decided to inspect the relevant documents *in camera*, even if this kind of check was not established in any law. The Court concluded that, given the importance of the criminal investigations underway (which involved murder), and given the evidential relevance of the documents, the Government's decision to refuse delivery was invalid. It thus ordered the Government to submit the documents to the investigating judges. The order was promptly complied with. This was the first time in Spanish history that a court invalidated a governmental decision of that sort.[49]

Courts are not only empowered to invalidate actions by the executive branch. They are also authorized to fix the compensation the State must pay to indemnify the individuals who have been harmed by its actions or omissions. The Constitution is quite generous in the way it proclaims the principle of State liability for damages. Article 106.2 provides that private individuals, under the terms established by law, shall be entitled to compensation for the harm they may suffer in their property or rights, except in cases of *force majeure*, whenever the harm derives from

---

[48]   For a criticism of the Constitutional Court's position, see ÁJ Gómez Montoro, 'El control jurisdiccional del Gobierno' in Aragón and Gómez Montoro (n 1) 489.

[49]   For an analysis of the judicial approach to official state secrets, see LM Díez-Picazo, *Sobre secretos oficiales* (Madrid, Civitas,1998).

the operation of public services. There is no need for there to be a malfunction of the administration: if an individual suffers a collateral damage that he is not legally obliged to bear, he is entitled to compensation, even if the administration has acted properly. Even the damages caused by the legislature may be indemnified. There has been debate about the precise limits of this doctrine, however. Some scholars have criticized the Supreme Court for having come too close to a regime of strict liability, which may have undesirable consequences.[50]

It should also be noted that all courts (not only administrative courts) can review the validity of regulations enacted by the executive branch. They can set aside the applicable regulation, if they find it to be legally or constitutionally infirm.[51] In addition to this general power of judicial review, some administrative courts can declare with general effects the invalidity of regulations. Interested parties may challenge the regulations, either directly or indirectly (in the context of a particular case). The advantage of these procedures is that a regulatory legal provision can be formally cancelled from the legal system, thus better protecting legal certainty.[52] As we will see in chapter eight, analogous procedures exist for the Constitutional Court to nullify, also with general effects, statutes and other norms that have the same rank as statutes.

The Court of Audit (Tribunal de Cuentas)

The Court of Audit is an even more specialized tribunal than administrative courts. It is regulated in a special organic statute.[53] Its mission, according to the Constitution (article 136), is to audit State accounts and supervise public financial management.

In order to ensure independence vis-à-vis the Government, the Constitution provides that the Court of Audit is directly answerable to the Cortes Generales. The organic statute, moreover, specifies that six

---

[50] See, eg E García de Enterría, *La responsabilidad patrimonial del Estado Legislador en el Derecho español* (Cizur Henor Civitas, 2007).

[51] See art 6, *Ley Orgánica 6/1985 del Poder Judicial*. On the power of courts to test the constitutionality of administrative regulations, see F Caamaño, *El control de constitucionalidad de disposiciones reglamentarias* (Madrid, Centro de Estudios Constitucionales, 1994).

[52] See arts 25, 26, 27 and 123, *Ley 29/1998, reguladora de la Jurisdicción Contencioso-Administrativa*.

[53] See *Ley Orgánica 2/1982 del Tribunal de Cuentas*.

members of the Court are selected by Congress (through a three-fifths super-majority), and six others by the Senate (through the same super-majority). Their term of office is nine years. The Court's members, moreover, are subject to the same regime of independence as regular judges.

Its jurisdiction extends to the public sector as a whole, including, for example, the local and regional public administrations. (The latter, however, can establish their own institutions of control, in addition to the Court). The Court is also empowered to control how private individuals have spent the public funds that were granted to them. Every year, the Court is to render general reports to the national Parliament and to the Autonomous Communities, explaining its findings and conclusions.

The Court has a dual function. First, it verifies whether the general budget of the State has been properly implemented by the executive branch, and whether the different public institutions have correctly managed their economic resources. It acts as the 'delegate' of Parliament when doing so. Second, the Court is also authorized to try cases of alleged violations of the laws, both by public officers and private individuals, in the management of public resources. It fixes the compensation to be paid by the violators for the damages produced. In so doing, the Court exercises a 'judicial function', though it is limited. The determination of the criminal responsibility of individuals who have breached the laws, for example, is in the hands of regular courts. The Court of Audit's decisions, moreover, can be appealed to the Supreme Court.

CONCLUSION

The executive branch is a powerful source of acts that can affect individual citizens in many different ways. It has been of great historical importance in all democratic countries for legal techniques to be gradually developed to control the excesses of that branch. The Spanish Constitution is fully committed to the view that all the actions of the executive branch must observe the law and may be challenged in court. It is necessary, however, for political mechanisms of control to be effective too, in addition to judicial remedies. Parliament is supposed to scrutinize the Government and the administration that the latter directs. In a parliamentary system where the executive branch can count on a stable majority in Congress, it is largely the task of minority parties in the opposition to be vigilant and critical. As was noted in chapter five, however, the capacity of the opposition to effectively control the Government is rather limited. It is not surprising that many issues have been judicialized, as a result of these limitations.

FURTHER READING

Aragón, M and Gómez Montoro, AJ (eds), *El Gobierno. Problemas constitucionales* (Madrid, Centro de Estudios Políticos y Constitucionales, 2005).

Bacigalupo Sagesse, M, *La discrecionalidad administrativa (Estructura normativa, control judicial y límites constitucionales de su atribución)* (Madrid, Marcial Pons, 1997).

Carmona Contreras, A, *La configuración constitucional del Decreto-ley* (Madrid, Centro de Estudios Políticos y Constitucionales, 1997).

Cruz Villalón, P, *Estados excepcionales y suspensión de garantías* (Madrid, Tecnos, 1984).

Díez-Picazo, LM, *Sobre secretos oficiales* (Madrid, Civitas,1998).

García de Enterría, E, *La responsabilidad patrimonial del Estado Legislador en el Derecho español* (Cizur Henor Civitas, 2007).

—— and Fernández, T-R, *Curso de Derecho administrativo* (Madrid, Cizur Menor, 2011).

Gutiérrez Gutiérrez, I, *Los controles de la legislación delegada* (Madrid, Centro de Estudios Constitucionales, 1995).

Jiménez Asensio, R, *Altos cargos y directivos públicos (Un estudio sobre las relaciones entre política y administración en España* (Oñati, IVAP, 1996).

Magide Herrero, M, *Límites constitucionales de las Administraciones independientes* (Madrid, INAP, 2000).

Sarmiento Ramírez-Escudero, D, *El control de proporcionalidad de la actividad administrativa* (Valencia, Tirant lo Blanch, 2004).

7

Regional Decentralization:
The Estado de las Autonomías

———❧———

**The Birth of the *Estado de las Autonomías* (State of Autonomies)
– General Principles of the *Estado de las Autonomías*: Unity,
Autonomy, Solidarity, Equality – The Constitutional Role of
Statutes of Autonomy – The Distribution of Powers between the
State and the Autonomous Communities – Cooperation and
Conflicts between the State and the Regions – The Financial
System of the Regional Governments – The Political System of
the Autonomous Communities – The Relationships between State
Law and Regional Law – The Debate about Asymmetry – The
Secessionist Challenge – Local Government – Conclusion**

In the last three chapters we have primarily focused on the political
institutions at the national level. We should now turn our attention to
the regional and local spheres. As was explained in the first chapter, one
of the most controversial issues on the constitutional table in 1977–78
was the definition of the new territorial structure that Spain needed.
That political power would have to be decentralized was a shared conviction among the framers. Several options were possible, however, as to
the degree and geographical reach of the devolution process. Should all
Spain be divided in self-governing Communities? Should all such
Communities have the same amount of powers? No completely worked-
out solution emerged from the constitutional debates. Title VIII of the
Constitution merely established a framework for the creation of
Autonomous Communities. Many choices were left open, as we will see.
To a large extent, the territorial question was 'de-constitutionalized' – it

was deferred to further processes of political negotiation.[1] As things developed, the transfer of political power from the State to the regions was finally applied to the whole Spanish territory. The process was gradual and asymmetric, however, as we will study.

Title VIII of the Constitution also includes provisions concerning local institutions, which were already in existence when the Constitution was being written. It does not say much about them, however. The big issue the framers discussed was regional autonomy. In line with this emphasis in the constitutional text, we first examine the rules and principles that apply to the Autonomous Communities, and then towards the end of the chapter we turn to consider the issue of local government.

THE BIRTH OF THE *ESTADO DE LAS AUTONOMÍAS* (STATE OF AUTONOMIES)

Spain is one of the oldest European nations, but its evolution towards a centralized form of political organization was a long and complicated one. The *Decretos de Nueva Planta* issued by King Philip V at the beginning of the eighteenth century were an important step in the process of dismantling the structures of regional power, including the local parliaments that were part of the old Medieval kingdoms. Philip V belonged to the Bourbon dynasty, which had carried out a programme of State centralization in France. Liberalism during the nineteenth century had a strong centralizing impulse too. Under its influence, codes were enacted to apply throughout Spanish territory – although parts of private law were preserved in some places. At the end of the nineteenth century, some regions insisted on recovering their traditional public institutions, or on creating new ones, to exercise self-government. In the Basque Country and Catalonia, the most industrially advanced regions of Spain at that time, nationalist movements emerged that fought for political autonomy. In 1895, the Partido Nacionalista Vasco was created in the Basque Country, and in 1901, the Lliga Regionalista was founded in Catalonia. Primo de Rivera's dictatorship in the 1920s repressed these nationalist movements, but they were again strong when the regime col-

---

[1] See P Cruz Villalón, 'La estructura del Estado, o la curiosidad del jurista persa' in P Cruz Villalón, *La curiosidad del jurista persa, y otros estudios sobre la Constitución* (Madrid, Centro de Estudios Políticos y Constitucionales, 1999) 381.

lapsed. The Second Republic, born in 1931, tried to accommodate the territorial problem through the enactment of statutes that devolved powers to specific Communities. Under the republican Constitution, Catalonia in 1932, and the Basque Country in 1936, were granted self-government, after referenda were held in those regions. A statute of autonomy for Galicia was also discussed, but the referendum took place just a few weeks before the Civil War started in July 1936. Since Galicia was soon occupied by Franco's forces, its statute of autonomy was never enacted. Franco's dictatorship put an end to the regional self-government that had been awarded to Catalonia and the Basque Country, and Spain was again a very centralized State, where all powers (legislative, executive and judicial) were concentrated on the national level. Regional languages and cultures, moreover, were persecuted.[2]

When the new constitutional text was discussed in 1977–78, political parties and public opinion were aware that one of the most challenging questions the nation faced was how to channel the aspirations of Catalonia and the Basque Country – and to a lesser extent Galicia – where nationalist sentiment was quite deep, while keeping Spain united around some common structures and principles. The framers knew that this was the hardest task they confronted. Title VIII of the Constitution, on the 'territorial organization of the State', together with some other constitutional clauses, is the answer the framers came up with.

Technically, the Constitution recognizes a 'right' to regional autonomy, a right which may or may not be exercised by the political representatives of the relevant provinces and municipalities. There is no constitutional requirement for all of Spain to be divided into Autonomous Communities. There is even no definition of which provinces are entitled to request the creation of an Autonomous Community. The Constitution merely refers to vague criteria related to historical, cultural, and economic factors (article 143). This freedom for the territories to form or refuse to form a Community is captured by the expression

---

[2] The only exception to the dictatorship's centralism concerned the province of Alava (one of the three provinces of the Basque Country), and Navarra. Because the so-called Carlist groups in these parts of Spain had given Franco military support during the Civil War, the dictatorship rewarded them and decided to maintain the institutional arrangements that these two provinces had traditionally enjoyed in fiscal and other matters (which we will examine later). The traditional institutions of the two other provinces of the Basque Country (Guipúzcoa and Vizcaya) were abolished.

'dispositive principle' (*principio dispositivo*), which is used by scholars to highlight the fact that political autonomy is just available to the regions, but is not compulsory.[3]

In practice, however, a consensus soon emerged that the most sensible course of action was to divide the whole Spanish territory into Autonomous Communities. The possibility of leaving certain parts of the country under the central government, while others enjoyed a measure of regional self-government, seemed dysfunctional to many. Actually, before the Statutes of Autonomy were enacted, provisional and rather rudimentary bodies had already been set up in 13 regions. The expectation developed that such bodies would be transformed into mature autonomous governments with the passage of the pertinent Statutes.

As a result of the process of devolution that the Constitution articulated, 17 Communities were finally created, covering the totality of Spanish territory. They are: Andalucía, Aragón, Asturias, Baleares, Canarias, Cantabria, Castilla-La Mancha, Castilla y León, Catalonia, Comunidad Valenciana, Euskadi (the Basque Country), Extremadura, Galicia, La Rioja, Madrid, Murcia and Navarra. In addition, two 'autonomous cities' in African territory were set up: Ceuta and Melilla. These cities are not Autonomous Communities, however, and their powers are more limited. They exercise no legislative authority, for example.

The degree of self-government granted to the Communities was not the same for all, however. In this connection, the Constitution distinguished two ways to achieve autonomy: a 'slow' one (regulated in article 143) and a 'fast' one (regulated in article 151). If the slow path was followed, the Autonomous Community would first achieve a relatively small package of competences (those enumerated in article 148). Only at a second stage (at least five years afterwards), the Statute of Autonomy would be amended to grant the Community additional competences (with the limit of those retained by the central government as provided by article 149.1). If, in contrast, the fast path was followed, the Autonomous Community would reach the highest level of self-government in a single step.

---

[3] For a comprehensive study of the origins and role of this principle in Spanish constitutional law, see E Fossas Espadaler, *El principio dispositivo en el Estado autonómico* (Madrid, Marcial Pons, 2007).

For the fast path to be taken, however, the procedural hurdles were more complicated than if the slow path was chosen.[4] The idea was to permit those regions in Spain that proved to be more intensely interested in self-government to obtain a higher level of autonomy than the rest – at least for a while.

This dualism was complicated, however, by the existence of a special rule in the Constitution (*Disposición Transitoria 2ª*), that applied to those territories whose citizens had already ratified a Statute of Autonomy in the past, through a referendum. This was an implicit but clear reference to Catalonia, the Basque Country and Galicia, which had held such referenda during the Second Republic. This special rule made things easier for such territories, since they could achieve the highest level of self-government through a procedure that was less complicated than the ordinary one.[5]

Obviously, Catalonia, the Basque Country and Galicia chose to avail themselves of the special rule. Andalucía, in its turn, wanted to have the highest level of autonomy from the very beginning, so it used the cumbersome procedure of article 151 to get there. Twelve regions (Asturias, Cantabria, La Rioja, Murcia, Comunidad Valenciana, Aragón, Castilla-La Mancha, Castilla y León, Canarias, Extremadura, Baleares and Madrid) took the slow track of article 143. They did so through a political process that was coordinated from above by the two main parties at the national level: UCD and PSOE. The remaining Community, Navarra, had access to autonomy through a special organic statute that was enacted by the Cortes Generales, after a negotiation with the Diputación foral of that province.

There were thus stark differences in the way the different Communities were formed. In the 1990s, however, the Statutes of Autonomy of the regions that had initially been awarded fewer competences were

---

[4] The fast way required the approval of the initiative by higher majorities (three-quarters of the municipalities affected, instead of two-thirds). Citizens in the region, moreover, were to be called to a referendum twice: first, to support the initiative; second, to ratify the text of the Statute of Autonomy passed by the Cortes Generales. In both cases, the majority of popular votes had to be supportive in all the provinces affected.

[5] Thus, the initiative to get a Statute of Autonomy enacted was not to be taken by the provinces and municipalities, but was to be directly exercised by the provisional autonomous government. No initial referendum was required, moreover, to support the initiative. The only referendum that was to be held was for citizens to ratify the Statute of Autonomy that would finally be approved by the Cortes Generales.

amended to expand their sphere of self-government. This equalization was not complete, as we will see, since some differences inevitably remained. Still, this trend caused the major nationalist parties in the Basque Country (PNV), Catalonia (CiU) and Galicia (BNG) to sign the so-called Declaration of Barcelona in July 1998, in order to reaffirm the special character of these three Communities. The Declaration was critical of the equalization process.[6] The situation changed again in 2006, when Catalonia obtained a new Statute of Autonomy that expanded its sphere of powers. Some Communities (Andalucía, notably) partially followed in the Catalan steps, and a new contrast was thus introduced. As we will explore later, there is ongoing debate in Spain about the pros and cons of these asymmetries.

GENERAL PRINCIPLES OF THE *ESTADO DE LAS AUTONOMÍAS*:
UNITY, AUTONOMY, SOLIDARITY, EQUALITY

In order to understand the workings of the system of Autonomous Communities, we should first examine some general principles the Constitution lays down. Article 2, which figures in the Preliminary Title, names the principles of unity, autonomy and solidarity. 'The Constitution', this article solemnly proclaims, 'is based on the indissoluble unity of the Spanish nation, the common and indivisible homeland of all Spaniards'. In the same Preliminary Title, article 8 mentions the armed forces, which are entrusted with the mission to defend the territorial integrity of Spain, among other things. They have to do so, of course, under the direction of the Government.

This unity, however, is to coexist with the appropriate degree of autonomy. The Constitution recognizes the 'right to autonomy' of the 'nationalities and regions' that Spain comprises (article 2). The reference to 'nationalities' (*nacionalidades*) is meant to be ambiguous. There was deep disagreement among the framers concerning the nature to be attributed to Communities like Catalonia, the Basque Country and Galicia. There was no doubt that such Communities exhibited linguistic and cultural features that made them special. More importantly, the population in the Basque Country and Catalonia was eager to be

---

[6] R Gunther, JR Montero and J Botella, *Democracy in Modern Spain* (New Haven, Yale University Press, 2004) 312.

awarded self-government.[7] It was not plausible to regard such Communities as ordinary regions. On the other hand, many people believed that only Spain is genuinely a nation. The expression 'nationality' tries to draw a bridge between these two positions. It captures the special character of some Communities, while it preserves Spain as the homeland of all citizens. Interestingly, however, the distinction between regions and nationalities has no technical legal consequences in the rest of the constitutional document. Title VIII, which lays down the more specific rules to create Autonomous Communities, no longer employs this distinction – though we can interpret the special rule that applied to Catalonia, the Basque Country and Galicia to facilitate their access to self-government (the *Disposición Transitoria 2ª* that was mentioned before) to be somehow related to that distinction.

Inevitably, there has been political controversy about the meaning and consequences of the term 'nationality', as used by the Constitution. Is there really a difference between a 'nation' and a 'nationality'? Could one say that Catalonia, the Basque Country and Galicia, for example, are genuine nations within a larger Spanish nation? The debate became more passionate in 2005 when the Catalan Parliament approved a proposal for a new Statute of Autonomy that declared Catalonia to be a nation. The proposal was amended by the Cortes Generales in 2006, but the Preamble of the final text that was enacted still made reference to the fact that the Catalan Parliament had defined Catalonia as a nation. The PP (Partido Popular) then in the opposition was very critical of the new Statute. By April 2006, it had collected four million signatures from citizens throughout Spain to petition the Government to hold a referendum in order to decide whether Spain would continue to be a single nation, based on equal rights. President José Luis Rodríguez Zapatero refused to call such a referendum. The PP then challenged the new Statute before the Constitutional Court. In its decision, the Court reasoned that, legally speaking, the only nation under the Constitution is Spain. It thus held that the Preamble of the Catalan Statute was to be deprived of interpretive force, to the extent that its reference to Catalonia as a nation might be taken to undermine that constitutional understanding (STC 31/2010).

[7] The nationalist movement in Galicia was dormant at that time. No regionalist party from Galicia was represented at the constituent assembly in 1977–78. It was some years later that a minority nationalist party emerged in Galicia: the Bloque Nacionalista Galego (BNG).

In addition to the principles of unity and autonomy, the Constitution also mentions solidarity. The Constitutional Court has specified that the Autonomous Communities must help each other, and must exhibit constitutional loyalty to the system as a whole (STC 64/1990). An important instantiation of solidarity is reflected in article 138.1 of the Constitution, which provides that the State shall guarantee the establishment of a just and adequate economic balance between the different areas of the Spanish territory. For these purposes, article 158 provides that the general State budget shall include funds to be assigned to the Autonomous Communities to guarantee a minimum level of 'fundamental public services' in all Spanish territory. A Fondo de Compensación Interterritorial, moreover, is to be set up, in order to correct inter-territorial economic imbalances and implement the principle of solidarity.

Unity, autonomy and solidarity are three fundamental principles announced in the Preliminary Title. Other principles in the document are relevant too, such as that of equality. 'All Spanish citizens', article 139.1 proclaims, 'have the same rights and obligations in any part of the territory of the State'. Literally read, of course, this principle makes no sense – if regional autonomy is to be preserved. The Communities are obviously allowed to exercise their powers in different directions. The rights and obligations of citizens, therefore, inevitably vary, depending on the regional laws that are applicable to them. The Constitutional Court has read the clause restrictively, to refer to basic rights and obligations only. This is consistent with another article in the Constitution (article 149.1.1), which empowers the central government to regulate the 'basic conditions' that guarantee the equality of all Spanish citizens in the exercise of constitutional rights and the fulfillment of constitutional duties. There is controversy in many cases, of course, as to whether a particular law enacted by the State is really necessary to ensure the basic conditions of equality, or is instead an unjustified infringement of regional autonomy. The Constitutional Court's case law on this matter is inevitably complex and casuistic.[8]

Connected to the principle of equality is the principle of economic unity, which is implicit in the Constitution when it provides that no authority can adopt measures that directly or indirectly create obstacles to the free movement of persons or goods in the national territory (arti-

---

[8] For a scholarly treatment, see MI González Pascual, *El proceso autonómico ante la igualdad en el ejercicio de los derechos constitucionales* (Oñati, IVAP, 2007).

cle 139.2). The Court has had to strike a balance here: on the one hand, the Autonomous Communities are authorized to enact their own legislation on economic matters; on the other hand, limits need to be established, to prevent the national market from being fragmented. The Court has thus held that 'equality in the basic conditions for exercising economic activities' is guaranteed by the Constitution (STC 88/1986). Again, this calls for a nuanced case law on what counts as 'basic conditions' of equality.[9]

THE CONSTITUTIONAL ROLE OF STATUTES OF AUTONOMY

The distribution of political power between the State and the Autonomous Communities makes Spain a decentralized polity. It resembles federal countries in many respects. An important feature that is idiosyncratic, however, is the key role of Statutes of Autonomy.[10] Such Statutes, as we know, are the legal instruments that give birth to the different Autonomous Communities. Each Statute defines the territory and chooses the name of the Community. It also sets out the institutions that will exercise the powers granted to it. If this were all a Statute of Autonomy did, it would be tempting to say that the Statute is a sort of 'Constitution' for the Community. Article 147 of the Constitution actually says that the Statute is 'the basic institutional norm' of each Community, which seems to suggest that it is something similar to the Constitution of a Member State of a federal polity.

But things are not exactly this way. The Statute of Autonomy is also part of the national legal system. The Constitution provides that the State will protect Statutes of Autonomy as part of its own laws (article 147). This makes sense if we realize that the Spanish Constitution, unlike Constitutions in federal polities, does not directly distribute competences between the central level and the regional level. It establishes the procedures to be followed for power to be devolved to the regions, and it fixes the limits to this devolution – the competences that the State must necessarily retain (those of article 149.1). But it is for each Statute

---

[9] On the principle of economic unity, see E Albertí Rovira, *Autonomía política y unidad económica* (Madrid, Civitas, 1995).

[10] The most comprehensive study on the role of Statutes of Autonomy within the Spanish legal system is C Aguado Renedo, *El estatuto de autonomía y su posición en el ordenamiento jurídico* (Madrid, Centro de Estudios Constitucionales, 1996).

of Autonomy to specify which competences are actually transferred to the respective Community. Since the competences not enumerated in the Statute remain in the hands of the State (as article 149.3 of the Constitution provides), the Statutes of Autonomy indirectly define the powers of the central government. The Statutes are thus part of national law, in addition to being the basic norms of the Autonomous Communities.

When it comes to the Spanish 'territorial Constitution', therefore, we have to put together the Constitution and all the different Statutes of Autonomy. It has thus been very common for scholars to say that the Statutes of Autonomy perform a 'constitutional function', that they are part of the 'constitutional bloc', that they have a 'constitutional nature', etc. This does not detract from the fact, however, that the Constitution is superior to them. The Constitutional Court is clearly authorized to pass judgment on any provision of a Statute of Autonomy that is challenged through the appropriate procedures.[11] In its decision on the 2006 Catalan Statute (STC 31/2010), the Court asserted that its authority of constitutional review is not extinguished when the Statute being challenged has obtained the support of the people in a regional referendum.[12]

It is important to highlight that Statutes of Autonomy somehow express the common will of the region that asks for self-government, and the national Parliament that finally grants it. The Constitution provides that the enactment and amendment of Statutes of Autonomy require the consent of the central government, expressed in the form of an organic law passed by the Cortes Generales. This makes sense, to the extent that those Statutes include provisions that affect the central government. This is clearly the case with the clauses that distribute competences, as we have just seen. When it comes to setting up the basic institutions of the Community, however, it is not obvious why the Cortes Generales should intervene. The Statutes of Autonomy have to respect the Constitution, of course, and the Constitutional Court can be petitioned to check their validity, but why should the central Parliament

---

[11] Article 27.2 of the *Ley Orgánica 2/1979 del Tribunal Constitucional* is explicit to this effect. It expressly includes Statutes of Autonomy within the list of norms that can be subject to a procedure of review by the Constitutional Court.

[12] In the Catalan case, the vast majority of citizens who participated voted in favour of the Statute: 74%. The turn-out was quite low for Spanish standards, however: around 49%.

have any say in the way the region has decided to rearrange its own political institutions? Regions could be given more freedom in this respect. This would require, however, amending the Spanish Constitution, for article 147.3 is categorical when it says that the reform of a Statute of Autonomy must obtain 'in any case' the approval of the Cortes Generales through an organic law.

On the other hand, the central government cannot unilaterally alter the Statutes of Autonomy once they are enacted. The region whose self-government is at stake must give its consent to any modification. This is a key safeguard to protect the sphere of powers of the Autonomous Communities.

For many decades, the Statutes of Autonomy confined themselves to the matters we have examined so far, as well as some other more specific matters that the Constitution mentions, concerning regional languages (article 3.2), flags (article 4.2) and the senators appointed by the regional parliaments (article 69.5). They were thus rather short legal documents. Some years ago, however, a completely new Catalan Statute of Autonomy was enacted in 2006, repealing the earlier one of 1979. The new text was much longer. One of the reasons for its length was that an attempt was made to define the competences granted to Catalonia in a very detailed manner. The idea was to reduce uncertainty and litigation through very specific clauses that clarified the meaning of the more abstract constitutional concepts. The other reason was that the new Statute included two themes that had been absent before.

The first theme was individual rights. A set of complicated issues arose, which the Constitutional Court was asked to decide. The basic question was whether a Statute of Autonomy can incorporate individual rights. In its decision (STC 31/2010), the Court held that, to the extent certain rights are at stake when an Autonomous Community exercises its powers, the Statute of Autonomy can include clauses to protect such rights. The legal force of the latter, however, cannot be the same as that of the fundamental rights enshrined in the national Constitution. They are to be understood, the Court said, as mere principles of public policy that need to be implemented through specific legislation.[13]

The other theme in the new Catalan Statute was expressed in a set of clauses that referred to the way various institutions of the central

---

[13] The Court had already admitted the incorporation of rights in Statutes of Autonomy in an earlier decision that concerned the Comunidad Valenciana: STC 247/2007.

government were to be structured. Provisions were included, for example, about the organization of courts, the General Council of the Judiciary, and national regulatory agencies. The provisions were fragmentary: they did not establish a complete regime for those institutions, but merely set forth various criteria or constraints. Such provisions, moreover, usually made reference to the pertinent legislation that the central government would have to enact in order to restructure the central institutions in light of the Statute of Autonomy. The debate was rather complex, but the question boiled down to this: may a Statute of Autonomy say anything at all about the institutions of the central government? The Constitutional Court basically said that the answer is no. The Statute of Autonomy has a limited geographical reach, and it is much more difficult to amend than ordinary legislation (including organic laws of the regular type). It is therefore inappropriate for a Statute of Autonomy to include provisions that affect the institutions of the central government. The Statute should focus on the regional institutions.

Another example of Statutes of Autonomy exceeding the limits of their authority, according to the Court, concerns transfers of water from one region to another. It is a principle of constitutional law, the Court has held, that it is for the central government to decide the distribution of water among the different territories in Spain (article 149.1.22). In recent years, however, several Statutes of Autonomies have been reformed to include provisions that set limits to the transfers decided by the State, or that establish some procedural requirements that must be observed by the State. The Court has declared those provisions unconstitutional.[14]

THE DISTRIBUTION OF POWERS BETWEEN THE STATE AND THE AUTONOMOUS COMMUNITIES

Let us now study how power in Spain has been distributed between the centre and the regions. The first thing to note is that, as a result of the creation of Autonomous Communities, legislative and executive powers have been decentralized. Judicial power, however, remains in the hands of the State: all courts in Spain belong to the national sphere. (Articles 149.1.5 and 117 of the Constitution are clear in this regard).

[14]   See STC 30/2011 (on the Statute of Autonomy of Andalucía); STC 32/2011 (on the Statute of Autonomy of Castilla y León); and STC 110/2011 (on the Statute of Autonomy of Aragón).

Legislative and executive powers have been distributed according to different techniques, depending on the field.[15] A first possibility is for the State to enact the pertinent laws, and for the Autonomous Communities to enforce those laws. This is what happens with labour law and penitentiary law, for example. It is important to note, in this connection, that the Constitutional Court has held that when the Constitution provides that the regional authorities may 'execute' State legislation, it refers to its administrative enforcement only. The power to execute does not include the power to issue regulations to implement the laws – unless the regulations are purely internal, to organize the administrative bodies in charge of enforcement (STC 18/1982, STC 31/2010).

A second technique entails a distribution of legislative authority over the same subject matter. Thus, the State is charged with the responsibility to enact laws that establish the basic framework in a particular domain (*'bases'*, *'legislación básica'*), while the Community is empowered to enact more detailed legislation, as well as to enforce it. The State, for example, is authorized to establish the basic norms regulating the health system, or the environment, while the rest of powers in these areas pertain to the Autonomous Communities. It has not been easy for the Court to define the scope of the 'basic' norms. The central government has some leeway, of course, but there must be limits to its power. The State cannot define as 'basic' any law it wishes to pass. The State laws, in particular, cannot be so detailed and exhaustive that the regions no longer have any margin for implementing their own policies. The Court has also held that the State should explicitly indicate which of the rules it enacts are to be regarded as 'basic' (unless it is easy to draw that inference). As a general principle, moreover, the basic norms should be expressed in the form of statutes enacted by the Cortes Generales (STC 69/1988). It is possible, however, for them to figure in administrative regulations too, if there are good reasons for the government to choose that source of law. It is even possible for the State to reserve for itself the execution of the laws in some cases, to guarantee basic conditions.[16]

Sometimes, the Constitution divides legislative power between the State and the Communities, but it does not confine the former to the

---

[15] For a detailed examination of the various techniques, see C Viver Pi-Sunyer, *Materias competenciales y Tribunal Constitucional* (Barcelona, Ariel, 1989).

[16] See, eg STC 86/89, which upheld the power of the State to issue administrative authorizations of insurance companies that operate throughout the Spanish territory.

task of laying down the basic framework. The State can pass legislation of a more specific sort. Taxes, for example, may be regulated by the State in a rather detailed manner, even if the regions are also assigned some legislative powers over them (article 137 of the Constitution).

In most fields, powers are shared between the State and the Autonomous Communities, following the techniques that have just been described. There are a few matters, however, that attract the 'exclusive' competence of the State. With regard to immigration and military affairs, for example, the State is given full authority. It is more doubtful, in contrast, that the Autonomous Communities can ever exercise competences that are truly exclusive, for the State can always resort to the so-called 'horizontal titles'. We already mentioned article 149.1.1, for example, which empowers the State to regulate the basic conditions that guarantee the equality of all Spanish citizens when exercising their constitutional rights and complying with their constitutional duties. The State's authority to establish the general ordering of the economy (which derives from article 149.1.13) is another horizontal title that can restrict the power of the Communities. The latter may have competence over tourism, say, but they need to respect the laws that the State may have chosen to enact, as part of its authority to regulate the economic order.

Many commentators have pointed out that the central government tends to exercise its horizontal powers in too expansive a manner, and tends to issue 'basic laws' that are too detailed and restrictive.[17] There has been debate, however, as to the best strategy to prevent this from happening. Some scholars plead the Constitutional Court to be less deferential to the State when reviewing its laws.[18] Others are more skeptical of the Court's capacity to curb the central government, and suggest that the solution lies in the Senate. They believe that if the Senate were reformed to become a genuine forum for voicing the interests and competences of the Autonomous Communities, the laws enacted by the State would be less intrusive.[19]

---

[17] See, eg R Jiménez Asensio, *La ley autonómica en el sistema constitucional de fuentes del Derecho* (Madrid, Marcial Pons, 2001) 190–246.

[18] See, eg Viver Pi-Sunyer (n 15) 29–33; and 'Soberanía, autonomía, interés general . . . y el retorno del jurista persa' (1989) 25 *Revista Vasca de Administración Pública* 91.

[19] This is, eg the position of E Aja, *El Estado autonómico. Federalismo y hechos diferenciales* (Madrid, Alianza Editorial, 2003) 247–53.

COOPERATION AND CONFLICTS BETWEEN
THE STATE AND THE REGIONS

Given that the State and the Autonomous Communities often share powers over a particular domain, it is not surprising that the need has been felt to establish mechanisms of cooperation. Actually, the Constitution sometimes grants the central government the power to 'coordinate' the policies in a given field (economic activity, scientific research, health-care, for example). The State can thus establish the appropriate mechanisms to ensure that the regions exercise their functions in ways that are consistent with certain criteria; that relevant information is shared; that the points of view of the diverse administrations are discussed in a common forum, etc. Different types of commissions have been created to facilitate cooperation. Some of them are of a multilateral character, as when the minister of the central government and the heads of the pertinent departments at the regional level meet to discuss common matters. Other Commissions are bilateral: they consist of representatives of the central government and of a single Autonomous Community. Agreements between the various executive branches are also signed to ensure cooperation in different fields.

So, for example, the State is in charge of laying down the basic framework of the health-care system, while the Autonomous Communities develop it and provide the necessary services. The central government must issue a decree specifying which services are covered by the free and universal health-care system. The list of services, however, is drawn by a Joint Commission that includes the Ministers of Health of the central and the regional governments.[20]

Another example of cooperation between the State and the regions concerns the European Union. Before the Spanish Government decides what positions it adopts in Brussels, the point of view of the Autonomous Communities needs to be heard. A forum has been created for these purposes: CARCE (Conferencia para Asuntos Relacionados con las Comunidades Europeas). Its goal is to ensure the participation of the Autonomous Communities in the decision-making processes at the European Union level.[21] A Joint Commission for the

---

[20] See arts 20 and 21, *Ley 16/2003 de cohesión y calidad del Sistema Nacional de Salud.*
[21] See *Ley 2/1997 por la que se regula la Conferencia para Asuntos relacionados con las Comunidades Europeas.*

European Union (Comisión Mixta para la Unión Europea), which comprises members of Congress and the Senate, is also relevant for these purposes.[22] This organ receives the legislative proposals of the European Union, and forwards them to the regional parliaments. The latter may issue reasoned reports on the application of the European Union principle of subsidiarity. It is the Joint Commission, however, that decides the final position of the Spanish Parliament. Sessions can also be held with members of the Spanish Government prior to a meeting of the European Council. The executive branches of the Autonomous Communities may request to be heard by the Joint Commission, to report on the impact that the laws and proposals by the European Union may have on their competences.

Commentators have insisted on the need to expand and improve these mechanisms of cooperation between the State and the regions, which are still underused.[23]

Conflicts, however, are inevitable. As we will see in the next chapter, the Constitutional Court plays a key role when disputes arise between the central government and the Autonomous Communities. Various procedures have been instituted for these purposes, as we will study.

It should be noted, finally, that article 155 of the Constitution authorizes the central Government to adopt extraordinary measures when an Autonomous Community does not comply with the duties that the Constitution or other laws impose, or when it acts in a manner that gravely runs against Spain's general interests. Before such measures are adopted, however, the Government must first address itself to the President of the Autonomous Community. If the latter fails to act as requested, the Senate must then intervene. The Government needs to obtain the approval of an absolute majority of senators. To enforce its measures, the Government can issue instructions directly to all the regional authorities. The scenario contemplated in this constitutional clause is very exceptional. As a matter of fact, the State has never resorted to this clause. In the context of the fiscal crisis that Spain is currently facing, however, a law has recently been enacted that imposes strict budgetary limits on the Autonomous Communities. This law, which implements the constitutional amendment adopted in September 2011, explicitly includes the extraordinary measures of article 155 within

---

[22] See *Ley 8/1994, por la que se regula la Comisión Mixta para la Unión Europea.*
[23] See, eg Aja (n 19) 207–44.

the menu of instruments that the central Government is authorized to resort to, in order to force a region to comply with its fiscal responsibilities.[24]

THE FINANCIAL SYSTEM OF THE REGIONAL GOVERNMENTS

In order to exercise their powers, the Autonomous Communities need to have some degree of liberty to tax and to spend, and they must be provided with sufficient resources. Article 156 of the Constitution guarantees the 'financial autonomy' of the Communities, while article 157 lists the sources of revenue they can rely upon. It is actually an organic law (the *Ley Orgánica 8/1980, de Financiación de las Comunidades Autónomas*, which has been amended several times), together with other more specific pieces of State legislation, that fixes the details of the financial system. The State has full authority to regulate this matter, but many of its laws are the upshot of agreements reached at a multilateral organ (the Consejo de Política Fiscal y Financiera), which includes representatives of the central government and of the Autonomous Communities.

The most important sources of revenue for the regions derive from the central government, which has transferred various State taxes to them (whether totally or partially). In addition, it assigns them funds out of the general budget. As was already mentioned, a small portion of the grants come from the Fondo de Compensación Interterritorial, which tries to correct economic imbalances between the regions.

The Autonomous Communities can also establish their own taxes, but these are of minor economic significance. The can borrow money, moreover, within certain limits. (In some cases, the loans need to be authorized by the central government).

The tendency has been for the central government to assign more and more State taxes to the Communities, while diminishing the funds that the latter receive out of the general budget. Importantly, the percentage of the income tax (*Impuesto sobre la Renta de las Personas Físicas*) that is allotted to the regions has increased over the years, and is now 50 per cent. The same is true of the value added tax (*Impuesto sobre el Valor Añadido*), the percentage of which is currently 50 per cent.[25]

---

[24] See art 26.1, *Ley Orgánica 2/2012, de Estabilidad Presupuestaria y Sostenibilidad Financiera*.

[25] See art 26, *Ley 22/2009*.

The laws often grant the Autonomous Communities legislative authority to regulate particular features of the taxes that are transferred to them. This authority has been quite large in some cases. Thus, the tax on inheritances and donations (the *Impuesto sobre Sucesiones y Donaciones*), is a State tax that the regions are allowed to partially regulate. Among other things, they can expand the list of fiscal benefits. Some Communities have been so generous in this connection that the tax has all but disappeared in their territories. Whether this is constitutionally acceptable is a matter of controversy. The Constitutional Court has allowed fiscal diversity as a natural result of the decentralized character of the political system, but it has placed limits, in the name of 'equality of citizens in their fundamental legal positions' (STC 150/1990). Arguably, it is against such basic equality for a national tax to be almost eliminated by some regional parliaments, while it is kept by others.

Similarly to what is the case with the national government, the regions must approve their budget every year. And the national Court of Audit is authorized to control the execution of the budget (article 153 of the Constitution).

In terms of the participation of the Autonomous Communities in the overall public expenses, the percentage in 2009 was 29.7 per cent, against 58 per cent for the central government and 12.3 per cent for the local entities.[26] Two of the most important services that Autonomous Communities provide are public education and health, which are key components of the social state. As a result of the financial situation that Spain currently faces, the capacity of the regions to fund these services has suffered significantly. The Communities have had to cut their expenses in these fields, and to ask the central government for help.

Finally, it is important to mention that the Basque Country and Navarra have special financial systems. The provinces in those regions have traditionally been in charge of collecting almost all the taxes, and have contributed a certain amount of money every year to the State. The Constitution preserves this traditional fiscal arrangement through a specific clause to this effect (*Disposición Adicional 1ª*). The Canary Islands, in turn, because of their geographical distance from the Spanish peninsula, are also granted a special fiscal treatment (*Disposición Adicional 3ª*).

---

[26] See 'Informe económico-financiero de las Administraciones territoriales, 2009' available at www.seap.minhap.gob.es.

THE POLITICAL SYSTEM OF
THE AUTONOMOUS COMMUNITIES

Each Community has organized its own system of government. However, the Statutes of Autonomy and the ordinary laws that develop them are quite similar in this regard. In all the regions a political regime has been designed that is very close to the regime that has been established at the national level.

The electoral laws, first, are very similar.[27] In all the regions a system of proportional representation has been adopted, which is based on the D'Hondt formula. In general, the distribution of parliamentary seats among electoral districts is sensitive to the size of the population. The Basque Country, however, is an exception, in that each of the three provinces elects the same number of representatives (25).

The regional parliaments are all unicameral. Their members enjoy inviolability for the opinions expressed when exercising their functions, but they are awarded no immunity – no parliamentary authorization is needed to charge them with a crime. Since immunity is a privilege that can harm the fundamental rights of ordinary citizens, the idea has prevailed that it should have a narrow scope: it ought to apply exclusively to the deputies and senators at the national level. On the other hand, the members of regional parliaments can only be arrested in the event of a flagrant crime.

The parliamentary mandate is four years. In some regions, it is possible to dissolve the chamber before its mandate expires. In practice, Catalonia, the Basque Country, Galicia and Andalucía hold their elections separately, while the other Communities share the same electoral cycle: they hold their elections the same day when the municipal elections are called by the central government every four years in May.

The democratic system in the regional sphere is of the parliamentary type, similar to the one that has been adopted at the national level. The President of the regional government is thus selected by the legislative assembly. He must be a member of that assembly, however. (No similar requirement exists on the national plane). Formally, it is the King that appoints the President of the Autonomous Community, but the actual

---

[27] The LOREG (*Ley Orgánica del Régimen Electoral General*), moreover, establishes some norms that apply to all types of elections.

decision is made by the regional parliament. As was already noted, the King's act must be countersigned by the President of the national (not the regional) Government. The members of the regional executive are freely appointed by its President.

Because the Government needs to maintain the support of a parliamentary majority, mechanisms of 'motion of censure' and 'question of confidence' are applicable, similar to those that operate in the national Congress. But whereas no Government at the national level has ever been brought down through these procedures, some regional governments have.[28]

In some Communities, the same person has served as President for very long periods: Jordi Pujol in Catalonia (1980–2003), Manuel Chávez in Andalucía (1990–2009) and Manuel Fraga in Galicia (1990–2005) are notable examples of this. Their long tenure led to a certain 'presidentialization' of the regional politics in those Communities. In all Communities, it must further be noted, the President is both the head of the executive branch, and the President of the Community as a whole – replacing the King, as it were. This gives the President some special symbolic authority.

In almost all the Autonomous Communities, the two largest political parties at the national level (PSOE and PP) are clearly predominant. One of these two parties always gets into the regional government, sometimes with the agreement of a small regional or nationalist party. The two exceptions are the Basque Country and Catalonia, that have been governed by nationalist parties (PNV and CiU, respectively) most of the time.[29]

Finally, it bears mentioning that some institutions that we examined in previous chapters have been replicated on the regional plane in some Communities. The Ombudsman, for example, as well as organs that perform similar functions to those of the Council of State and the Court of Audit, are present in many regions.

---

[28] C Aguado Renedo, 'Algunas cuestiones problemáticas acerca de los ejecutivos de las Comunidades Autónomas' in M Aragón and ÁJ Gómez Montoro (eds), *El Gobierno. Problemas constitucionales* (Madrid, Centro de Estudios Políticos y Constitucionales, 2005) 582.

[29] For a detailed picture of the evolution of the party system in the regional sphere, see Gunther, Montero and Botella (n 6) 313–21.

THE RELATIONSHIPS BETWEEN STATE LAW AND REGIONAL LAW

As we saw earlier, the Statutes of Autonomy perform a complex role within the legal system. The relationships between State law and regional law are also intricate. After having examined the institutional aspects of the territorial organization, we can now enter a more detailed discussion of these legal matters.

The Equal Rank of State and Regional Legislation

The first thing to note is that both the regional parliament and the national Parliament must respect the distribution of legislative authority that derives from the applicable Statute of Autonomy. If a law fails to observe that distribution, it is unconstitutional. The reason for this is that the Constitution charges Statutes of Autonomy with the task of defining the competences that are allotted to the region, thus indirectly defining those that remain in the hands of the State. This being so, a violation of the pertinent Statute of Autonomy amounts to a breach of the Constitution too.[30]

The Constitutional Court has emphasized the equal rank of State law and regional law. Which of the two laws is to prevail in the event of a clash depends on whose competence it is to regulate a particular subject matter. Suppose, for example, that the State is empowered to lay down the basic regulation in a given area, while the Autonomous Communities are to dictate the more detailed legislation. If a conflict arises between the two normative pieces, it is first necessary to decide whether or not the law the State has enacted can be qualified as truly 'basic'. If the answer is yes, the State has acted within the bounds of its authority, and its law does prevail over regional law. If, on the contrary, the State law is too detailed and constraining, the State has exceeded its regulatory powers. Regional law is then to prevail.[31]

---

[30] Article 28.1 of the *Ley Orgánica 2/1979 del Tribunal Constitucional* expressly instructs the Constitutional Court to measure the constitutional validity of laws against the Statutes of Autonomy.

[31] The Court has thus rendered inoperative article 149.3 of the Constitution, which provides that State law 'shall prevail over regional law, in the event of a con-

Only the Constitutional Court, moreover, is authorized to review the validity of regional statutes (or norms of equivalent rank): they have the same 'jurisdictional privilege' as national statutes. Ordinary judges cannot set them aside on their own authority. Even when a regional statute seems to contradict the basic legislation enacted by the State, it is for the Constitutional Court to hold that there is such a contradiction and that the regional statute must yield (STC 163/1995).

Also, if the Constitution establishes that a certain matter is to be regulated by 'statute', both national and regional statutes can satisfy that requirement. It all depends on which level of government has been awarded the competence to regulate that matter. The fact that national statutes are promulgated by the King, while regional statutes are promulgated by the President of the Autonomous Community (in the King's name), is absolutely irrelevant in this connection, of course.

As we will see in chapter eight, however, there is a difference between national and regional statutes when it comes to their constitutional review: while it is not possible for the Constitutional Court to suspend the application of a national piece of legislation that has been challenged, it is possible for the Court to do so in the case of regional laws.

The Principle of *Supletoriedad*

There have been some complications, however, as a result of the so-called *principio de supletoriedad* (principle of supplementarity).[32] Article 149.3 of the Constitution provides that, 'in any case, State law will supplement regional law'. This principle makes sense, once we understand the gradual and asymmetric process of devolution of political powers to the regions in Spain. At the very beginning, some Communities had been established, while others were still in the process of being created. Later, when all the Spanish territory had been divided into regions, some Communities had acquired more legislative powers than others, as was already explained. To the extent this diversity is maintained in some fields, the State is obviously entitled to issue laws that apply to the terri-

flict, when the matter regulated does not pertain to the exclusive competence of the regions'.

[32] For a focused study on this principle, see J Tajadura Tejada, *La cláusula de supletoriedad del Derecho estatal respecto del Derecho autonómico* (Madrid, Biblioteca Nueva, 2000).

State Law and Regional Law

tories with a lower level of self-government. What the *principio de supleto-riedad* says is that such laws will also be applicable to the regions that have been granted legislative authority in the relevant field, in the event of a gap. That is, if the region entitled to regulate a matter has not yet exercised its legislative power, or the law it has passed is insufficient, the State law can be applied to fill the vacuum.

The Constitutional Court, however, has restricted the role of this principle (see SSTC 118/1996, 61/1997). It has held that, once all the regions have assumed legislative powers in a particular domain, the State has no longer any title to issue a law in that domain. The *principio de suple-toriedad* provides no such title. In other words, the State cannot pass a law whose only goal is to fill the gaps that regional law may exhibit. Should a gap emerge, it should be filled up following the traditional rules of interpretation and application of the law (analogy, general principles, presumption in favour of liberty, etc).The State is not to assume the burden of enacting laws just in case the regions fail to fully exercise their own competences.[33]

Altering the Statutory Distribution of Competences through Special Laws: Article 150 of the Constitution

We have so far referred to the Constitution and the Statutes of Autonomy as the normative package that distributes legislative authority between the central government and the regions. We should now note that article 150 of the Constitution establishes three ways in which the central government can unilaterally alter that distribution. The first two ways entail an enlargement of the sphere of autonomy of the regions. The third way, in contrast, means a restriction.

First, the State may decide to enlarge the sphere of powers of all or some Communities through the passage of a *ley marco,* a framework statute (article 150.1). This is an ordinary statute, enacted by the Cortes Generales, that transfers legislative powers to the regions. The statute establishes the principles, basic conditions and guidelines that must be

---

[33] It is interesting to compare this approach with the so-called 'Sewel Convention' in the United Kingdom which allows the Scottish Parliament to pass consent motions allowing Westminster to continue to legislate on its behalf. See P Leyland, *The Constitution of the United Kingdom. A Contextual Analysis* (Oxford, Hart Publishing, 2012) 250 and 263.

observed. In addition to the checks provided by courts, the statute can specify the ways the Cortes Generales can control the conformity of the regional laws to the criteria laid down in the enabling statute. As an example of this technique, we can mention the laws that assign certain State taxes to the Autonomous Communities. As was already explained, it is often the case that the Communities are authorized to regulate certain aspects of the tax that has been conveyed to them.

Second, the State can choose a more intense measure to increase regional authority (specified in article 150.2). It can enact an organic statute that transfers legislative and executive powers to the Autonomous Communities, without establishing a basic framework. The financial resources that are necessary to exercise the delegated powers are also included. The State can fix the forms of control it retains, however. It is important to note that this mechanism can have a broad impact, for the competences that can be transferred include competences that the Constitution attributes to the central government in article 149.1. That is, the mechanism can go further than a Statute of Autonomy can. The only limitation is that the competence 'must be of a nature that makes it susceptible to being transferred', the Constitution says. This is a vague standard, but the implication is that there are certain functions that the State must necessarily keep under its control.

Through these two types of measures, the regions acquire more powers than are granted to them in their respective Statutes of Autonomy. But while the powers enumerated in a Statute of Autonomy cannot be unilaterally withdrawn by the State, these other powers can.

The third measure (regulated in article 150.3) goes in the opposite direction. The State is authorized, if the general interest so requires, to pass a 'law of harmonization' (*ley de armonización*), establishing some principles that the laws enacted by the regions must comply with. For such a law to be passed, both Congress and the Senate, by an absolute majority of their members, must declare that the harmonizing measures are indeed necessary to preserve the general interest. The Constitutional Court has been very restrictive as to the circumstances under which such laws can be passed. The general interest, it has reasoned, can normally be preserved through the ordinary competences that the State is assigned (such as the competence to establish the basic regulation in various fields). The Court thus invalidated the only harmonizing law that has so far been approved, the LOAPA (*Ley de Armonización del Proceso Autonomico*): STC 76/1983.

THE DEBATE ABOUT ASYMMETRY

As has been noted several times, the Spanish process of decentralization has been gradual and asymmetric: different regions have been treated differently at different stages with regard to their sphere of self-government. The debate is still open about the desirability of equalizing the competences of all the Autonomous Communities.[34]

It should be noted, first of all, that symmetry is impossible in some specific areas. The Constitution, for example, provides that Castilian is the official language, and that the other languages in Spain (such as Catalan, Euskera and Galician) are also official in the respective Autonomous Communities (article 3). Obviously, laws need to be passed to regulate linguistic matters. Both the central government and the Communities have competences to exercise in this area. An asymmetry naturally emerges between those regions where only Castilian is spoken, and those others where another language is also official (Catalonia, Comunidad Valenciana, Baleares, the Basque Country, Navarra and Galicia). The former have no legislative powers concerning languages (or only very marginal ones), while the latter do. Different linguistic policies have been implemented by those communities where a local language coexists with the Castilian language. When it comes to teaching in public schools, in particular, some Communities, such as Catalonia and Galicia, have established a system of 'language immersion', under which the local language occupies centre stage, while in others, such as the Basque Country, two separate lines of schools have been arranged, depending on the language professors employ in their teaching.[35]

Another source of asymmetry concerns private law. As was already indicated, liberalism in Spain triggered a process of codification throughout the nineteenth century. Many fields were subjected to common rules as a result of it, but some pockets of private law were preserved in some regions, and were maintained even under Franco's dictatorship. The Constitution ascribes the power to lay down private law rules to the central government, but it permits the Autonomous Communities to 'preserve, modify and develop' their own laws in the

---

[34] For a comparative perspective on the Spanish debate on asymmetry, see E Fossas and F Requejo Coll (eds), *Asimetría federal y estado plurinacional: el debate sobre la acomodación de la diversidad en Canadá, Bélgica y España* (Madrid, Trotta, 1999).

[35] Gunther, Montero and Botella (n 6) 322–25.

field, if such laws exist (article 149.1.8). Obviously, only those regions where local private law was not eliminated in the past are empowered to issue this type of updating legislation.

Another factor that makes complete symmetry impossible concerns the fiscal system and local institutions that have traditionally existed in the Basque Country and Navarra. Since the Constitution includes a clause to guarantee these special arrangements, which are linked to 'historic rights' (*Disposición Adicional 1ª*), another difference inevitably arises.[36]

Beyond these matters, however, there seems to be flexibility: the Spanish *Estado de las autonomías* may develop towards homogeneity, or it may retain asymmetries among the regions in a number of fields. What can be said, for or against these different possibilities?

It is sometimes said that all the Communities should have the same legislative powers, so that citizens are treated equally. This position seems to rest on a conceptual confusion, however. Whether or not the regions should have the same sphere of powers is not immediately connected to the principle of equality among citizens. Suppose a particular Community prefers to have a lower level of autonomy than the others. It is not obvious why honouring the equality of citizens should mean that a higher level of autonomy should be forced on that Community.

It seems more plausible to argue that, to the extent possible, each Community should be free to determine the scope of regional self-government it wishes to enjoy. This idea has some interesting consequences. On the one hand, the nationalist parties are wrong, one could maintain, when they claim that the regions with a strong national identity should have more competences than the rest. What if a Community that has no specific national identity wants to achieve the same degree of self-government as those that do exhibit such identity? In what ways are the 'national' Communities harmed when 'non-national' Communities are granted the same level of autonomy as they are? It is sometimes said that they are harmed symbolically, for the system as a whole sends the message that all the Communities are the same. But this answer is not very attractive. If, indeed, 'national' Communities are different than the rest, there is no need to award them more powers for

---

[36] On the constitutional meaning of these 'historic rights', see M Herrero de Miñón, *Derechos Históricos y Constitución* (Madrid, Taurus, 1998), and FJ Laporta and A Saiz Arnaiz, *Los derechos históricos en la Constitución* (Madrid, Centro de Estudios Políticos y Constitucionales, 2006).

symbolic purposes. The same amount of powers can be exercised differently. After all, we are all equal at the individual level, but we do not feel that this equality makes it difficult for each of us to define the kind of life we want to live, which may be wildly different from that of others. It would be absurd to say that, in order to make it clear that I am different from you, I should have more rights.

The other side of the coin, of course, is that those Communities that would like to have more responsibilities than the rest should not be denied the additional powers they seek, on the grounds that other Communities don't want them. Catalonia, the Basque Country and Navarra, for example, were authorized to have their own police, as the Constitution permits (article 149.1.29). It would have been inappropriate to deny such regions this possibility on the sole ground that the other Communities were not initially interested in it. (Some of them are now interested, however). Quite tellingly, in the middle of the recent economic crisis in Spain, a number of regional politicians have suggested that they would like their Communities to give parts of their authority back to the central government. Technically, this would require amending the Statutes of Autonomy of those regions. But apart from the legal complications involved, this move illustrates that some Communities do not feel strongly about keeping their powers – much less about seeking ways to expand them. If so, asymmetry appears as an acceptable upshot of the diverse preferences of the different Communities.

The problem, however, is that asymmetry brings with it some important costs. First, there is a limit to how much diversity the State can cope with. Imagine, in an extreme scenario, that each region had its own specific level of autonomy. It would be very difficult for the central government to make decisions. It would have to be sensitive to the particular list of competences each Community was authorized to exercise. If some measure of asymmetry is inevitable, there is good reason to channel it into different groups or categories, rather than allowing each Community to have its own list of competences.

The second problem that arises as a result of asymmetry is analogous to the so-called 'West Lothian question' that has become a constitutional issue in the United Kingdom since the introduction of devolution.[37] Suppose some Autonomous Communities are granted legislative

---

[37] See Leyland (n 33) 272–74.

powers over a particular field, while others are not. This means that the regional parliaments in the first group will issue the laws that apply to those territories, while the national Parliament will enact the law that will be operative in the rest of the country. The question is: should all the members of the national Parliament participate in the decision-making process that leads to the adoption of the national law? If all of them do, the national representatives of the regions that belong to the first group are then given more power than they should get. The citizens of the Communities they represent have two votes: through their regional representatives, they determine the content of the regional laws that will apply to them and through their representatives at the national level they also help shape the national law for the other Communities. They govern themselves, and they govern others at the same time. A clear example of this problem concerns fiscal matters: the representatives of the Basque Country and Navarra vote for laws at the national Parliament that are not entirely applicable in their territories. There is no easy solution to this problem. The traditional understanding in Spain is that the members of the national Parliament represent all Spanish citizens, and not only their constituencies in a particular electoral district. If we think this traditional conception is too formalistic, however, some rule should be adopted to address the problem that asymmetry generates. Maybe the national Parliament should have the power to decide in each case whether the law to be discussed will apply to all the regions, or will instead apply to some of them only. Which Members of Parliament would be entitled to participate in the legislative process would be determined accordingly. The rule seems plausible, but many details need to be worked out. For the moment, however, there is no political discussion in Spain over this tricky problem.[38]

The third problem concerns the Senate. Under the current institutional arrangements, the Senate is a very marginal organ, as we know. There has been constant talk about reforming the Senate, to transform it into a chamber that represents the interests of the Autonomous Communities. There seems to be an agreement that the Senate is a rather useless institution, if kept in its present form. There is more controversy about the direction the reform should take. The Senate must be changed in light of the developments in the system as a whole. If the

---

[38] Some scholars have made reference to this problem in the general media, however. See, eg LM Díez-Picazo, 'El Estatuto de Cataluña y la West Lothian question', *El País*, 18 November 2005.

system is strongly asymmetric, in particular, it is harder for the Senate to be the voice of the Communities: some Communities will be affected by a piece of legislation under discussion, while others will not, depending on the specific sphere of competences that has been awarded to each of them.

The method used to select the senators is also related to the kind of decentralized political system we wish to have.[39] If all the senators were selected by the regional parliaments, or by the regional governments, as some scholars have proposed, the regional elections would become 'nationalized'. The debates would not focus on local problems. They would instead be strongly influenced by political developments at the national level. The reason is that the votes in the regional elections would have an impact on the composition of the Senate, since the regional parliament or government would send new senators. The capacity of the national Government to have its programmes enacted into law would be at stake, therefore, depending on the results of such elections. Certainly, it is already the case that the regional elections have a national dimension to them. This is especially so when they are held together with the local elections – which is true of all Autonomous Communities, except Catalonia, the Basque Country, Galicia and Andalucía. But the nationalization of regional political life would be reinforced to a large degree if the senators were appointed by the regional institutions.

To make matters more complex, the nationalist parties are not especially worried about the future of the Senate. Those parties are already present in Congress, where they can play their cards to protect the interests and competences of the Autonomous Communities they represent. When the governing party at the State level needs the support of smaller groups to ensure the passage of legislation, the two main nationalist parties from Catalonia and the Basque Country are often asked to provide the necessary votes. Given the open-ended character of the Spanish Constitution when it comes to the territorial distribution of power, the nationalist parties can use their votes to press for legislative changes that actually expand the sphere of self-government of the Autonomous

---

[39] Two main models have been proposed: under a first model, the regional parliaments elect the senators. Under a second model, the regional governments do so. For a debate on the pros and cons of these two models, see E Aja, E Albertí Rovira and JJ Ruiz Ruiz, *La reforma constitucional del Senado* (Madrid, Centro de Estudios Políticos y Constitucionales, 2005).

Communities. What these parties really worry about, therefore, when general elections take place is whether or not one of the two large parties will get an absolute majority in Congress. To a certain extent, when no party has an absolute majority, Congress becomes a 'territorial' chamber of sorts.

THE SECESSIONIST CHALLENGE

An important factor that introduces further complexity in these matters is the existence of an increasing number of citizens and political representatives, both in the Basque Country and in Catalonia, that advocate secession from Spain. They are still a minority, it seems, but it is a large and probably expansive one. A recent poll indicated that 24 per cent of citizens in the Basque Country are in favour of independence, against 33 per cent that support the current status of the Basque Country as an Autonomous Community, and 32 per cent that would favour a federal solution.[40] In Catalonia, a poll showed that 34 per cent of Catalans prefer secession over other alternatives, while 25.4 per cent would like Catalonia to remain an Autonomous Community, and 28.7 per cent are in favour of a federal arrangement. If a referendum on Catalonia's independence were held, however, 51.1 per cent would vote yes, and only 21.1 per cent would vote no.[41]

It is against this background that one has to read the political developments that have taken place in these two regions in the last years. Thus, in the Basque Country, a very controversial initiative was taken in 2003 by the regional President, Juan José Ibarretxe, when he submitted to the Basque Parliament a *Propuesta de Estatuto Político de la Comunidad de Euskadi.* Article 1 of this proposal invoked the right of the Basque territories and their citizens to 'decide in a free and democratic manner their own organizational and relational framework', and established a 'Basque Community freely associated to the Spanish State'. The other articles regulated the terms of the new organization in ways that collided with the Spanish Constitution in many respects. The central Government challenged the proposal before the Constitutional Court, but the Court held that it was not possible under Spanish law for a mere

[40] Universidad del País Vasco, *Eurobarómetro. Mayo 2012*, 39.
[41] Generalitat de Catalunya, Centre d'Estudis d'Opinió, *Baròmetre d'Opinió Política. 2ª onada 2012*, 34 and 36.

legislative proposal to be invalidated. Only the laws finally enacted can be annulled.[42] The Basque Parliament, where the nationalist forces held a majority of seats, proceeded to vote in favour of this proposal, against the opposition of the two non-nationalist parties, PP and PSOE. The proposal was then sent to the Spanish Cortes Generales. José Ibarretxe was able to appear before Congress to defend his plan in February 2005. A vote was soon taken and the proposal was rejected – it was not even admitted for further discussion.

Ibarretxe's next step, after his party (PNV) won the elections again in 2005, was to suggest the regional legislative assembly to pass a law providing for the organization of a referendum to decide on the future of the Basque Country. The law was finally enacted (*Ley 9/2008*), providing that a referendum would be held on 25 October 2008. Basque citizens were to be asked (a) whether they approved of starting a process to end violence through dialogue, if ETA (the terrorist group) expressed its clear will to end violence forever, and (b) whether they approved of starting a process whereby all Basque political parties would negotiate a democratic agreement on the right of the Basque Country to decide, an agreement that would be submitted to a referendum by the end of 2010. This second question was not very clear, to say the least. In any case, the law was soon challenged on constitutional grounds by the central Government. The Constitutional Court was quick to render its decision, declaring the law invalid (STC 103/2008). Basically, the Court found that the regional parliament had no authority to regulate referenda, and that, in any event, it was always necessary for the State to authorize a referendum. The Court also held that the question to be submitted to the people in this case amounted to a proposal to amend the Spanish Constitution. For such an amendment to be passed, the procedural steps of article 168 of the Constitution would have to be followed, the Court reasoned.

Since then, two important events have taken place: after the elections of March 2009, the Basque Government was placed in the hands of a non-nationalist party (PSOE) for the first time, after an agreement was reached with PP. And ETA announced in October 2011 that it would put a definitive end to its criminal activities. Whether the secessionist forces will be stronger or weaker in this new atmosphere remains to be seen.

---

[42] ATC 135/2004.

With regard to Catalonia, the developments in the last years are also complex. The new Statute of Autonomy that was enacted in 2006 was partially invalidated by the Constitutional Court (STC 31/2010). The latter's decision produced an uproar in Catalan public opinion. A huge demonstration took place in July 2010, to protest against the judicial ruling. In November, regional elections were held, which the main nationalist party (CiU) won. A new Government led by President Artur Mas decided to centre its strategy on economic matters. It proposed a new fiscal arrangement for Catalonia, similar to the one that the Basque Country and Navarra already have. The central Government expressed its rejection of such a plan. A massive demonstration was held in Barcelona, on 11 September 2012, under the banner 'Catalonia, the next European State'. The event hit the headlines of the major international newspapers. The movement in favour of Catalan independence was so strong, that President Artur Mas decided to call early elections, to be held in November 2012. Things are very uncertain at the time of writing.

LOCAL GOVERNMENT

Let us now focus on local authorities, which form the third level of government, under the State and regional governments. As we noted at the beginning of this chapter, the Constitution includes some provisions in this connection. Article 137 recognizes the 'autonomy' of municipalities and provinces. In addition, the Constitution also mentions the islands – implicitly referring to the Canary and Balearic archipelagos. The Constitution, moreover, permits the establishment of other local authorities that are created by putting various municipalities together. The *comarcas* that have been formed in some regions (in Catalonia, for example) are an instance of this. But while municipalities, provinces and islands have a constitutionally protected existence, these other entities owe their existence to other norms, and can thus be more freely repealed.

The Constitution protects local autonomy, but it is a different kind of autonomy than that awarded to the regions. First, local entities have a more restricted domain to enact public policies. Ordinary laws enacted by the State and the regions constrain the powers of local governments in important ways. The State is entitled to establish the basic normative framework on local matters (by virtue of article 149.1.18 of the Constitution), while the regions can develop the relevant State laws through more detailed legislation.[43] Second, and related to this, the local authorities are not granted legislative powers. The ordinances they enact are not 'statutes' or norms of equivalent rank. Their status within the legal system is lower, and must therefore respect the legislation that has been produced by the State and by the regions. Consistent with this, they are subject to review by ordinary courts – not by the Constitutional Court.

This does not mean, however, that local ordinances are to be treated as if they were ordinary administrative regulations issued by the executive branch. The Constitutional Court has held that the general doctrine on *reservas de ley,* which requires administrative regulations to be based on sufficiently precise statutes, cannot be extended automatically to local regulations (STC 233/1999). Two arguments have been made to justify a relaxation of the general doctrine. First, local entities must enjoy a certain margin of manoeuvre when issuing norms, if the constitutional principle of local autonomy is to be respected. Second, some local norms are passed by democratically elected bodies. At the municipal level, in particular, the assemblies are directly elected by the people. The enabling statutes issued by the central or the regional Parliament must therefore open up some space for democratic self-government to develop in the local sphere.

As we will see in the next chapter, moreover, even the legislation enacted by the State and the regions can be challenged by the local authorities before the Constitutional Court under some conditions, if it breaches the constitutionally guaranteed sphere of local autonomy.

Furthermore, both municipalities and provinces must enjoy sufficient resources to exercise their functions, the Constitution provides in article 142. Those resources come from their own taxes, as well as from funds that are transferred to them by the State and the regions. All the details are regulated in a State law.[44]

We should next fix our attention on municipalities and provinces, which are the most relevant local institutions.

---

[43] The most important law in this field is *Ley 7/1985, Reguladora de las Bases del Régimen Local.*

[44] See *Ley Reguladora de las Haciendas Locales.*

Municipalities

Municipalities are run by the *ayuntamientos* (the local councils). They comprise an *alcalde* (the mayor), and an assembly of *concejales* who are directly elected by the people every four years. Political participation is slightly lower than in general elections. The turn-out was 66.16 per cent in 2011, 63.97 per cent in 2007, and 67.67 per cent in 2003.[45] The political system at this local level is a form of parliamentary regime like the one we encounter on the State and regional planes. There are some interesting variations, however. The threshold to get representation, for example, is 5 per cent of the popular vote, which is higher than the 3 per cent threshold that applies to the national Congress. It should also be recalled that foreign citizens who reside in Spain can participate in the municipal elections – to vote, and to run for office – under conditions of reciprocity.

Another difference relates to the selection of the mayor. An absolute majority of the assembly members is required to appoint the mayor. If no such majority obtains, however, the head of the political party that attained the largest number of popular votes is automatically proclaimed mayor.[46] No such solution applies at the national or regional level. Incidentally, it is interesting to note that, because some municipalities are very small, the law even lays down the rule to be followed in the event that two or more parties garner the same number of popular votes: the tie is resolved by lot.

Also, as is typically the case under parliamentary systems, the assembly can file a 'motion of censure' against the mayor. The motion is 'constructive' –an alternative candidate needs to be presented, and an absolute majority of votes is required. As is true in the national and regional contexts, the law makes it difficult for the head of the executive to be removed. A special clause applies, however, which is idiosyncratic to local government: if the proponents of the motion include councillors who are – or have been – members of the mayor's political group, or if they include councillors who have abandoned the political group they belonged to at the beginning of the assembly's mandate, the required majority for the motion to succeed is then increased corre-

---

[45] Information available at www.infoelectoral.mir.es/min.
[46] See art 196, LOREG.

spondingly.[47] This is a measure to counteract the consequences of so-called *transfuguismo,* which takes place when representatives change their political affiliations after they are elected. As will be recalled, the Constitutional Court has ruled that representatives do not lose their seats when they are expelled from their parties. The clause in the law we are referring to respects this holding, but establishes a higher majority for a motion to succeed, so that changes in political party affiliations cannot easily destabilize the local government.

The other mechanism we examined when we studied the national Government, the 'question of confidence', is available in local politics too. The mayor may submit such a question to the assembly. The difference, however, is that this motion does not refer to a general programme or declaration, but to specific ordinances that the mayor wishes to get approved. Such ordinances can relate to the budget, fiscal matters, urban planning and internal organization. When one of these ordinances has been rejected by the assembly, the mayor can then submit a 'question of confidence'. The mayor succeeds if the pertinent ordinance gets passed. If not, he resigns and a new mayor is chosen.[48]

Mayors, however, are not given the powerful weapon of dissolving the assembly before the four-year mandate expires. Municipal elections take place the day same throughout all the Spanish territory.

The laws establish some special rules for the smallest municipalities. When a village includes fewer than 250 citizens, for example, the electoral system is not proportional, but majoritarian.[49] It is also possible in some very tiny places, especially if there was a traditional practice to that effect, for citizens to run the local government directly, instead of choosing representatives. (This system is called *concejo abierto*).[50]

A couple of rules illustrate the need that has been felt to establish more constraints in the local sphere than at the national or the regional level. The first rule establishes that those who owe money to the municipality – and who have received the pertinent judicial order to pay – are not eligible to become councillors or mayors.[51] The goal this rule pursues may be legitimate, but its potential impact on marginal groups

[47] See art 197, LOREG.
[48] See art 197*bis*, LOREG.
[49] See art 184, LOREG.
[50] See art 29, *Ley 7/1985, Reguladora de las Bases del Régimen Local.*
[51] See art 177, LOREG.

seems disproportionate. Access to democratic office should be less restrictive, arguably.

The other rule provides that the national Council of Ministers, with the approval of the Senate, can decide to dissolve a local government that has gravely harmed the general interests, in violation of its constitutional obligations.[52] This rule has been applied once: in April 2006, the governing body of the town of Marbella (in the province of Málaga) was dissolved by the Council of Ministers, on the grounds that many of its members were involved in corruption crimes. A provisional body was appointed to rule the town, until the regular elections were held in 2007 and normalcy was restored.

Provinces

The other local entity we should briefly refer to is the province. There are 50 of them in Spain. Each province encompasses a territory that is the result of combining several municipalities. Provinces have a double nature, however. On the one hand, they are an association of municipalities. On the other hand, they are the basic units for the central government to organize its own activities from a territorial point of view. The emergence of Autonomous Communities, however, has eroded the role of the provinces for State purposes. The *gobernadores civiles* (civil governors) that traditionally ruled the provinces, for example, have been replaced by *delegados del gobierno* (delegates of the Government) that exercise their powers in the regions. (In each province, there is a *subdelegado del gobierno* that is under the authority of the regional *delegado del gobierno*).

In contrast to the Autonomous Communities, the provinces were already in existence when the Constitution was enacted in 1978. This is the reason why no law was passed to establish them. What the Constitution does provide is that an organic statute is needed if the existing limits of the provinces are to be altered in the future (article 141.1). The clear implication is that the limits can be changed, but the provinces must remain in existence. A special arrangement has been established, however, when an Autonomous Community comprises a single province (this is the case of Asturias, Cantabria, La Rioja, Madrid, Murcia and Navarra). In such cases, the organs of the Community absorb the functions of the organs of the province.

---

[52] See art 61, *Ley 7/1985, Reguladora de las Bases del Régimen Local.*

The province as a local entity is run by the Diputación Provincial. It consists of an assembly, elected by the municipal councillors, and a President chosen by the assembly. The democratic legitimacy of the Diputación Provincial is thus indirect: it derives from the local councils, in contrast to the direct democratic character of the latter.

Finally, it is important to mention that the Basque Country has a distinctive regional and local organization. Its provinces (Álava, Vizcaya and Guipúzcoa) have retained a set of traditional institutions and powers that both the Autonomous Community and the State must respect. The *Disposición Adicional 1ª* of the Constitution preserves the 'historical rights' of such provinces. Importantly, the provinces are in charge of collecting almost all the taxes. The Community then pays the central Government a certain amount of money, which comes from the provinces, to cover the general expenses incurred by the State, and to make the appropriate contribution to guarantee solidarity with other regions in Spain.[53] Through their assemblies, moreover, the provinces can issue fiscal norms that receive the same treatment as statutes (that is, only the Constitutional Court, not ordinary courts, can declare their invalidity). A similar arrangement exists in Navarra. The difference, however, is that this Community is based on a single province. The Community and the province are thus fused, and the fiscal norms are technically statutes issued by the regional parliament.[54]

CONCLUSION

There was no doubt among the constitutional framers in 1977–78 that the most challenging task they had to confront was the establishment of a decentralized system of government. That Catalonia and the Basque Country, in particular, were to be granted a measure of political autonomy was not questioned by the main political parties. What was not clear, however, was the amount of autonomy that was to be granted to them, and the extent to which other regions in Spain should participate in the devolution process. As things turned out, all of Spain was finally divided into Autonomous Communities. After almost three decades of

---

[53] See *Ley 12/2002, por la que se aprueba el concierto económico con la Comunidad Autónoma del País Vasco.*

[54] See *Ley 28/1990, por la que se aprueba el convenio económico entre el Estado y la Comunidad Foral de Navarra.*

incremental developments, the new territorial structure has affirmed itself: both citizens and political representatives take for granted the existence of a regional level of government, that needs to interact with the national one. There is no realistic possibility for this structure to be eliminated –at least for many decades.

There is a generalized sentiment, however, that the Constitution has only been a partial success in this area. On the one hand, there is much room for technical improvements to ensure a better cooperation between the Communities and the central government. On the other hand, if the ultimate goal of the *Estado de las Autonomías* was to find a solution to the 'Catalan and the Basque problem', the goal has not been fully achieved. The social and political forces that favour secession from Spain have expanded throughout the years, and tensions have inevitably arisen. It is hard to maintain and reconstruct a quasi-federal system, if secession is endorsed by an increasing number of citizens in some parts of the country. The regional question was the hardest issue to come to terms with during the transition to democracy, and this remains the hardest constitutional issue that Spain will face in the coming years.

FURTHER READING

Aguado Renedo, C, *El estatuto de autonomía y su posición en el ordenamiento jurídico* (Madrid, Centro de Estudios Constitucionales, 1996).

Aja, E, *El Estado autonómico. Federalismo y hechos diferenciales* (Madrid, Alianza Editorial, 2003).

Aja, E, Albertí Rovira, E and Ruiz Ruiz, JJ, *La reforma constitucional del Senado* (Madrid, Centro de Estudios Políticos y Constitucionales, 2005).

Fossas Espadaler, E, *El principio dispositivo en el Estado autonómico* (Madrid, Marcial Pons, 2007).

Fossas, E and Requejo Coll, F (eds), *Asimetría federal y estado plurinacional: el debate sobre la acomodación de la diversidad en Canadá, Bélgica y España* (Madrid, Trotta, 1999).

García Morales, MJ and Roig Moles, E, 'The Spanish "Autonomic State"' in Rose, J and Traut, J (eds), *Federalism and Decentralization* (Berlin, LIT Verlag, 2001).

González Pascual, MI, *El proceso autonómico ante la igualdad en el ejercicio de los derechos constitucionales* (Oñati, IVAP, 2007).

Gunther, R, Montero, JR and Botella, J, *Democracy in Modern Spain* (New Haven, Yale University Press, 2004) ch 6.

Hopkins, J, *Devolution in Context: Regional, Federal and Devolved Government in the European Union* (London, Cavendish, 2002).

Jiménez Asensio, R, *La ley autonómica en el sistema constitucional de fuentes del Derecho* (Madrid, Marcial Pons, 2001).

Muñoz Machado, S, *Derecho Público de las Comunidades Autónomas* (Madrid, Iustel, 2007).

Viver Pi-Sunyer, C, *Materias competenciales y Tribunal Constitucional* (Barcelona, Ariel, 1989).

8

The Constitutional Role of Courts

Jurisdictional Exclusivity and Unity – Impartiality, Independence, Legality and Responsibility – The Democratic Legitimacy of Judicial Decisions – The Government of Judges – Prosecutors and the Jury – Why a Constitutional Court? – Composition – Jurisdiction of the Court – The Court's Performance: Tensions with the Political Branches and the Ordinary Judiciary – Conclusion

I N A DEMOCRATIC State that is based on the rule of law, it is not easy to strike the right balance between two competing sets of considerations when designing the judiciary. On the one hand, courts ought to be awarded a certain measure of independence, so that they can decide controversies in the light of the law, without suffering external pressures. This independence is especially important when courts are empowered to review the legality of decisions made by the governmental institutions. On the other hand, courts must be subject to certain constraints, so that the case law they generate is ultimately in keeping with the considered judgments of the democratic institutions. It is not easy to harmonize these different requirements.

In this chapter we will study the role of courts. One of the characteristic features of the judiciary in Spain is its dualist structure. As has been noted in earlier chapters, a specialized constitutional tribunal has been established to guarantee the supremacy of the Constitution. Only this tribunal, in particular, can invalidate statutes passed by Parliament (or any other norms that have the same rank as statutes).

In the discussion that follows, we will first examine the organization of the regular courts, as well as the constitutional principles that are relevant to their functions. A brief reference will be made to the role of public prosecutors and juries. We will then proceed to study the Constitutional Court. We will explore the main reasons why this special institution was established, and will study the different types of cases it handles. As we will see, tensions have sometimes emerged between the Constitutional Court and the political branches, as well as with the ordinary judiciary.

PART I: THE ORDINARY JUDICIAL BRANCH

The structure and functions of ordinary courts are regulated in an organic statute, the *Ley Orgánica 6/1985 del Poder Judicial* (hereinafter: LOPJ), which implements the principles laid down in the Constitution.

The first important thing this statute does is to establish the different courts in Spain, and to distribute judicial authority among them. The judicial map the LOPJ has defined basically mirrors the territorial organization of the country. We thus find courts at each municipality (Jueces de paz), at each province (Audiencias Provinciales, Juzgados de lo Mercantil, Juzgados de lo Penal, Juzgados de lo Social, Juzgados de Vigilancia Penitenciaria, Juzgados de Menores, Juzgados de lo Contencioso-Administrativo), at each Autonomous Community (Tribunales Superiores de Justicia), and for the whole national territory (the Audiencia Nacional, and the Supreme Court).[1]

All these organs make up the judiciary, which is part of the apparatus of the State. The Autonomous Communities, as we already know, do not have their own courts. They have a very marginal intervention in the judicial sphere. The regional parliaments, for example, can propose names to occupy one-third of the vacancies at the civil and criminal chamber of the Tribunal Superior de Justicia. The General Council of the Judiciary elects one of the three names proposed, for each vacancy.[2]

---

[1] There is also an intermediate level between the municipalities and the provinces: the *partido judicial*. This unit, which only exists for purposes of the judicial organization, comprises several municipalities. The courts at this level are the Juzgados de Primera Instancia e Instrucción, which have jurisdiction in civil and criminal matters. In addition, some courts are specialized in domestic violence: Juzgados de Violencia sobre la Mujer.

[2] See art 330, LOPJ.

The number of judges has increased in the past years. In 2011, the number reached 5,047. Interestingly, the vast majority of the new judges are women. In 2011, for example, 99 of the junior judges that were recruited were women, while only 35 were men. That year, 49 per cent of the total number of sitting judges were women. In the highest courts, however, the presence of women is still very low. On the Supreme Court, for instance, 68 judges in 2011 were men and only 10 were women.[3]

JURISDICTIONAL EXCLUSIVITY AND UNITY

The Constitution establishes several important principles with regard to the judiciary. Article 117 starts by saying that justice is administered by judges and magistrates that make up the judicial power. A particular function, that of 'administering justice', is thus assigned to a specific set of institutions: courts. Administering justice (that is, adjudication or *jurisdictio*) consists of having a public official resolve a dispute between two parties, by means of a binding decision that rests on the pertinent body of law. This task is entrusted to the courts, which are run by *jueces y magistrados* (judges and magistrates).[4]

As a result of this constitutional link between the jurisdictional function, on the one hand, and the network of courts, on the other, two important consequences follow. The first is that, as a general rule, only courts that belong to the ordinary judicial branch may be assigned the job of administering justice. The exceptions to this rule are grounded in the Constitution itself. Thus, the Constitutional Court, the Court of Audit, the Tribunal de la Vega Valenciana and the Consejo de Hombres Buenos de Murcia (two traditional tribunals in charge of conflicts over water), are examples of institutions that exercise a jurisdictional function and are nevertheless outside the network of ordinary courts. The

---

[3] See Consejo General del Poder Judicial, 'Memoria sobre el estado, funcionamiento y actividad del Poder Judicial y de los Juzgados y Tribunales en el año 2011' 435, 436, 554, available at www.poderjudicial.es/cgpj.

[4] Judges and magistrates are two categories within the civil servant career, the latter having a higher status than the former. We can leave aside this distinction for purposes of our discussion here. In addition to these public servants, the judiciary also comprises *jueces de paz* (justices of the peace), who are elected by the local councils (*ayuntamientos*) and serve four-year terms. They are not required to hold a law degree.

legitimacy of their existence is not problematic, however, since it is covered by specific clauses in the Constitution (articles 159, 136, and 125, respectively).

Another partial exception to the general rule, which is also specifically mentioned in the constitutional text, concerns military tribunals. These are not part of the ordinary judiciary, but their decisions can be reviewed by one of the chambers of the Supreme Court (the fifth chamber). Military tribunals are thus not totally detached from the ordinary judiciary. The Constitution, moreover, limits the jurisdiction of such tribunals to matters that strictly pertain to the military domain, as well as to cases that arise under a state of siege (article 117.5).

The link between the jurisdictional function and ordinary courts has another aspect: as a general rule, the only responsibility judges can be asked to exercise is that of administering justice. This ensures that judges will not be overburdened with non-jurisdictional tasks that might make it harder for them to adjudicate cases in an effective manner, or that might entangle them with matters that could put their independence at risk. The Constitution only permits an exception to this general rule when the task assigned to judges is instrumental to the protection of rights. The role of judges when they participate in the 'electoral administration', or when they run the Civil Register, are two prominent examples of non-jurisdictional tasks that the Constitution permits by way of exception.

The Constitution also enshrines the principle of 'jurisdictional unity' (article 117.5), which is closely related to what we have just seen. It requires that there be a single set of courts with jurisdiction over all persons. No group of individuals, that is, should be entitled to special courts. This principle of unity is a historical reaction against the privileges that some social groups enjoyed in ancient times. The Constitution expressly prohibits 'courts of exception' (article 117.6). The principle of unity, however, is not breached when the case load is distributed among courts in accordance with the subject matter involved. In this connection, it is important to indicate that there are four 'jurisdictional orders' within the Spanish judiciary: civil, criminal, social and administrative. Consistent with this division, there are four chambers within the Supreme Court, which distribute their work accordingly. (In addition, there is the fifth chamber we already mentioned, to review decisions rendered by military tribunals). On some levels, in addition, there is further specialization (in cases involving family law, penitentiary law, and violence against women, for example). All these divisions of labour are compatible with the principle of jurisdictional unity. Another consequence of the principle of unity, as has already been noted, is that there is no division of judicial power between the State and the Autonomous Communities. All courts belong to the State level.

IMPARTIALITY, INDEPENDENCE, LEGALITY AND RESPONSIBILITY

The Constitution lays down a further set of principles that are strongly interrelated: impartiality, independence, legality and responsibility.

Impartiality is not explicitly mentioned in the constitutional text, but it is implicit in the very notion of adjudication.[5] The courts that are charged with the jurisdictional task must proceed in an impartial manner. For these purposes, the laws provide that judges can be recused, or must disqualify themselves, in certain circumstances.[6] A prejudiced judge, or one who is involved in a conflict of interest, ought not to decide a case. Precisely in order to reduce the risk of bias, the laws also place some limitations on the activities of judges. The Constitution, for example, expressly prohibits them from belonging to political parties or trade unions, though it permits the creation of judicial associations (article 127.1). The LOPJ, in turn, establishes a strict regime of incompatibilities, which makes it impossible for judges to exercise any other office or profession, except teaching, researching and publishing.[7]

To secure impartiality, it is also important for rules to be laid down in advance for purposes of determining which courts are going to decide a given case. This requirement is captured by the 'right of access to the ordinary judge predetermined by the law', guaranteed in article 24.2 of the Constitution. The law must use general terms to specify the courts that will hear the disputes. It is constitutional, however, for the law to provide that certain crimes are to be tried by a central court, such as the Audiencia Nacional, if those crimes have characteristics that justify that special treatment, such as their social impact or geographical reach (STC 199/1987). The Audiencia Nacional, for example, investigates and tries

---

[5] R Jiménez Asensio, *Imparcialidad Judicial y Derecho al Juez Imparcial* (Cizur Menor, Aranzadi, 2002).

[6] See arts 217–28, LOPJ.

[7] See art 389, LOPJ.

cases involving terrorism, among others. This has given the judges on this court high public visibility.

It is necessary, moreover, for judges to be independent, and thus protected against external pressures, particularly from the political branches. In this connection, the Spanish system makes judges part of a bureaucratic body whose members have tenure until the age of retirement fixed by the law. Judges 'may only be dismissed, suspended, transferred or retired on the grounds, and subject to the guarantees, provided by law', article 117.2 of the Constitution declares. The only exception to the rule of indefinite tenure concerns the judges that are appointed for limited (though renewable) terms, to fill up vacancies.[8] Once those positions are finally occupied by permanent judges, recruited according to the ordinary procedures, the temporary judges have to step down. Their independence is thus likely to be weaker, given their lack of indefinite tenure. Unfortunately, there are a great number of them: in 2011, 190 new temporary judges were appointed, and 1,261 were reappointed, for the 2011–12 judicial year.[9] The Minister of Justice has recently expressed his willingness to reduce this number, replacing those judges with permanent ones.

To safeguard judicial independence, moreover, certain delicate decisions concerning the administrative status of judges are placed in the hands of bodies that are insulated from the executive branch. The General Council of the Judiciary plays a key role in this regard, as we will see later.

Judicial independence, interestingly, also shields judges from any pressures from their judicial peers. Article 12 of the LOPJ, in this connection, provides that the highest courts can only correct the lower courts' interpretation and application of the law through the system of appeals. No judicial institution can issue instructions on the law for lower courts to follow.

Independence and impartiality are instrumental to the goal of making sure that the law is correctly applied to disputes. The judge is to be impartial and independent so that the controversies that are brought to him or her are effectively resolved in accordance with the law. The judge is thus exclusively subject to 'law's empire' (*el imperio de la ley*), as the Constitution puts it. The expression 'law' is to be given a broad meaning

---

[8]   See art 298.2, LOPJ.

[9]   See Consejo General del Poder Judicial (n 3) 82.

in this context. It embraces all sources of the law, not only the written ones. Customs and general principles are certainly included.

The view is often held in Spain that judicial independence protects judges from the case law established by the Supreme Court. Such case law, it is commonly asserted, is not strictly binding, and judges can therefore choose to disagree with it. It is true that lower court decisions can ultimately by quashed by the highest courts. But as a matter of principle, there is no legal duty to follow vertical precedents. Lower judges can go their own ways.[10]

Some scholars, however, have argued against this traditional thesis.[11] In any modern State, they claim, the law will inevitably exhibit gaps and contradictions, and will give rise to interpretive uncertainties. The Supreme Court is to play a crucial role in settling the disagreements that emerge among lower courts in many cases. In order to protect legal certainty and equality under the law, the Court's holdings should be understood to bind lower courts. What needs to be done is to introduce reforms that allow the Supreme Court to focus on a smaller number of cases, so that it can be more careful and consistent when it works out its jurisprudence from one legal problem to the next.

The Constitution also mentions the principle of 'judicial responsibility'. Independence does not mean that judges are immune from all kinds of legal consequences if they make mistakes or otherwise cause damages. This is, of course, a delicate matter. The laws establish different types of responsibility: disciplinary (when administrative rules are breached), civil (when there has been a judicial error, or damages have been caused some other way), and even criminal.

It should be noted, in particular, that judges commit the crime of *prevaricación* if they knowingly render a decision that is clearly illegal, or render such a decision through serious negligence or inexcusable ignorance.[12] This crime has given rise to great controversies in some

---

[10] See, eg LM Díez-Picazo, *Régimen constitucional del poder judicial* (Madrid, Civitas, 1991). For a collection of essays on this topic, edited by the General Council of the Judiciary, see *La fuerza vinculante de la jurisprudencia* (Madrid, Consejo General del Poder Judicial, 2001).

[11] See, eg I de Otto, *Derecho constitucional. Sistema de fuentes* (Barcelona, Ariel, 1988) 287–303. For my own views on this question, see V Ferreres Comella, *El principio de taxatividad en materia penal y el valor normativo de la jurisprudencia* (Madrid, Civitas, 2002) 153–231, where I give arguments to support the binding character of the Supreme Court's rulings.

[12] See arts 446 and 447 of the Criminal Code.

instances. The most recent case concerns Judge Baltasar Garzón, who had served as an investigating judge (*juez de instrucción*) of the Audiencia Nacional for many years, until he was expelled from the judiciary. The Supreme Court found him guilty of *prevaricación* in one case. Two criminal actions had actually been brought against Judge Garzón, concerning the lawfulness of his decisions. In one case, the Judge had decided to allow the police to intercept the conversations between some prisoners and their lawyers, in the context of a criminal investigation involving money-laundering and corruption activities where a political party (PP) was implicated. The Supreme Court found that this decision was clearly illegal, and that the judge had committed the crime of *prevaricación*.[13] The other case had to do with Judge Garzón's decision to open criminal investigations against those responsible for the killings committed against republicans during the Civil War, as well as under Franco's dictatorship. It was controversial whether such a judicial move was correct, in light of the amnesty law that had been enacted in 1977, during the transition to democracy. The Supreme Court, however, concluded that, even if wrong, Judge Garzón's decision was not so patently erroneous as to make him criminally liable for having rendered it.[14]

An association has asked the Council of Ministers to pardon Garzón, who has garnered popularity among large sections of Spanish public opinion. This is the Judge, it should be recalled, who prosecuted former President of Chile, Augusto Pinochet, in 1998. He also played a key role in the judicial investigations against ETA terrorists, as well as against governmental officials who had organized the 'dirty war' against terrorism.

In any event, these criminal charges against Judge Garzón illustrate the difficulty of making the existence of the crime of *prevaricación* compatible with the principle of judicial independence. The Supreme Court has insisted in its jurisprudence that for this crime to be committed, it is not sufficient for the judge to interpret the law incorrectly. The interpretation needs to be clearly wrong, completely indefensible, impossible to support on any legal argument. How to apply these vague criteria, of course, is a hard question. This uncertainty can produce a chilling effect on judges, who might prefer to err on the safe side, and thus abstain from offering readings of the law that could end up being too heterodox in the eyes of the Supreme Court.

[13] See decision 9 February 2012.
[14] See decision 27 February 2012.

THE DEMOCRATIC LEGITIMACY OF JUDICIAL DECISIONS

We should briefly reflect on the democratic sources of the legitimacy of the judicial power. How are courts linked to popular will?

With respect to the procedures to appoint judges, the democratic input is of marginal importance. The regular way to enter the judiciary in Spain is through an exam that is administered by technical, non-political Commissions. Some high appointments to the judiciary, however, are made by the General Council of the Judiciary, as we will see later. Some democratic inputs are introduced this way, given the parliamentary method to select the members of the Council.[15]

A more intense source of democratic legitimacy is connected to the way judges perform their functions. An important rule is laid down in the Constitution in this regard: judges must always reason their decisions (article 120.3). Judges must always explain, therefore, how their legal opinions in the particular cases flow from the general rules embodied in the law. When the decisions patently derive from a statutory provision enacted by Parliament, their democratic legitimacy reaches the highest level. If, in contrast, there is reasonable controversy about how to read the relevant provision, the chain through which democratic legitimacy is transferred is weaker. Judges must then struggle to justify why they think their interpretive conclusion is better than the rival ones. Dissenting opinions can be published, moreover.[16] All this facilitates a certain dialogue about the law, which is also to be appreciated from a democratic perspective.

In this connection, it is interesting to mention that those who deny the binding force of the legal doctrines established by the Supreme Court often appeal to democratic considerations to justify their position. They argue that the Supreme Court cannot be given the power to issue binding doctrines, for that would be equivalent to granting the Court the power to issue legal norms, and it is not acceptable for a non-democratic institution to do that.

It can be countered, however, that if judges were bound to follow the interpretations fixed by the highest courts, the democratic conversation would be improved. After all, the political branches can more easily

---

[15] On this source of democratic legitimacy, see L López Guerra, 'La legitimidad democrática del juez' (1997) 1 *Cuadernos de Derecho Público* 43.

[16] See art 260, LOPJ.

enter a dialogue with the judiciary as to what to do with the existing laws, if there is a relatively consistent reading and application of those laws by the judiciary, instead of a chaotic collection of different positions. Whether a statute needs to be changed or repealed depends, in part, on how it is being interpreted by judges. Parliament cannot easily decide what to do when it cannot take for granted that what the Supreme Court is saying is the right interpretation of the current law is actually the interpretation that the rest of the courts are following.

THE GOVERNMENT OF JUDGES

The Spanish Constitution distrusts the executive power when it comes to governing judges. This is the reason why it establishes a special institution, the General Council of the Judiciary, drawing inspiration from the French and Italian systems.[17]

The Council comprises 20 members, who then appoint the President of the Supreme Court. The latter will also preside over the Council. According to the Constitution (article 122), the 20 members are to be appointed as follows: 12 from amongst judges and magistrates (*entre jueces y magistrados*), four by a three-fifths majority of Congress, and four by a three-fifths majority of the Senate. The law implementing this provision in 1985 established that the first group of 12 members were to be judges, but were not to be elected *by* judges, but by Congress (six of them) and the Senate (the other six). There was a huge controversy about this law, and objections were raised on constitutional grounds. The Constitutional Court upheld the law against the challenges that were launched (STC 108/1986). An amendment was introduced some years later (in 2001), establishing a mixed solution: the 12 members are still appointed by the parliamentary chambers, but the list of candidates is now drawn by judges.

The members of the Council occupy their offices for a limited five-year period, which is non-renewable. All of them are appointed at the same time, which is not a very reasonable arrangement. Every time a new Council is appointed, too many plans are conceived from scratch. The organ lacks institutional memory.

---

[17] On the origin and justification of this institution, see MJ Terol Becerra, *El Consejo General del Poder Judicial* (Madrid, Centro de Estudios Constitucionales, 1990).

To guarantee its institutional autonomy, the Council prepares its own budget, which is automatically included in the general budget of the State that the Government sends Parliament for its approval.

The Council is in charge of various tasks. One of them is to write reports on certain legislative proposals and other matters that affect the judiciary. Every year, it has to send a report to the Minister of Justice, concerning the material needs of the administration of justice, and a more general report to the Cortes Generales. Its most important responsibility, however, is to make various administrative decisions that affect courts: selecting and educating judges; making judicial appointments; deciding promotions; inspecting the courts; granting judges administrative permissions for various matters; imposing disciplinary sanctions on judges who violate the laws. These are all delicate decisions that it might be too risky to charge the executive branch with. The Council, which is insulated from that branch, seems to be better equipped to handle such matters. Its decisions, moreover, can be reviewed by the Supreme Court by way of an appeal.

It should be indicated that judicial promotions, though decided by the Council, are almost always the result of the mechanical application of the criteria established by the law. Seniority is the basic standard that is employed. Only exceptionally does the Council have discretion to choose whom to appoint, from amongst the various candidates that meet the legal requirements. This is so, for example, with respect to Supreme Court judges, as well as the Presidents of Tribunales Superiores de Justicia or of the Audiencias Provinciales.

The Council, however, is not responsible for all the matters that affect judges from an administrative point of view. Several courts have their own governmental units too (made up of judges), which take care of less important administrative tasks.

The executive branch, moreover, retains its competences over the material aspects of the administration of justice, as well as the staff (excluding the judges) that serves it. These competences may be transferred to the Autonomous Communities, and they have generally been. Since such competences do not affect judges directly, but merely involve the material and personal resources that serve judges, the Constitutional Court has found no problem in this devolution of authority (SSTC 56/1990, 62/1990).

Whether it has been a good idea, all things considered, to create the General Council of the Judiciary is a matter for controversy, however.

The complex distribution of responsibility between the Council and the Minister of Justice (as well as the regional governments) has made it more difficult for public opinion to identify whom they have to blame for the malfunctioning of the administration of justice. In addition, some recent scandals have gravely affected the image of the Council. Its President, Carlos Dívar, was forced to resign in June 2012, under the accusation of having used public funds to pay for his private expenses in hotels and restaurants during long weekends. Other members of the Council are also suspected of having benefited from public resources in inappropriate ways. The question has been raised in the media whether it is really necessary to have such a large body to deal with judicial matters. Since the Constitution clearly fixes the number of counsellors, it is impossible to reduce the composition of the Council without amending the Constitution. But a proposal is currently being considered to reduce the number of full-time members, so that the rest are only expected to participate in a few important meetings. This would diminish the economic costs of the institution, and might enhance its efficiency.

Another problem that has arisen concerns the high level of politicization of the Council. The political parties exert a powerful influence over its members in some cases. If the idea is that some decisions concerning judicial promotions, for example, ought to be taken in a relatively democratic fashion, it is not obvious why the Council is necessary at all. Instead of having Parliament elect the members of the Council, who will then make the relevant judicial appointments under the influence of the political parties, it would be more transparent for Parliament to make the appointments directly. The Council, after all, does not exist in most European countries. The fact that the President of the Council is, at the same time, the President of the Supreme Court, introduces an additional factor of complexity. It is not a reasonable arrangement for the same person to wear these two hats: one hat as the President of an institution that is basically political (the Council), and the other hat as the Chief Justice of the Supreme Court, which is expected to be neutral and detached from politics. Public opinion gets certainly confused about the responsibilities that the President of the Council bears.

PROSECUTORS AND THE JURY

We should now say a few words about two other institutions that are mentioned in the Constitution in the same title devoted to the judicial power, but which are not judicial institutions properly so-called: the Office of the Public Prosecutor (Ministerio Fiscal), and the jury.

Prosecutors, the Constitution proclaims, have as their mission

> that of promoting the operation of justice in the defence of the rule of law, of citizens' rights and of the public interest as safeguarded by the law, whether *ex officio* or at the request of interested parties, as well as that of protecting the independence of the courts and securing through them the satisfaction of the social interest (article 124.1).

This is a rather broad definition. Although the main task of prosecutors is carried out in the context of criminal cases, the laws require their participation in other procedures too (such as civil cases involving minors, for example).

Prosecutors are organized hierarchically. At the apex sits the Fiscal General del Estado, who is appointed by the Government after having heard the General Council of the Judiciary. The Fiscal General is relatively protected from the Government, since he serves a term of four years, during which he cannot be freely removed. When a new Government is installed, however, a new appointment is made.[18] The Government can suggest the Fiscal General to take a particular action, but the latter may reason his decision not to do so. The higher authorities within the organization of prosecutors can instruct the lower authorities how to proceed with the cases, and how to interpret the relevant laws. The Constitution, however, seeks to strike a balance between this hierarchical principle and the countervailing principles of 'legality and impartiality' (article 124.2). This is not an easy equilibrium. The law, for example, provides that a prosecutor may express his disagreement with the orders and instructions received from above. In such cases, the higher authority that insists on the original ruling must reason its decision. The dissenting prosecutor may be replaced by another one to pursue a particular case.[19]

[18] See art 31, *Ley 50/1981, del Estatuto Orgánico del Ministerio Fiscal.*

[19] On the role of public prosecutors, and their interactions with other governmental institutions, see the comparative study by LM Díez-Picazo, *El poder de acusar* (Barcelona, Ariel, 2000).

It is important to emphasize that prosecutors are not ordinary parties to the cases they handle, for they must seek the correct application of the law in an impartial and objective manner, without being tied to any partial interest. In criminal cases, for example, they may refuse to bring charges against someone, if they think there is no case under the law, while other parties may decide to go forward. It is important to note, in this regard, that prosecutors have no monopoly as accusers: any citizen in Spain, even if not affected by the underlying action as a victim or in any other manner, is entitled to bring criminal charges. The Constitution actually includes an explicit clause protecting this *actio popularis* right (article 125). In some politically relevant cases, individual citizens or associations have exercised this right, to start criminal proceedings against relevant public figures. It was an association, for example, and not the public prosecutor, that accused Judge Baltasar Garzón of having rendered clearly mistaken judicial decisions for which he deserved punishment. Political parties too have sometimes exercised the *actio popularis*. Recently, for example, a political party represented in the national Parliament (UPyD) brought criminal charges against the chief executives of BANKIA, an important financial institution that was bailed out by the Spanish Government in the middle of the economic crisis.

The other institution that needs mentioning is the jury, which the Constitution conceives as an instrument for citizens to participate in the administration of justice (article 125). The jury is limited to certain types of criminal cases, enumerated in the pertinent law. For many years this constitutional clause was not implemented through the appropriate legislation. The resulting gap provided an example of an 'unconstitutional omission'. Finally, in 1995, the law regulating the jury was enacted.[20]

The jury is composed of nine lay people, but a professional judge presides over them. The judge does not participate in the deliberations of the jury, however. It is noteworthy that the judicial decision based on the verdict can be appealed to a higher court on several grounds, both when it convicts and when it acquits. The judicial checks on the jury are thus quite broad. It is also interesting to point out that the verdict by the jury must be properly reasoned, whether it is favourable or unfavourable to the accused. This is to honour the general requirement that the Constitution establishes in article 120.3. The Constitutional Court has had to specify the manner in which this requirement is to be applied to

[20] *Ley Orgánica 5/1995, del Jurado.*

juries. Although it has conceded that the kind of reasoning to be expected from them cannot be exactly the same as that of professional judges, the Court has been quite strict. It once upheld, for example, a judicial decision that had quashed a verdict of acquittal on the grounds that the verdict was not sufficiently reasoned. Three members of the Constitutional Court dissented, however. They insisted that the jury need not reason why it finds a person not guilty (STC 169/2004).

PART II: THE CONSTITUTIONAL COURT

Let us now turn our attention to the Constitutional Court. Title IX of the Constitution is specifically devoted to this tribunal. An organic statute, the *Ley Orgánica 2/1979 del Tribunal Constitucional* (hereinafter: LOTC), provides the detailed regulation.[21]

In what follows, we will first enquire into the reasons why such a court was established. We will then proceed to study its composition and functions. We will finally say something about the tensions that have emerged between the court and the other branches.

WHY A CONSTITUTIONAL COURT?

The constitutional framers in 1977–78 easily agreed that a Constitutional Court had to be created.[22] This is not surprising. First of all, various European nations at that time already had such an institution. In particular, Germany, France and Italy did, which were the three countries whose political systems were most influential in the framing of the

[21] The most important commentary on the LOTC is JL Requejo (ed), *Comentarios a la Ley Orgánica del Tribunal Constitucional* (Madrid, Tribunal Constitucional, 2001). For an interesting and influential set of studies, by a former Vice-President of the Court and the current Secretary General, on the theoretical foundations of this institution, see F Rubio Llorente and J Jiménez Campo, *Estudios sobre jurisdicción constitucional* (Madrid, MacGraw-Hil, 1998). Information about the Court can be obtained from its website (www.tribunalconstitucional.es), which also publishes its decisions (some of them translated into English). Every year, the Court issues a useful report (*Memoria*) with information and statistics about the different types of cases it has dealt with.

[22] See P Pérez Tremps, *Tribunal Constitucional y poder judicial* (Madrid, Centro de Estudios Constitucionales, 1985) 97–109.

Spanish Constitution. The reasons that are usually offered to justify the centralization of judicial review of legislation in a single body were applicable to Spain too: legal certainty is deemed to be better protected if a single tribunal is in charge of checking ordinary law against constitutional norms, instead of conferring that power on all courts. To the extent, moreover, that statutes are enacted by a democratic Parliament, the general feeling is that their validity should only be reviewed by a special institution whose members are selected in more democratic ways than ordinary judges are. The justices of the Constitutional Court, moreover, tend to be prestigious jurists who exhibit diverse professional backgrounds. Some of them are former judges and prosecutors, while others are former lawyers, professors, or public servants. This professional diversity is a desirable feature of a tribunal that has to speak to complex constitutional issues.[23]

Secondly, Spain had already set up a Constitutional Court during the Second Republic. At that time, Spain was one of the few countries (together with Czechoslovakia and Liechtenstein) that followed the so-called 'Austrian' (Kelsenian) model of constitutional review.[24] General Franco's dictatorship abolished this republican institution, but it served as a historical precedent for the constitutional framers in 1977–78.

Thirdly, the ordinary judges that had been appointed under Franco's dictatorial regime were not replaced when democracy came, in spite of the fact that the liberal–democratic commitments of many of them were rather weak. Given this historical circumstance, it made no sense to grant regular courts the power to check the validity of the laws enacted by the new democratic Parliament. The framers preferred to ascribe the task of legislative review to a separate body, whose members would be selected by the political branches.

For all these reasons, the framers easily agreed to set up a Constitutional Court in Spain, as part of the new political order.

---

[23] For a general discussion of the potential advantages of constitutional courts, see V Ferreres Comella, *Constitutional Courts and Democratic Values. A European Perspective* (New Haven, Yale University Press, 2009).

[24] For a general study of the emergence of the 'European model' of judicial review between the First and the Second World Wars, with a specific examination of the Spanish version of it as it operated during the Second Republic, see P Cruz Villalón, *La formación del sistema europeo de control de constitucionalidad (1918–39)* (Madrid, Centro de Estudios Constitucionales, 1987).

COMPOSITION

The Constitutional Court comprises 12 members, all of whom must be prestigious jurists with at least 15 years of professional experience. Four of them are selected by Congress, four by the Senate, two by the Government, and the other two by the General Council of the Judiciary. Parliament has thus an important say in the appointment process: most judges on the Court (8 out of 12) are chosen by it.[25]

In spite of this strong link between the Constitutional Court and Parliament, it is impossible for a transient majority to appoint a Court of its liking. A super-majority of three-fifths is necessary for both Congress and the Senate to nominate the justices. This means that the governing majority must negotiate the names of the candidates with the main party in the opposition. The two appointments in the hands of the General Council of the Judiciary must also be made by a super-majority of three-fifths, which requires some consensus among its members.[26]

In order to enhance the transparency of the appointment process, a reform was introduced in 2007 to require parliamentary hearings to be held with the judicial candidates, before a vote is taken in Congress and the Senate.[27] These hearings, however, have nothing to do with the procedures that develop in the United States Senate. The candidates are not asked any difficult questions. The legislative chamber simply rubber-stamps the agreements that have already been reached by the leaders of the main political parties. The hearings have proved to be rather useless.

Unlike ordinary judges, the members of the Constitutional Court do not serve indefinitely until retirement age, but for a fixed period of nine years. Every three years, there is a partial renewal of the Court. For these purposes, the 12 justices are distributed in three different groups,

---

[25] With respect to the Senate, the LOTC was reformed in 2007 to permit the legislative assemblies of the Autonomous Communities to propose the names of possible candidates. The Senate was to choose the constitutional justices from among the lists provided by the Communities. The Constitutional Court, however, has introduced an important qualification: if the candidates proposed by the Autonomous Communities fail to obtain the required super-majority of three-fifths, the Senate is free to select others (STC 49/2008).

[26] The Constitution does not impose this super-majoritarian requirement on the Council. The LOPJ does, in art 107.2.

[27] See art 16.2, LOTC.

depending on the institution that appointed them (Congress; the Senate; the Government and the General Council of the Judiciary). The justices can only be reappointed after a partial renewal of the Court has taken place. Only once, so far, has a judge been reappointed.[28]

It is probably a bad idea for reappointment to be allowed. It would be much better for the law to exclude this possibility. Judicial independence would be better served. In any case, the members of the Constitutional Court are protected in their functions as ordinary judges are. Thus, they can only be removed on the specific grounds provided by the law. Actually, the Constitutional Court itself is in charge of applying them.[29] As far as criminal liability is concerned, moreover, only the Supreme Court can establish it.[30] The Constitutional Court, it should be added, has financial autonomy to protect its independence: the Court defines its own budget, which is automatically made part of the general budget that the Government submits to the Cortes Generales.[31]

One of the justices is appointed President of the Court. Another is appointed Vice-President.[32] The election is made by the justices themselves. They serve for three-year terms (which can be renewed once). One of the important attributions of the President, apart from organizing the agenda of the Court and taking care of its administrative matters, is to break the ties when votes are taken.[33] This puts him or her in a very delicate position when a highly controversial case is to be decided. The fact that dissenting opinions can be published gives high visibility to the President's vote. In 1983, for example, the Court had to examine a governmental *decreto-ley* that expropriated an important set of banks and industries that were in crisis. The Court was divided equally, and the vote of the President was decisive to uphold the decree (STC 111/1983). Similarly, he had to cast the decisive vote in a controversial decision that ruled that a new statute liberalizing abortion was partially unconstitutional (STC 53/1985).

---

[28] Javier Delgado Barrio became President of the Supreme Court in 1996, after he stepped down from the Constitutional Court. In 2001 he was again appointed judge of the Constitutional Court.

[29] See arts 10 and 23, LOTC.

[30] See art 26, LOTC.

[31] See art 10.3, LOTC.

[32] The President presides over the Court as a whole, as well as the first chamber. The Vice-President, in turn, presides over the second chamber.

[33] See art 90.1, LOTC. The Vice-President also has this power in his capacity as President of the second chamber.

In recent years, it is sad to say, the two big political parties have not shown much institutional respect for the Court: they have failed to observe the constitutional timetable for making the congressional and senatorial appointments. The LOTC provides that judges will continue to exercise their functions when their term expires, until the vacancies are filled. The delays, however, have been so long in recent times, that the LOTC has been amended (in 2010) to provide that the justices will not serve the ordinary nine-year term, but a shorter term, if their appointments were delayed. One is authorized to have doubts about the constitutional validity of this provision. The Constitution, after all, clearly says that the judges will serve a nine-year term. It is not obvious why the new appointees should suffer the consequences of the scandalous failure of political parties to fill the vacancies in time.

JURISDICTION OF THE COURT

The Court decides different types of cases, through different kinds of procedures: it controls the constitutionality of legislation; it decides conflicts between certain public institutions and it examines complaints for violations of fundamental rights. For these purposes, the Court is divided into two chambers (Salas) of six judges each. The latter are further organized in two sections (each comprising three judges).[34]

Constitutional Review of Legislation

The Court, first of all, has the authority to pass judgment on the constitutionality of statutes. This is the most important function that has historically led to the creation of constitutional tribunals in Europe. The Court has a 'monopoly' when it comes to legislative review: only this

---

[34] Depending on the cases, the Court decides en banc (*Pleno*), or through its chambers or sections. Until the 2007 reform of the LOTC, the basic division was roughly this: the Court as a whole exercised constitutional review of legislation and resolved conflicts of competences; the chambers were concerned with deciding individual complaints for violation of fundamental rights; and the sections were responsible for admissibility decisions over the latter. Under the new regime, there has been a delegation of tasks from the Court as a whole to the chambers, and the sections have been given wider discretion to reject complaints. There is no subject matter division of labour between the two chambers.

special body is entitled to hold a legislative provision to be invalid on constitutional grounds.

It should be recalled that this monopoly applies equally to the statutes enacted by the national Parliament and to those enacted by the regional legislative assemblies. This monopoly also applies to other sources of law that are not statutes, but get the same treatment: *Decretos-leyes, Decretos legislativos,* parliamentary standing orders, Statutes of Autonomy, and international Treaties.[35]

Different procedures can be employed to trigger legislative review: constitutional challenges, constitutional questions, and preventive control.

Constitutional Challenges

Constitutional challenges (*recursos de inconstitucionalidad*) can be initiated by the President of the Government, the Ombudsman, 50 deputies or 50 senators.[36] Through this procedure, laws are attacked in the abstract (within three months of their official publication). In practice, the 50 deputies or 50 senators belong to the parliamentary opposition: they disagree with the majority and, since they take the statute to be problematic from a constitutional point of view, they decide to bring an action to the Court.

When the law has been enacted by the national Parliament, the regional governments or their legislative assemblies can also file constitutional challenges.[37] Such challenges are normally related to federalism questions. But the Court has interpreted the standing rules broadly: if the law has some connection to the sphere of responsibilities of the regional government, a constitutional attack can be launched on other grounds too (STC 56/1990). So, for example, the regional parliament of Navarra was granted standing to question a law that restricted the fundamental rights of foreign citizens (STC 236/2007).

When a State law is attacked, it is not possible for the Court to issue interim measures, such as suspending the application of the law (ATC

---

[35] A reform of the LOTC enacted in 2010, moreover, extended this special treatment to the fiscal norms issued by the provincial territories of the Basque Country.

[36] See arts 31–34, LOTC.

[37] In this case, the deadline of three months can be extended to nine months, if a bilateral Commission composed of State and regional representatives meets to negotiate an agreement.

90/2010). This is sometimes problematic. The PSOE, for example, has recently challenged a *decreto-ley* that establishes a fiscal amnesty for a limited period of time. Unless the Court proceeds very quickly, the fiscal amnesty will have produced all its effects by the time the decision is handed down. If interim measures were permitted, such an outcome would be precluded. In contrast, when laws enacted by the Autonomous Communities are brought to the Court by the central Government, the latter can *require* the Court to suspend the law automatically.[38] This asymmetry in the system is deemed to be unfair by the Autonomous Communities. Even if the Court can lift the suspension after five months have elapsed since the challenge was filed, the Court sometimes maintains it for many years, until the decision on the merits is finally made.

Once the challenge has been received, the Court notifies it to a set of institutions: Congress, the Senate and the Government. If the law has been enacted by an Autonomous Community, the regional government and parliament are also notified. This way the Court will hear the point of view of those who are expected to defend the statute against the constitutional attack.

The effects of the Court's decision are *erga omnes*: they bind all branches of government. If the statutory provision under examination is found to be unconstitutional, it is declared invalid.[39] Normally, this means that the provision gets eliminated from the legal system. Sometimes, however, the Court thinks it better to 'save' the provision: it establishes the conditions under which it can remain in the legal system. A law, for example, that guaranteed foreigners who do not understand Castilian (Spanish) the right to a translator when they are under arrest, was found wanting by the Court. Spanish citizens, the Court reasoned, should also be granted that right, in the rare event that they do not understand Castilian. The law was not struck down, however. Instead, the Court held that the law should be interpreted broadly, to benefit Spaniards (STC 74/1987). In other cases, the Court has deferred to a future moment the effects of a declaration of unconstitutionality (see, for instance, STC 195/1998).

A complex issue concerns the retroactive effects of a Constitutional Court's opinion declaring a statute unconstitutional. What happens with

---

[38] See art 30, LOTC, and art 161.2 of the Constitution.
[39] See art 39.1, LOTC.

the past official actions that enforced the statute? The LOTC explicitly provides that past judicial decisions cannot be revised, if they achieved *res judicata* finality. This rule has an exception, however: if the statute imposes criminal or administrative sanctions, the past judicial decisions can be revised.[40] The Court has held that the same scheme should be extended to administrative decisions: if they achieved finality, they should only be open to revision if a sanction was imposed. The taxes paid by citizens, for example, cannot be recovered, once the deadline for attacking the administrative decision has expired. (See, for instance, STC 45/1989).

Constitutional Questions

A second avenue to get the Court to exercise legislative review is the constitutional question procedure (*cuestión de inconstitucionalidad*).[41] When ordinary judges handling disputes entertain doubts about the constitutionality of the relevant law, or are convinced that the law is unconstitutional, they are required to certify a question to the Constitutional Court. The proceedings in the instant case are suspended until the latter addresses the matter. There is thus a division of labour between the Constitutional Court and ordinary judges. The procedures that the Court follows, and the effects of its decisions, are basically the same as those that apply to abstract constitutional challenges.

Judges may raise questions at the request of a party to the case, or *sua sponte*. If they refuse to certify a question that a party has requested, they have to explain the reasons why (STC 35/2002). The decision not to raise a question cannot be appealed, but if the case proceeds and gets to a higher court, the parties can again make their request.

Only when judges are performing an adjudicative function, it should be noted, can they petition the Court through this mechanism. As was mentioned before, judges sometimes carry out functions that are not 'jurisdictional'. Judges, for example, may be in charge of the Civil Register. Some years ago, a judge who had to administer the marriage of a same-sex couple raised a question to the Court concerning the 2005 law that allows same-sex marriages. The Court declared the question inadmissible, for the judge was not adjudicating any case, but was merely

[40]   See art 40.1, LOTC.
[41]   See arts 35–37, LOTC. For a comprehensive treatment, see JM López Ulla, *La cuestión de inconstitucionalidad en el Derecho español* (Madrid, Marcial Pons, 2000).

carrying out an administrative task. Only judges who are doing a jurisdictional job can petition the Court through the constitutional question mechanism. (ATC 505/2005).

Interestingly, the law provides that, before an ordinary judge sends a statute to the Constitutional Court for its review, he must try to find an interpretation of that statute that makes it consistent with the Constitution.[42] That is, if the applicable legal provision can be read in different ways, the judge must choose that reading that harmonizes it with constitutional principles. The Court should intervene only when this attempt at *interpretación conforme* has been unsuccessful. This does not mean, of course, that judges are entitled to distort a statutory provision through interpretive means. The constitutionally inspired reading of the statute should not be at odds with its clear textual meaning and the underlying legislative intention. As the Court has held, the judge should not use the Constitution to support an interpretation of the statute that is *contra legem* (STC 138/2005). The problem, however, is that it is not always easy to determine whether a particular reading of the statute is still possible as a fair interpretation of it or is, on the contrary, so strained a reading that it should count as a prohibited, *contra legem* interpretation.

An important question arose soon after the Court was set up in 1980: what about statutes that were enacted *before* the Constitution of 1978 entered into force? What happens if there is a contradiction between an old statute and the new Constitution? May ordinary judges set aside the statute on their own authority, or are they required to certify a question to the Constitutional Court? The latter held that judges have a choice: they can directly disregard the statute by themselves or, in case of doubt, they can send it to the Constitutional Court for its review (STC 4/1981).

Preventive Review of International Treaties

In addition to constitutional challenges and questions, a third procedure exists, in order to check international Treaties (article 95.2 of the Constitution).[43] Once Treaties are signed by Spain, but before they are finally consented to, the Court can be requested to determine whether they respect the Constitution. Congress, the Senate and the Government

---

[42] See art 5.3, LOPJ.
[43] See, also, art 78, LOTC.

can petition the Court to rule on the issue. A parliamentary minority, however, is not entitled to do so, a feature of the system that has attracted criticism.[44]

This procedure to control Treaties is currently the only instance of a priori review of legal norms that exists in Spain.[45] The justification for this mechanism is that it is particularly useful to clarify the underlying constitutional issue before Spain ratifies a Treaty that will affect third parties on the international level. If the Court rules that there is an incompatibility, the Treaty cannot be ratified, unless the Constitution is first amended. This procedure has been used twice, in connection with the 1992 Maastricht Treaty (Declaration 1/1992), and the 2004 Treaty establishing a Constitution for Europe (Declaration 1/2004).

It should be mentioned, however, that the Court is also entitled to review a Treaty once it has been ratified, through an ordinary constitutional challenge or question. The preventive mechanism complements, but does not replace, the general procedures that are available to impugn the validity of statutes and legal norms of equivalent force.

Conflicts

A second head of jurisdiction relates to controversies between public institutions.[46] The most important disputes arise in the area of regionalism. So-called 'conflicts of competences' are likely to arise between the two levels of government (or, less often, between different regions). Almost always, the conflict is 'positive', in that both governments claim authority over a disputed subject matter. In such cases, the conflict can be initiated by one of the executive bodies involved. The Court declares who is competent to decide the matter under dispute.[47]

The conflict can also be 'negative', which means that both organs assert that they lack competence over a particular matter. Such conflict

---

[44] See, eg A Remiro Brotons, *La acción exterior del Estado* (Madrid, Tecnos, 1984) 218–20.

[45] In the past, organic laws and Statutes of Autonomy could also be reviewed before their promulgation. This preventive mechanism was abolished in 1985, through a reform of the LOTC.

[46] See arts 59–75*quinque*, LOTC.

[47] When the source of the controversy is a statute (or any other norm that has the same rank), the Court follows the same procedure that applies to constitutional challenges.

may be instituted by the State executive (but not by a regional executive), or by an affected person, who has obtained a negative response by the two governmental levels. Negative conflicts are extremely rare.

As already noted, an important asymmetry is built into the Spanish system of constitutional justice. Article 161.2 of the Constitution permits the national Government to cause a regional regulation or act to be automatically suspended, by filing a challenge before the Constitutional Court.[48] The regional regulation or act can be suspended for a maximum period of five months. The Court can then decide whether or not to maintain the suspension for a new period, depending on the balance of the interests and risks. In contrast, no such automatic suspension can be obtained by the regional authorities when they go to the Court and impeach the State's actions. They can only obtain a suspension if irreparable harms could otherwise be produced. And, very importantly, no such suspension is possible if the regulation being attacked is a national statute or law of statutory rank.

The Court has also been given the authority to settle controversies between various organs at the national level. Only the Government, Congress, the Senate and the General Council of the Judiciary are relevant for these purposes, however.[49] In a parliamentary democracy, it is unlikely that deep tensions will emerge between these institutions. As a matter of fact, only in very few cases have controversies been filed. The Senate, for example, once refused to honour the Government's decision to expedite the legislative procedure to enact a particular law. As a reaction, a conflicts procedure was instituted, and the Court held in favour of the Government (STC 234/2000).

A third kind of conflict, which is also of marginal importance, was introduced in 1999, to protect local autonomy. When municipalities or provinces consider that a statute (or another norm of equivalent rank) enacted by the State or a region violates their constitutionally protected 'local autonomy', a certain number of them can bring an action to the Court. As a result of this procedure, the Court declares whether local autonomy has been breached. The Court can also fix the consequences for the situations that have arisen under the law that has been attacked. In a separate procedure, the Court will declare the unconstitutionality of the law, if a violation of local autonomy has been found.

---

[48] The challenge can actually be based on any constitutional ground – not necessarily a ground that is linked to the distribution of competences.

[49] In addition, the Court of Audit can request the Cortes Generales to file a conflict.

Complaints for Violation of Fundamental Rights

A third function of the Court is linked to fundamental rights. As we will see in the next chapter, some of these rights (those mentioned in articles 14–30.2 of the Constitution) benefit from a special procedural guarantee: public actions (or omissions) that violate them can be attacked through a 'complaint' (*recurso de amparo*) that is lodged before the Constitutional Court.[50] The actions that can be impugned in this way may originate in the executive, the judiciary or a parliamentary assembly.[51] A special type of *amparo*, which is decided through expedited procedures, is the *amparo electoral*, which applies to violations produced in the electoral context.

Standing is given to the persons who claim to have been harmed as a result of an infringement of fundamental rights. The Ombudsman and the Office of the Public Prosecutor are also granted standing, but they rarely bring cases.

Before an *amparo* is filed, however, the plaintiff must exhaust all judicial remedies. That is, he must first seek legal protection from the ordinary judiciary, if it is available under the pertinent procedural laws. The Constitutional Court therefore acts a 'special court of appeals'. It is the really supreme judicial body in Spain, for it can quash the decisions of any other court – even the Supreme Court. It cannot decide, however, all the factual and legal issues that a case poses. Its *amparo* jurisdiction is limited to checking whether the relevant fundamental right has been infringed. If it concludes that there has been such a violation, it so declares, and it normally invalidates the action that has caused the violation. It can also establish measures to restore the right.

It is important to note that in the vast majority of cases, the action that is found to offend a fundamental right rests on an incorrect interpretation and application of the relevant body of law. The law as such is fine, but the public authorities have not read it in a proper way, or have exercised their discretion in the wrong direction. Sometimes, however, it is the applicable statutory provision that is at fault, in that it violates a fundamental right. If the Court so concludes, it suspends the procedure,

---

[50] See arts 41–58, LOTC.

[51] Laws enacted by a legislative assembly cannot be directly challenged through this procedure, however. Only decisions that do not have the form of a law can be attacked.

and declares the statute's invalidity in a separate decision that will produce general effects.

THE COURT'S PERFORMANCE: TENSIONS WITH THE POLITICAL BRANCHES AND THE ORDINARY JUDICIARY

The Constitutional Court was conceived as a novel institution, which would transform Spanish legal practices. Tensions with the political branches, as well as with the ordinary judiciary, were thus to be expected.

The Constitutional Court and the Political Branches

With respect to the political branches, the main source of controversy has been the Court's power to strike down laws. Maybe because the Court has been aware of this, it has tended to focus on rather 'technical matters' when invalidating statutes. An important part of its jurisprudence in the field of legislative review has been devoted to the problem of defining the boundaries between different sources of law (ordinary statutes, organic statues, *decretos-ley,* parliamentary standing orders, etc). Another significant part of its case law has centred on the legislative conflicts between the State and the Autonomous Communities, an area where there is usually a clash of parliamentary wills, and the Court is asked to decide who is competent to regulate what. Even the opinions in the field of fundamental rights have often addressed rather technical questions, such as, for example, whether a criminal law on terrorism was sufficiently precise (STC 89/1993), or whether the statutory definition of 'flagrant crime', for purposes of police searches in private homes, was in accordance with the constitutional meaning of this term (STC 341/1993).

Of course, the Court's decisions can have significant political consequences, even if the reasons for invalidating legislative enactments are rather technical. Thus, the Court's decision invalidating the statute that defined 'flagrant crime' too broadly, for purposes of police home searches, caused the resignation of the Minister of the Interior who had sponsored it. Actually, in an act of pressure, the latter had publicly announced that he would resign if the law were invalidated. So the Court's ruling had an important political effect, even though its justification was rather technical. Similarly, the most controversial decision in recent years involved the 2006 Catalan Statute of Autonomy, which was partially struck down by the Court, as was mentioned in the previous chapter. To a large extent, the reasons for the Court's decision were technical. Yet, a huge demonstration, led by the most prominent political and social figures in Catalonia, took place in Barcelona, to protest against the Court's decision.

There certainly have been decisions striking down laws in morally controversial matters. The abortion case is the most prominent example (STC 53/1985). In spite of the public criticisms that the decision generated, some of them voiced by leading political figures such as the Vice-President, Parliament accepted the constitutional ruling, and changed the law accordingly.

In general, the Court gets into a difficult position when cases become politicized. The degree to which this happens depends, in part, on who invokes the Court's jurisdiction. There is a clear contrast in this respect between the parliamentary opposition (50 deputies or 50 senators) bringing a constitutional challenge against a law, on the one hand, and an ordinary judge certifying an issue to the Court, on the other. In the first case, the Court is closer to the terrain where political battles are fought. A decision upholding the statute will count as a political victory for the Government and a defeat for the opposition, while a decision against the statute will be read in the opposite way. It is interesting to note, in this connection, that when the Government is supported by an absolute majority in Congress, the number of challenges against legislation is higher than when the Government lacks such a majority and needs to negotiate with other parties. A study covering the period from 1980–2000 found that nearly seven per cent of the laws were attacked by the main party in the opposition when there was a majority Government, while only two per cent of them were attacked when there was a minority Government.[52]

All this does not mean, however, that when ordinary judges raise questions to the Constitutional Court, there is no potential conflict with the political branches. The latter may be very upset if an important piece of legislation is struck down, even if the parliamentary minority cannot

---

[52] P Magalhães, 'The Limits of Judicialization: Abstract Review and Legislative Politics in the Iberian Democracies' (PhD dissertation, Ohio State University), cited in R Gunther, JR Montero and J Botella, *Democracy in Modern Spain* (New Haven, Yale University Press, 2004) 124–25.

claim a victory. Actually, sometimes ordinary judges have asked the Court to intervene in connection with statutes that no important political party has chosen to challenge – either because all of them support the statute, or because it would not be very popular to insist on certain criticisms. Thus, both the majority and the parliamentary opposition were in favour of a legal provision enacted in 1995 that makes it a crime for someone to deny or justify past genocides, or to defend political regimes that committed such acts.[53] When criminal charges were brought against a person who sold books that denied the existence of gas chambers in Nazi concentration camps, the criminal court in Barcelona that handled the case decided to certify a question to the Constitutional Court, on the grounds that the applicable provision offended freedom of speech. The Court's decision (STC 235/2007) declared the relevant law to be unconstitutional in part. It held that it is possible to criminalize speech that seeks to *justify* past genocides, but not speech that simply *denies* their commission.

Similarly, the Criminal Code was amended in 2004 in order to establish harsher penalties for certain crimes of domestic violence, but it did so in a way that treats the convicted persons differently depending on their gender – men receive higher penalties than women for the same kind of conduct. The law was voted unanimously in Parliament. Given this unanimity, and given that it is not very popular to challenge a law whose explicit goal is to reduce the level of violence against women, no constitutional challenge by political actors was to be expected. Instead, a significant number of ordinary judges in charge of enforcing the new provision concluded that it was unduly discriminatory, and chose to petition the Court to review it. In a very controversial decision, however, the Court upheld the new law (STC 59/2008).

Overall, it is fair to say that the Court's performance as a counterweight to the parliamentary majority at the national level has been marginal. The Court has been so overwhelmed with its *amparo* jurisdiction that it has not had much time and energy left to decide constitutional challenges and questions against statutes. The Court has usually taken a long time (up to 8, 9, 10, and even 11 years in some instances) to render a decision.[54] As a result of these extraordinary delays, it is often the case that the law has already been repealed or modified by Parliament when the Court finally lays down its decision (which gives rise to the some-

---

[53] See art 607.2, Criminal Code.
[54] See, eg SSTC 194/2000, 10/2002, 193/2004, 138/2005, 111/2006.

times difficult question whether a decision is still necessary, given that the law that was attacked no longer exists).

There is a general consensus among experts that the Court should play a more prominent role as guardian of the Constitution against the legislature. The problem for a long time was that the Court's workload in the *amparo* jurisdiction was huge. The 2007 reform of the LOTC introduced a revolutionary change, for it granted the Court much more discretion to decide which *amparo* cases to take. Only those cases that exhibit a 'special constitutional transcendence' are admissible. The Court has tried to specify the criteria to determine this broad concept (see STC 155/2009). The basic idea is that complaints are sufficiently relevant when they create an opportunity for the Court to establish doctrine on a new problem, or to clarify, qualify, or change the existing doctrine; when they illustrate the existence of contradictions among courts, or a refusal by some judges to follow the Court's doctrines; or when the legal problem the complaint raises has a broad social, economic or political impact. It is to be hoped that, as a result of this reform, the Court will be able to concentrate its efforts on legislative review in the coming years.

The Constitutional Court and the Ordinary Judiciary

When it comes to the ordinary judiciary, in contrast, the main tensions have been produced by the Constitutional Court's decisions rendered in *amparo* cases. One of the Court's historical missions has been to instil the new constitutional values into the legal minds of ordinary judges. In this connection, the *amparo* jurisdiction has played a key role. It has allowed the Court to illustrate in specific disputes how the law must be applied in light of constitutional liberties. But defining the scope of the *amparo* jurisdiction has been extremely hard.

The Court is supposed to confine its attention to the question whether the action complained of has caused an infringement of fundamental rights. It has no jurisdiction to check whether the ordinary courts have properly decided the factual and ordinary legal issues that the case poses. In practice, however, it has been difficult to specify the boundaries that define this division of labour.[55] And this difficulty has produced

---

[55] For a systematic study of the tests and doctrines that the Court has constructed in order to define its own jurisdiction vis-à-vis ordinary courts, see the collection of

institutional frictions. The question has been raised whether ordinary judges are bound by the Court's rulings, if the latter has overstepped the limits of its jurisdiction.

The Court, for example, addressed the question as to when exactly the action to bring criminal charges against someone has the effect of interrupting the applicable statute of limitations (STC 63/2005). The thesis it maintained ran counter to the dominant case law of the Supreme Court. It is not clear whether this is really a matter for the Constitutional Court to decide, or is instead an ordinary legal question of statutory interpretation. Both the prosecutors and the Supreme Court decided not to apply the new doctrine.[56] Interestingly, the legislature entered this debate in 2010, and amended the Criminal Code in a direction that basically endorsed the Supreme Court's position.

Similar tensions arose in the past concerning the amount of damages that must be granted to public figures whose fundamental right to privacy is found to have been infringed. The Constitutional Court once quashed a Supreme Court's ruling on the amount of compensation to be awarded to the plaintiff (STC 186/2001). The Supreme Court expressed its strong disagreement with that decision.

All these boundary problems and tensions are probably inevitable in a system that superimposes a new Constitutional Court on the extant Supreme Court. What happened in 2004, however, was more extraordinary – almost surrealist. To make the story short, the facts were basically these. A lawyer who wanted to challenge the way the Constitutional Court appoints its own legal staff brought an action before the third chamber of the Supreme Court (which specializes in administrative law). Since he did not succeed there, he afterwards lodged a complaint before the Constitutional Court itself, asking all judges, on impartiality grounds, to abstain from participating in the case, and to request the Government to create a new Constitutional Court that would be in an impartial position to decide. The Court rejected the complaint, giving reasons why it was not possible for it to do what the plaintiff had asked. This was not the end of the story, however, for the plaintiff then went to the first chamber of the Supreme Court (which deals with 'civil

---

articles edited by C Viver Pi-Sunyer (former Vice-President of the Constitutional Court), *Jurisdicción constitucional y judicial en el recurso de amparo* (Valencia, Tirant lo Blanch, 2006).

[56] See *Instrucción* 5/2005, issued by the Fiscalía General del Estado, and decision by the Supreme Court (second chamber), 24 March 2006.

matters'), seeking damages against the judges of the Constitutional Court, on the grounds that their decision to reject his constitutional complaint was based on insufficient reasons, and that this had caused him a moral harm: he no longer trusted courts! Incredibly, the Supreme Court agreed, and ordered each constitutional judge to pay €500 to the plaintiff.[57] Although the Supreme Court made clear that it had no jurisdiction to review the validity of the order to reject the complaint, it insisted that it had jurisdiction to impose liability for damages on the judges who issued it. The Constitutional Court made a public statement criticizing the decision. What is more, the judges themselves filed an *amparo* against the decision! (The Constitutional Court has not yet decided it). This episode has seriously poisoned the relationships between the two high courts in Spain, and has introduced an additional element of complexity in the system. The legislature has had to step in, to make clear that the Constitutional Court's decisions cannot be checked by any other judicial body. For these purposes, the LOTC was reformed in 2007 to authorize the Court to invalidate any act that undermines its own jurisdiction.[58]

Some frictions between the Supreme Court and the Constitutional Court are probably inevitable. They have occurred in other European countries too. But things have gone too far in Spain, unfortunately, as this sad story reveals.

CONCLUSION

Courts are key institutions in any polity that is based on the rule of law. They are needed to perform a function that is crucial for the stabilization of rules, and for the protection of the rights and interests that those rules embody. Courts must be designed in such a way that this function can be properly carried out. Judicial independence is an ingredient of the rule of law ideal: judges must be protected against the pressures of those who may be harmed by the correct interpretation and enforcement of the existing rules. If the rules need to be changed, the democratic procedures should be employed.

---

[57] See decision 23 January 2004.
[58] See art 4.1, LOTC.

When it comes to interpreting the Constitution, things get more complicated. The Constitution expresses fundamental principles and values that are widely shared in the polity, but whose specific meaning is often controversial. The democratic branches, it seems, should participate in the process of constructing the meaning of the constitutional text – a text that is not easy to modify. The judiciary, moreover, should be structured in the right way to enter into dialogues with the political branches concerning the Constitution. In light of all these considerations, Spain decided to follow in the steps of several European countries that had created a specialized constitutional tribunal, with the exclusive authority to declare the invalidity of statutory enactments. This institutional choice has its pros and cons, some of which we have explored in this chapter. The Spanish case has a mixed lesson to offer. The constitutional court has been a good instrument for purposes of spreading among ordinary judges the new principles and values announced in the Constitution. It has acted, however, as an insufficient check on the legislature. The worst part of the picture, probably, concerns the profound tensions that have arisen between the Constitutional Court and the Supreme Court. A better interaction of the two courts is deeply needed.

FURTHER READING

Carrillo, M, *La tutela de los derechos fundamentales por los tribunales ordinarios* (Madrid, Centro de Estudios Constitucionales, 1995).

Cruz Villalón, P, *La formación del sistema europeo de control de constitucionalidad (1918–39)* (Madrid, Centro de Estudios Constitucionales, 1987).

De Otto, I, *Estudios sobre el Poder Judicial* (Madrid, Ministerio de Justicia, 1989).

Delgado del Rincón, LE, *Constitución, Poder Judicial, y responsabilidad* (Madrid, Centro de Estudios Políticos y Constitucionales, 2002).

Díaz Revorio, FJ, *Las sentencias interpretativas del Tribunal Constitucional* (Valladolid, Lex Nova, 2001).

Díez-Picazo, LM, *Régimen constitucional del poder judicial* (Madrid, Civitas, 1991).

——, *El poder de acusar* (Barcelona, Ariel, 2000).

Ferreres Comella, V, *Constitutional Courts and Democratic Values. A European Perspective* (New Haven, Yale University Press, 2009).

Guarnieri, C and Pederzoli, P, *The Power of Judges: A Comparative Study of Courts and Democracy* (Oxford, Oxford University Press, 2002).

Jiménez Asensio, R, *Imparcialidad Judicial y Derecho al Juez Imparcial* (Cizur Menor, Aranzadi, 2002).

López Ulla, JM, *La cuestión de inconstitucionalidad en el Derecho espanō* (Madrid, Marcial Pons, 2000).

Mieres Mieres, LJ, *El incidente de constitucionalidad en los procesos constitucionales* (Madrid, Civitas, 1998).

Pérez Royo, J, *Tribunal Constitucional y división de poderes* (Madrid, Tecnos, 1988).

Pérez Tremps, P, *Tribunal Constitucional y poder judicial* (Madrid, Centro de Estudios Constitucionales, 1985).

——, *El recurso de amparo* (Valencia, Tirant lo Blanch, 2004).

Rubio Llorente, F and Jiménez Campo, J, *Estudios sobre jurisdicción constitucional* (Madrid, MacGraw-Hil, 1998).

Terol Becerra, MJ, *El Consejo General del Poder Judicial* (Madrid, Centro de Estudios Constitucionales, 1990).

Tomás y Valiente, F, *Escritos sobre y desde el Tribunal Constitucional* (Madrid, Centro de Estudios Constitucionales, 1993).

Urías, J, *La tutela frente a leyes* (Madrid, Centro de Estudios Políticos y Constitucionales, 2001).

9

Fundamental Rights

———»·•·«———

The Structure of the Bill of Rights – Legal Mechanisms for Protecting Rights – Restriction and Suspension of Fundamental Rights – Who is Entitled to Fundamental Rights? – Are Private Individuals Bound by Fundamental Rights? – Fundamental Rights in an Activist State – Conclusion

I N THIS FINAL chapter, we will study the legal regime that applies to fundamental rights in Spain. We will examine, in particular, the structure of the Bill of Rights included in the Constitution, and the mechanisms that have been set up to protect those rights. Attention will also be paid to the rules and principles that govern the restriction and the suspension of rights. We will then proceed to discuss three important questions: who is entitled to rights; how do rights operate in the private sphere; and what role should an activist State play in this field.[1]

THE STRUCTURE OF THE BILL OF RIGHTS

Title I of the Constitution concerns itself with rights, as well as principles and duties. It is a rather long list, which is divided into different sections. The structure of the Title is a bit complicated – unnecessarily so, as we will see. It comprises five chapters, dealing with issues of nationality and the status of foreigners (Chapter I), rights and liberties (Chapter II), principles on social and economic policy (Chapter III),

---

[1] The most comprehensive treatment of fundamental rights in Spain is LM Díez-Picazo, *Sistema de derechos fundamentales* (Cizur Menor, Aranzadi, 2008).

mechanisms to guarantee rights and liberties (Chapter IV) and suspension of rights (Chapter V).

Fundamental Rights, and Social and Economic Principles

The first thing to bear in mind is that the Constitution establishes two different legal regimes, depending on the interests being protected. As a result of this dual scheme, the fundamental rights that figure in Chapter II (articles 14–38) are more strongly protected than the principles on social and economic policy (*principios rectores de la política social y económica*) that are enumerated in Chapter III (articles 39–52). Article 53 specifies what these differences are.

When it comes to rights, article 53 says that they are 'binding on all public authorities'. This means that there is no need for ordinary laws to be passed to guarantee a fundamental right: the Constitution directly protects it. This idea was especially important at the beginning of the democratic era, when some of the rights announced in the Constitution, which had been ignored under the dictatorship, had not yet been regulated by the legislature. The Constitutional Court insisted on their direct applicability. For many years, for example, there was no statute implementing the right to conscientious objection to the military service. The Constitutional Court held that this did not mean that such right could not be exercised. Since the Constitution enshrines the right to conscientious objection in article 30.2, the executive branch and the courts were bound to respect the core of it (STC 15/1982). Nowadays, almost all rights have been developed through the pertinent laws, but some of them have not. Article 20.1 of the Constitution, for example, guarantees the right of journalists to the confidentiality of their sources, but no law has yet been passed to specify this right. Judges have therefore had to apply the Constitution directly, and have balanced the interests at stake on a case-by-case basis.

Another rule that article 53 establishes is that only statutes may regulate the exercise of fundamental rights. This means that the popularly elected Parliament must necessarily intervene to specify the scope of the right, and to lay down the pertinent conditions and restrictions. Administrative regulations are only admissible if they play a marginal role – they are merely to work out the details of the relevant statutes.

The legislature, moreover, must respect the 'essential content' of the right, article 53 says. There has been a complex scholarly discussion about the meaning of this expression, as we will see. But it is a clear indication that the legislature is not free to impose any limitations or restrictions it wishes. Again, this was particularly important during the first years of the new constitutional order. Some of the laws inherited from the past were too restrictive in their regulation of rights. The law on associations, for example, or the law on labour strikes, had to be partially invalidated and reconstructed by the Constitutional Court, to ensure the direct effect of the Constitution in this field (see, for instance, STC 11/1981).

Hence, fundamental rights get a high level of protection. The social and economic principles included in Chapter III, in contrast, benefit from a less robust regime. Article 53 specifies that such principles are to inspire the legislation that is enacted, as well as judicial and administrative practice, but they are not directly enforceable. The Constitution explicitly says that the social and economic principles 'can only be invoked before the ordinary courts in accordance with the laws that develop them'. Note that the implementation of those principles is not reserved to statutory sources of law. Administrative regulations have thus a wider space to occupy, than it is the case when fundamental rights are at stake.

That ordinary courts must apply the social and economic principles in accordance with the pertinent laws, however, does not mean that there is no possibility at all for a statute or regulation to be struck down on the grounds that it clearly fails to protect those principles. The Constitutional Court may be asked to review the validity of a piece of legislation that is claimed to disregard the social and economic goals the Constitution sets forth. But the Court will be extremely deferential to the legislature in such cases, since the idea of an 'essential content' is not applicable in this context. The Court must therefore grant the political branches ample room for manoeuvre. As a result, citizens have to rely on non-judicial mechanisms, such as petitioning the Government or filing a complaint with the Ombudsman, to press the State to implement a programme that supplies the necessary services to realize the social and economic principles. Participation in the relevant administrative processes where decisions and regulations are made is also especially important. The Constitution makes an explicit reference to this kind of participation when it deals with consumer protection in article 51, for example.

There is thus a significant contrast between the legal regime that applies to the rights of Chapter II and that of the social and economic principles specified in Chapter III. This contrast has an important connection with the distinction between civil and political rights, on the one hand, and social and economic rights, on the other. But there is no perfect coincidence. The right to form trade unions and to strike (article 28), the right to work (article 35) and the right to collective bargaining (article 37), for example, are all fundamental rights under the Constitution, and yet they are of a social and economic character. The contrast between rights and principles is also linked to the distinction between negative and positive rights. But, again, there is no perfect congruence. The right to free education, for example, figures in the Constitution as a fundamental right (article 27), not a social principle, in spite of its clearly being a positive right that requires the State to act. The same is true of the right of prisoners to obtain paid employment and social security benefits, which appears in article 25.2 as a fundamental right.

Constitutional Duties

In addition to the fundamental rights and social and economic principles we have so far examined, Title I of the Constitution enumerates some duties that citizens must comply with.[2] These are the duty to defend Spain, which includes performance of the military service (article 30.1 and 2); the duty to pay taxes (article 31), and the duty to work (article 35). The Constitution also allows the legislature to impose a civilian service for the general interest, and to establish certain obligations on citizens in the event of a grave risk, catastrophe or public calamity (article 30.3 and 4). In all these cases, the Constitution reserves the regulation to the pertinent statutes. The specific obligations that flow from these general duties are to be fixed by the legislature.

It is not clear what the justification is for the Constitution to include duties. In part, a republican tradition is being followed, which insists on the idea that citizens must make certain sacrifices for the common good. The government must respect individual liberties, but individuals must

---

[2] See F Rubio Llorente, 'Los deberes constitucionales' (2001) 62 *Revista Española de Derecho Constitucional* 11.

also contribute to the general welfare. In addition, the insertion of certain duties in the constitutional text resolves any doubts about the legal validity of certain measures that might otherwise be questioned, on the grounds that they impose heavy costs on private individuals.[3]

The duty to defend Spain is probably the most salient constitutional duty. It is partially honoured through the establishment of a system of obligatory military service, to be performed by those citizens that are selected in accordance with the law. Since 2001, however, the military service has been 'suspended' indefinitely, which is an indirect way of eliminating an institution that the Constitution explicitly imposes. This removal is constitutionally problematic, however. The Constitution seems to make compulsory military service a central part of the duty to defend Spain. The legislature has some margin of discretion as to who is required to perform this service, and what are the circumstances under which an exemption applies – apart from those that refer to conscientious objection. But this margin is not so large as to permit the legislature to totally dismantle the institution. Arguably, a constitutional amendment should have been passed to do away with compulsory military service.

With respect to the duty to contribute to public expenses through the tax system, it is obvious that the particular taxes to be paid are defined in the various laws that make up that system. Article 31.3 explicitly provides that only statutes may fix the concrete fiscal obligations individuals must honour. This does not mean, however, that the legislature is totally free to define the tax system. Arbitrary fiscal exemptions, for example, would be invalid.

There has been great controversy, recently, with regard to a temporary fiscal amnesty that the Government has announced, as part of a larger package of measures it seeks to implement in order to deal with the current economic crisis. For citizens to benefit from the amnesty, they have to pay a 10 per cent tax on their unreported assets. No penalties will be exacted. Deputies belonging to the PSOE parliamentary group have brought an action before the Constitutional Court against the *decreto-ley* that regulates this temporary amnesty. One of the grounds they have articulated in their brief invokes the constitutional clause that imposes on citizens the duty to pay taxes. They acknowledge that a fiscal amnesty is not unconstitutional per se. It must, however, respect the

---

[3] Ibid 18–19.

principle of proportionality, they contend. A tax of 10 per cent on unreported income is too low. In many cases, that amount is less than the
amount of interests the taxpayer would have had to contribute, as a
result of his delay in paying. So, they argue, it is not that the Government
imposes a lower tax than the tax that should have been satisfied. It actually pardons the tax entirely. It is difficult to predict what the Court will
say in this case. Quite likely, however, the law will have produced all its
effects before the Court finally renders its opinion.

With regard to the constitutional duty to work, things are a little mys-
terious. It is not clear what the implications of this duty established in
article 35 are. It is obvious that the State cannot force anyone to work.
The very same article provides that individuals are free to choose their
profession or trade. Not even prisoners can be subjected to forced
labour, as the Constitution explicitly indicates in article 25.2.

In addition to these duties, the Constitution also refers to individual
obligations in connection to education. It proclaims that the basic education is compulsory (article 27.4). With respect to the family, moreover,
the Constitution mentions the duties of parents toward their children
(article 39.3), and the family duties to take care of citizens of advanced
age (article 50).

Institutional Guarantees

Title I of the Constitution seems to protect 'institutions', in addition to
the rights, principles and duties that are linked to individual persons.
The Constitution, for example, includes references to the 'autonomy of
universities' (article 27.10), social security (article 41) and professional
organizations (article 52). These are institutions whose existence, arguably, the Constitution guarantees. The institution of marriage, in addition, can be taken to be implicit in the right to marry that article 32
proclaims.

There has been a considerable amount of controversy concerning the
role and force of these 'institutional guarantees'. The basic idea seems
to be that the Constitution protects these institutions less strongly than
it protects rights. While the legislature has to be more careful when
imposing restrictions on rights, it has more leeway when it regulates an
institution: the only requirement is for the institution to be maintained,
and to be 'recognizable' as such. The Constitutional Court, however, has

made matters more complex by taking some institutions to be linked to fundamental rights. It has thus held that universities have a fundamental right to autonomy. This has helped blur the distinction between rights and institutions. In any event, the Court has upheld many restrictions on university autonomy, such as rules fixing the maximum number of students universities may have, or the method of selecting professors, even if a fundamental right is supposed to be at stake (STC 26/1987).

The idea that there are constitutionally guaranteed institutions has led some people to argue that the 2005 law that permits same-sex marriage is against the Constitution. Marriage, they say, is no longer 'recognizable' as a result of the changes that the law has introduced. Heterosexuality is an essential feature of marriage, they argue. Indeed, the PP (Partido Popular) launched a constitutional attach against the law, partly on this ground. The Constitutional Court, however, has recently upheld the law (STC 198/2012). The Court has reasoned that the Constitution does not prevent the legislature from moving beyond the traditional conception of marriage as the union of a man and a woman.

LEGAL MECHANISMS FOR PROTECTING RIGHTS

Let us now focus on fundamental rights, and on the various devices that the Constitution sets up to ensure their protection. We have already examined the general features of their legal regime, in contrast to that which applies to social and economic principles. The system of protection is complex, however, to the extent that different rules have been constructed for different groups of fundamental rights. There are thus further distinctions to be drawn, within the domain of rights.

The first distinction concerns the need for an organic statute to develop the fundamental right at stake. As we saw in chapter three, organic statutes are based on a broader parliamentary consensus than ordinary statutes: an absolute majority of members of Congress (not a simple majority) is needed to approve and modify them. There was some controversy in the first years after the enactment of the Constitution as to which rights should benefit from this special protection, since article 81 is ambiguous when it refers to 'fundamental rights and public liberties'. Should all the rights and liberties of Chapter II be covered? The Court held that a restrictive interpretation was to be preferred, in order to expand the field for the principle of simple majority, which the Court took to be the normal rule in a democracy. Since Chapter II is divided into two Sections, and the first Section is entitled 'on fundamental rights and public liberties', the Court concluded that only that section is to be developed through organic statutes. So only the rights mentioned in articles 15–29 are covered.

The second distinction refers to the procedures that need to be followed to modify the Constitution. As was explained in previous chapters, two tracks are established in the Constitution for the introduction of amendments, depending on the subject matter that is affected. Article 168 requires that the more burdensome procedure be applied when the reform affects Title I, Chapter II, Section I. In other words, an amendment that touches the rights enumerated in articles 15–29 requires the more complicated procedure. The other rights trigger the easier procedure regulated in article 167. So this distinction, for purposes of constitutional reform, is congruent with the first one we have just seen, concerning the requirement that organic statutes be enacted.

The third distinction is related to the constitutional complaints procedure (*amparo*) that we studied in chapter eight. Not all the rights can be protected through this mechanism, which allows individuals to bring cases to the Constitutional Court. As article 53.2 specifies, only the right to equality (article 14), the rights of Chapter II, Section I (that is, articles 15–29), and the right to conscientious objection to the military service (article 30.2) are covered. Similarly, only these rights (with the exception of the right to conscientious objection) are constitutionally entitled to an expedited and summary procedure before ordinary courts. Different laws have been enacted to satisfy this constitutional requirement. In private law, labour law, criminal law and administrative law, various special procedures have been regulated to make it possible for individuals to go to the courts to complain of a violation of fundamental rights. Such procedures focus on the alleged violation – so the impact of the judicial decision is limited to that issue. And the proceedings are expected to be faster, and to be given priority over other cases. Individuals, however, may choose to institute an ordinary procedure, where all relevant legal issues can be fully addressed.[4]

So there are important differences between various subgroups of rights under the Spanish Constitution. It is debatable, however, whether

---

[4] On the role of ordinary judges in these special procedures, see M Carrillo, *La tutela de los derechos fundamentales por los tribunales ordinarios* (Madrid, Centro de Estudios Constitucionales, 1995).

the complexity of the system is worth the price. The requirement that certain rights be implemented through 'organic statutes', for example, has generated many technical legal problems, as was already noted in chapter five. The Constitutional Court has held that only the basic features of a right must be governed by an organic statute – other aspects are to be addressed by ordinary legislation. This vague distinction has inevitably led the Court to a rather unpredictable jurisprudence as to what falls under each category.

Another problem is that there are strong internal connections between rights that happen to be placed in the different subgroups. The right to conscientious objection to the military service, for example, is not within the list of rights that need to be regulated by organic statute, but it is obviously connected to the right to liberty of conscience (article 16), which is part of that list. The Constitutional Court has had to address the matter. In a rather convoluted opinion, it held that, in spite of the underlying links, no organic statute is required to regulate the right to conscientious objection to the military service, which appears in the Constitution as an autonomous right (STC 160/1987). The problem is that two years before, the Court had asserted that physicians who object to performing an abortion on conscientious grounds are protected by the constitutional guarantee of liberty of conscience (STC 53/1985). This entails that an organic statute is necessary to govern the conditions for physicians to object, while an ordinary statute is the appropriate law to govern the conditions for those who refuse to perform military duties. It is difficult to see the justification for this contrast.

The connections between rights also create problems when determining the availability of the constitutional complaints procedure. Thus, the rights to collective bargaining and to adopt measures of collective conflict appear in article 37, which is not covered by the complaints procedure, but they are linked to the right to trade union activity and the right to strike, which are mentioned in article 28 and are thus covered. The Constitutional Court has held that, given these connections, the former rights benefit from the complaints procedure, but only if trade unions are involved. (See, for instance, STC 105/1992).

The decision by the framers to create subgroups of rights and to establish different regimes of legal protection may lead interpreters to believe that some rights are substantively more important than others, depending on the group they belong to. This would not be a plausible position to hold, however. In many European countries that share the same culture of rights as Spain, the list of fundamental rights gets a more homogeneous treatment, when it comes to the mechanisms for their protection. The requirement that some rights, but not others, be covered by organic statutes is quite idiosyncratic to Spain. We do not find it in most countries. The same is true of the establishment of two groups of rights for purposes of constitutional amendments, or the adoption of a complaints procedure. These institutional arrangements are rather exceptional. It would thus be too parochial for Spain to draw important substantive differences among rights on the basis of these institutional features.

If we inspect which rights have been included in the privileged list, moreover, the framers would not seem to have done a great job in some instances, if we took their classifications to mirror the degree of importance of the rights at stake. Human dignity and the free development of one's personality, for example, are announced in article 10 as part of the 'foundation of the political order'. One would expect this foundational principle to belong to the privileged set, but it does not: no organic statute is required to specify it, the easy procedure to amend the Constitution is applicable, and it furnishes no basis for a constitutional complaint before the Court. Similarly, although the right to equality mentioned in article 14 is protected through the constitutional complaint procedure, it does not benefit from the two other devices: no organic statute is required, and the easy amendment procedure is to be followed.

One of the most salient exclusions from the privileged set concerns private property, which is mentioned in article 33, and does not benefit, therefore, from the complaints procedure. Could one point to this exclusion as evidence that private property deserves less protection than other rights, when it clashes with public interests? Again, this would not be a convincing argument. After all, human dignity is also left out of the complaints procedure, as we have just seen, and yet it is regarded as the foundation of the political order. Whether or not private property is more likely to yield to countervailing interests should be the result of substantive analysis, not of a formalistic classification.

Actually, the exclusion of private property from the complaints procedure may have had a negative effect. The Constitutional Court has had few opportunities to speak about private property, since only constitutional challenges and questions, but not complaints lodged by citizens, can be filed when such a right is at stake. If the Court had had more occasions to address private property issues, it would have generated a more refined jurisprudence than it has been able to.

RESTRICTION AND SUSPENSION OF FUNDAMENTAL RIGHTS

The Constitution implicitly allows for rights to be restricted, and explicitly allows for them to be suspended. While it is difficult in some cases to decide whether a restriction is so intense that it really amounts to a suspension of the right, different rules apply.

Restriction of Rights

From a conceptual point of view, the content of a right must be determined before the restrictions that may be imposed on it can be evaluated. Each right has its own scope, which depends on the semantic content of the constitutional clause that carries it. It is obvious that freedom of speech has nothing to do with committing suicide, for example. In this sense, all rights have limits – they do not cover everything. The fact that we distinguish diverse rights implies that each has its own field of operation.

Some rights are 'absolute', within their limits. The interests they protect can never be overridden by other considerations. Thus, the right not to suffer torture, which is guaranteed in article 15 of the Constitution, is absolute. The right does have limits: it does not include the right not to suffer the inconveniences of a noisy city, to give an obvious example. What the right protects, however, it protects in a categorical manner. No exceptions are allowed, no matter how weighty other interests may seem to be. We should bear in mind, in this regard, that article 10.2 of the Constitution requires Title I to be interpreted in the light of human rights covenants ratified by Spain, the most relevant of which is the European Convention on Human Rights. The case law produced by the European Court of Human Rights in Strasbourg is thus to be taken into account by the Spanish judiciary. And since the European Court has held that the right not to suffer torture is absolute, the same understanding is to be followed in Spain.[5]

---

[5] See, eg the Judgment of 1 June 2010, in the case of *Gäfgen v Germany* App no 22978/05 (2011) 52 EHRR 1. The European Court insists that the ban on torture is

Whether a right is absolute in this sense ultimately depends on substantive argument. If the relevant textual clause is formulated in a categorical manner, there seems to be an indication that the right it embodies is absolute. But this textual indication is only prima facie. There may be good substantive reasons to take the right to be open to restrictions, and thus not absolute. The Constitution, for example, proclaims that the home is inviolable. In a very categorical way, article 18.2 announces that 'no entry or search may be made without the consent of the occupant or a judicial warrant, except in cases of flagrant crime'. So with the only exception of flagrant crime, a judicial warrant is required for a forceful entrance into one's home. Does this mean, then, that a fireman needs to get a judicial warrant to enter a house and extinguish a fire? Obviously not. The Constitutional Court has held that there is an implicit exception to the rule established in article 18.2: entrance is authorized in the event of state of necessity (STC 22/1984). Taking the right to be absolute would generate results that are difficult to accept from a substantive point of view.

Although some rights are absolute, most of them are not. They can be restricted in the name of interests that are external to them. The Constitutional Court has embraced the principle of proportionality, which permits restrictions if they are necessary to achieve a legitimate goal, and the result is a balanced one, in light of the interests at stake. The Court has basically followed the version of the principle of proportionality developed in Germany, which includes three steps in the analysis: it is necessary to ask, first, whether the restriction is useful to achieve a legitimate goal; second, whether the restriction is necessary, in that no more moderate measure could be chosen to sufficiently satisfy that goal; third, whether the costs that the restriction entails are offset by the benefits that are to be achieved (STC 66/1995).[6] It is important to note that the work of Robert Alexy has had a huge impact among Spanish constitutional scholars. The principle of proportionality has been understood, to a large extent, in accordance with the account that this German scholar has developed in his writings.[7]

absolute: even in the most difficult circumstances, such as the fight against terrorism and organized crime, and irrespective of the conduct of the person concerned, no torture is allowed (para 87).

   [6] The origin and the evolution of this doctrine in the jurisprudence of the Spanish Constitutional Court are traced in M González Beilfuss, *El principio de Proporcionalidad en la jurisprudencia del Tribunal Constitucional* (Cizur Menor, Aranzadi, 2003).

   [7] The classic book (in its English version) is R Alexy, *A Theory of Constitutional Rights* (Oxford, Oxford University Press, 2002). C Bernal Pulido has further helped

There was some controversy in the first years as to whether the fundamental rights enumerated in the Constitution could only be restricted in the name of other fundamental rights. The Court, however, soon permitted restrictions to be based on the need to protect interests other than rights (STC 11/1981). Public interests, in particular, are relevant. The most obvious example is the State's interest in investigating crimes, which justifies measures that restrict the liberty and privacy of individuals. The Constitution itself sometimes explicitly mentions public interests as grounds for restricting rights. Article 21.2, for example, provides that meetings and demonstrations in public places may be prohibited if there are good reasons to believe there is a risk for 'public order'. And article 77 protects the institutional autonomy of Parliament when it provides that no petitions can directly be submitted to it by demonstrators. Article 105, in turn, grants citizens a right of access to public archives and registers, but it explicitly names national security and the interest in investigating crimes as grounds for denying access. The Constitution, moreover, establishes certain limitations on the rights of several officers, such as judges, prosecutors, military personnel, to secure the well-functioning and the neutrality of the judiciary and the public administration.

Furthermore, the fact that the European Convention on Human Rights permits restrictions that are necessary in a democratic society to protect morals, public order and national security, among other interests, has helped the Constitutional Court reject the thesis that only rights can justify the restriction of rights. The Court has taken the Convention into account when defining the public interests that may justify a limitation on freedom of speech, for example (STC 62/1982).

The role of the 'essential content' guarantee has also been a matter of debate. To simplify the discussion, some scholars are of the view that even restrictions that may be justified in order to serve other rights or public interests may be declared unconstitutional if they destroy the heart of the right. The scope of the right, as they conceive it, is composed of two circles: the outer circle defines the 'normal' content of the right, and it can be reduced, if good reasons are supplied on the basis of the principle of proportionality. The inner circle, however, defines the nucleus of the right, which cannot be eroded or destroyed. Other

increase Alexy's influence in the Spanish-speaking world, with his book *El principio de proporcionalidad y los derechos fundamentales* (Madrid, Centro de Estudios Políticos y Constitucionales, 2003).

scholars, in contrast, believe that the 'essential content' does not guarantee anything that is not already guaranteed by the principle of proportionality. What it does is to remind interpreters that, as the restrictions under review get closer and closer to the core of the right, the reasons to justify further restrictions need to be increasingly weighty.[8]

The Constitutional Court, in its turn, has defined the 'essential content' through two complementary strategies (STC 11/1981). The first appeals to interests: the essential content is destroyed if the interests that the right protects can no longer be served, as a result of unreasonable restrictions. This line of argument easily connects the essential content to the principle of proportionality. After all, the best way to decide whether the restriction is unreasonable is to apply the proportionality test. The second strategy is more conceptual: the Court has said that if the restrictions are such that the right can no longer be recognized as falling under the pertinent category, the essential content has been violated. There are features, in other words, that must be present for the right to be recognized as such, and not to be degraded into something else. This line of reasoning detaches the essential content from a proportionality analysis, and refers interpreters to the consensus among jurists, as well as ordinary citizens, as to what are the paradigmatic traits of a right that should always be present (or, what are the paradigmatic instances of a particular right being violated). The Court has not come up with a definitive theory on this, but it seems to evolve to an understanding that centres on interests, rather than concepts, and on the principle of proportionality as the guiding tool. Concepts are necessary to fix the provisional image of a right, but when restrictions are imposed and conflicts emerge, proportionality appears to be the key principle.

Suspension of Rights

We have so far discussed the possibility for rights to be restricted. We should now turn to a different kind of measure, which entails the 'suspension' of rights. Article 55 of the Constitution allows the executive branch to suspend certain rights, in special circumstances. There are two possible regimes in this regard.

[8] For a detailed discussion on the essential content guarantee and its connection to the principle of proportionality, see J Jiménez Campo, *Derechos fundamentales. Concepto y garantías* (Madrid, Trotta, 1999), and M Medina Guerrero, *La vinculación negativa del legislador a los derechos fundamentales* (Madrid, McGraw-Hill, 1996).

The first one is 'collective suspension'. When the Government declares a state of siege or exception, a list of rights may be suspended. In chapter six, we studied the procedures that need to be followed for such a state to be declared, and the fundamental rights that may be suspended in such circumstances.

The second exceptional regime is 'individual suspension'. It refers to the measures that may be taken against specific persons in connection with investigations of the activities of 'armed bands or terrorist groups'. We should bear in mind that the constitutional framers did their job in a complicated political and social atmosphere, charged with the anger caused by the actions of diverse groups of terrorists, the most important of which was ETA. Until very recently (October 2011), ETA was active and caused many deaths. The laws suspending rights have been in operation to facilitate police investigations. Only three fundamental rights, however, may be suspended: the right of the arrested person to be brought to a judge no later than 72 hours since the arrest (article 17.2); the right to the inviolability of one's home (article 18.2) and the right to the secrecy of private communications (article 18.3). The Constitution, moreover, lays down some rules to prevent governmental abuses. First, it requires that the specific types of measures to be enforced by the executive branch be established through an organic statute. Second, courts must intervene to check the validity of the actions taken. Third, appropriate forms of parliamentary control must be organized. Fourth, the unjustified or abusive employment of suspension measures will produce criminal responsibility, as a violation of the rights and liberties recognized by the laws.

The Constitutional Court has had to determine the constraints the laws must observe when regulating suspension measures (see, generally, STC 199/1987). Importantly, it has interpreted the scope of the exceptional regime in a restrictive manner: it has held, in effect, that the 'armed bands' the Constitution refers to in article 55.2 are to be understood as equivalent to 'terrorist groups'.

The Court has also imposed other limitations. In 1984, for example, a law was enacted that allowed the detention period to be extended – with judicial authorization – for seven additional days. The Court thought the extension was excessive, and declared the law invalid. Under the current law, the extension –also to be authorized by judges – is much more limited: 48 hours.[9] The Court's holding illustrates that even measures that

---

[9] See art 520*bis*, *Ley de Enjuiciamiento Criminal*.

suspend rights must conform to the principle of proportionality, which is the principle that applies to the restrictions of rights in normal circumstances.

With regard to the suspension of privacy rights, the laws permit the police to enter someone's home, in order to detain a suspected terrorist. Courts must be informed immediately. Similarly, the Minister of the Interior or the General Director of State Security is authorized to order the interception of private communications. Judges must also be informed immediately, to confirm or revoke the measures taken. The Constitutional Court has upheld these legal provisions, if understood in a restrictive manner: only in the event of urgent necessity may the executive authorities act in that way. Otherwise, they must seek the pertinent judicial warrant. The current law satisfies this requirement.[10]

There is another measure that is also provided by the law and which is not taken to be a 'suspension' of a fundamental right, but a mere 'restriction'. A detained person can be held *incommunicado* for a brief period of time, during which he can have no contact with other people. There is no possibility for the arrestee and his lawyer to have a reserved meeting, during that period of time. The lawyer, moreover, is appointed by the State.[11] These measures are not limited to suspected terrorists, but most often they are applied to them. Their rationale is to prevent arrestees from sending information to other people, which would frustrate police investigations. The Constitutional Court has upheld this legal regime, but has required that the decision to hold the arrested person *incommunicado* must be immediately submitted to the competent judges, who must confirm or reject it (STC 199/1987).

In another opinion (STC 196/1987), the Court specified the reasons why it is constitutional for the law to provide that the detained person cannot choose his lawyer while being held *incommunicado*. First, the European Convention on Human Right recognizes in article 6 the right of the 'accused' person to a lawyer of his own choosing, but no such right is extended to the 'arrested' person. Secondly, the essential content of the right is not violated, since the arrested person obtains legal assistance to protect his interests during detention – which is a less complex situation than that of a trial. Although the 'normal content' of the right of the detained person includes his liberty to select the lawyer, the 'essen-

---

[10] See arts 553 and 579, *Ley de Enjuiciamiento Criminal.*
[11] See art 520, *Ley de Enjuiciamiento Criminal.*

tial content' of the right – its core – does not. Thirdly, the Court found the restriction of the normal content of the right to comply with the principle of proportionality. The goal the law seeks is legitimate, and the means it employs are proportional, for as soon as the arrested person is no longer *incommunicado*, he recovers his freedom to select a lawyer.

Some judges on the Court dissented, however. They argued that choosing one's lawyer is no less important during detention than at trial. They claimed, moreover, that it would have been more reasonable to punish the lawyer who acts illegally, rather than deny the arrestees the right to choose one. A lawyer appointed by the detainee, moreover, is incapable of frustrating the *incommunicado* character of the arrest: no meeting between detainee and counsel is possible, after all. The dissenting justices on the Court were especially worried that the restrictive measure is to be applied not only to people suspected of terrorist crimes, but to other people involved in more ordinary crimes too. The law, moreover, does not allow for decisions to be made on a case-by-case basis: if a judge decides to hold someone *incommunicado*, the loss of the right to choose counsel follows automatically.

WHO IS ENTITLED TO FUNDAMENTAL RIGHTS?

We have so far referred to individuals as holders of fundamental rights. We must now refine this general idea. Two issues are of special importance: are foreigners to be treated like citizens, when it comes to fundamental rights? Are legal persons entitled to such rights?

Citizens and Foreigners

The first issue concerns the relevance of citizenship. Article 13.1 of the Spanish Constitution proclaims that foreigners shall enjoy the public freedoms guaranteed in Title I, under the terms to be laid down by Treaties and the law.[12] Article 13.2 of the Constitution then establishes an exception: only Spaniards, it says, shall be entitled to the rights recognized in article 23 (that is, the right to political participation and the right

---

[12] The statute that regulates this matter in a systematic fashion is *Ley Orgánica 4/2000, sobre derechos y libertades de los extranjeros en España y su integración social.*

of access to public office). This exception, in turn, is qualified by a further exception: a Treaty or a law may establish that foreigners may vote and stand as candidates in municipal elections, in accordance with the principle of reciprocity.

The Constitutional Court has made clear that, with the only exception of the rights recognized in article 23, all the rights and liberties that figure in Title I are applicable to foreigners (STC 107/1984). The laws and Treaties may establish a different treatment, but they cannot completely deny foreigners those rights and liberties. Article 13, the Court insists, is the provision that addresses the issue, and the only exception it allows is that of article 23. This means, therefore, that we should pay no attention to whether the clauses embodying the different rights refer to 'Spanish citizens' or to 'all persons'. Such language is ultimately irrelevant, since the clause that must be consulted, in order to determine the rights of foreigners, is article 13. This certainly makes sense. The Constitution says in article 14, for example, that 'Spaniards' cannot be discriminated against on grounds of race or gender, among other grounds. It would be implausible to point to the expression 'Spaniards' to conclude that foreigners can be discriminated against on grounds of race or gender. When it comes to deciding the rights of foreigners, article 13 is controlling, not article 14. Similarly, foreigners can enjoy the right to free movement within Spain, with limitations, even if article 19 refers to 'Spaniards' exclusively (STC 94/1993).

What is possible, however, is for distinctions to be drawn between Spaniards and non-Spaniards, if those distinctions are reasonable. When engaging in this analysis, the Court has paid some attention to whether the constitutional clause carrying the right refers to 'Spaniards' or to 'all persons'. In some instances, no distinctions are allowed, since the right at stake is so strongly connected to human dignity that citizenship is absolutely irrelevant. The right to life and to physical integrity is a prominent example. In other cases, the treatment afforded by the law may be different, if it is based on an objective justification. Even here, a core of the right needs to be protected.

In general, the Court has been eager to scrutinize with rigour the reasons advanced by the Government to justify its legislative choices. It has struck down statutory provisions, for example, that required foreigners to obtain an administrative permission to exercise the right of assembly, and that allowed the Council of Ministers to suspend the activities of associations most of whose members were foreigners (STC 115/1987).

More recently, the Court has invalidated a law that required foreigners to be legally resident in Spain before they could exercise their rights to assembly, to association, to non-elementary education, to trade union activity and to free legal assistance (STC 236/2007).

When dealing with citizenship, it is noteworthy that the Constitution is silent about the criteria that must be met for someone to be regarded as a Spanish citizen. The legislature is thus free to regulate this matter. The Constitution does lay down two rules, however. First, it provides that no person of Spanish origin may be deprived of his or her nationality. Only those who become Spaniards at a later stage, therefore, may lose their nationality according to the law. Second, the State may enter dual nationality Treaties with Latin American countries or other countries that have special links with Spain. In such places, Spaniards may become naturalized without losing their nationality of origin, even if those countries do not recognize a reciprocal right to their own citizens.

In addition to these rules, there is another constraint that the legislature must observe. According to the Constitutional Court, the status of citizenship cannot be fragmented. That is, one is either a Spanish citizen, or one is not. It is not possible for someone to be a Spaniard for some legal purposes, while not for others. The Court's holding was a response to the Government's attempt in 1992 to avoid reforming the Constitution in order to ratify the Maastricht Treaty. Indeed, the Government had argued that it was possible to take foreign EU citizens that reside in Spain as 'Spanish citizens', for purposes of municipal elections. The Court asserted that this was an unacceptable fiction. The Constitution, which reserved the right to run for office exclusively to Spaniards, had to be amended. Only thus could foreign EU citizens who reside in Spain be permitted to exercise that right, as the Maastricht Treaty required (DTC 1/1992).

Finally, it bears emphasizing that whatever rights and guarantees the Constitution extends to all foreigners have to be understood as forming a layer of protection that does not detract from the stronger protection that the European Union grants its own citizens. Citizens of the different countries that belong to the Union must be treated by the Spanish authorities in accordance with the rules and principles that have been constructed by the European Union in order to ensure equal treatment.

Legal Persons

A second problem to consider is whether legal persons are also covered by the Spanish Bill of Rights. There is no general clause in the Constitution that addresses this question. The Constitutional Court has drawn inspiration from a provision in the German Constitution (article 19.3) that extends fundamental rights to legal persons, if the nature of the right at stake so permits. Indeed, some articles in the Spanish Constitution can only make sense if we understand them to cover legal persons. The rights concerning associations (article 22) and trade unions (article 28) are good illustrations of this. The Constitution, moreover, explicitly grants legal entities the right to set up schools (article 27.6). Other rights, in contrast, are obviously reserved to natural persons, such as the right to life, or the right not to be tortured, for instance. Beyond these clear cases, doubts arise. The Court has decided the issue on a case-by-case basis. Among the rights it has held to be applicable to legal persons are the right to equality, the right to judicial protection, the right to the inviolability of domicile and, more controversially, the right to honour (STC 139/1995). It has excluded the right to privacy, however, which is in some conflict with the Court's having included the right to the inviolability of the home (STC 137/1985). Recently, in 2010, the Criminal Code has been reformed to extend criminal liability to legal entities. This must entail that legal persons will benefit from the rights that the Constitution bestows upon those who are charged with crimes.

What about public institutions? Can they hold fundamental rights? There seems to be a paradox in the State having rights against the State. The Court, however, has admitted this possibility, with regard to the procedural rights of public entities that are parties to judicial proceedings. It has also suggested the extension of freedom of speech to public bodies that run television or radio media (STC 64/1988). It bears mentioning in addition, that the Constitution protects, in article 27.10, the autonomy of universities, both private and public ones. As was already noted, the Court has characterized this autonomy as an expression of a fundamental right (STC 26/1987).

ARE PRIVATE INDIVIDUALS BOUND
BY FUNDAMENTAL RIGHTS?

Let us now focus on the other side of the coin: who is bound by fundamental rights? The big issue here is whether private individuals are so
bound. It is plain that certain rights are only for the State to honour. The
right, for example, not to be punished for actions that were not defined
as crimes when they were committed exclusively applies to the State,
since only the State exercises the power to punish. The right to be compensated for takings of property for the public interest is also for the
State to observe. But many other rights are susceptible to being extended
to private individuals – thus acquiring 'horizontal effect', as the expression goes.[13]

In Spain, there is some scholarly and judicial consensus that fundamental rights do play a role in the private sphere. Some constitutional
rights must constrain the actions of private individuals, for otherwise
they would have a very marginal effect. The rights to reputation and to
privacy, which are explicitly referred to in the Constitution as 'limits' on
freedom of speech and information (article 20.4), are usually mentioned
to illustrate the idea that individuals must respect the constitutional
rights of other individuals when they exercise their own liberties. In the
context of labour relationships, moreover, the Constitution enshrines
some rights that workers are entitled to invoke in their interactions with
employers. The right to strike, for example, is clearly for employers –
and not only for the State – to respect. As the Constitutional Court has
held, the employer would violate the right to strike if he sanctioned the
workers on strike, or replaced them with other workers, or resorted to
lock-out measures as a response (STC 11/1981).

There is more controversy as to the technical way in which this general idea is to be translated into practice. Do rights bind private actors
directly? Or do they bind them only indirectly, through the legislation
enacted by the State, and through the judicial doctrines that lay down
more specific rules to coordinate the liberties and the interests of the
parties to a private–law relationship? The Constitutional Court has
tended to avoid this debate. One factor pushes in the direction of the

---

[13] On the justification of horizontal effect, see V Ferreres Comella, 'Do
Constitutional Rights Bind Private Individuals?' SELA paper (2001), available at
www.law.yale.edu/intellectuallife/sela2001.

'indirect effect' theory: as was mentioned in the previous chapter, the *amparo* procedure before the Constitutional Court can only be activated when *public* entities are deemed to have violated a fundamental right. But this factor is neutralized by another consideration that goes in the opposite direction: special procedures have been created for ordinary courts to safeguard in an expedited fashion fundamental rights, in the context of private law and labour law, as required by article 53 of the Constitution. We can only make sense of such procedures if we understand them to be based on the assumption that fundamental rights do bind the private actors involved, and bind them in a direct way. The defendant in such procedures can be a journalist, or an employer, for example. The role of ordinary courts is to protect the constitutional rights at stake, against those private actors. If they fail to do that, the door of the Constitutional Court may then be open to the plaintiff, who may file a complaint, if the pertinent conditions are met.

Another facet of the debate is more substantive: how differently do rights operate when they are alleged against private individuals, instead of governmental institutions? The fact that private parties to a relationship may both hold fundamental rights against each other makes the situation special. The constitutionally protected claims of A against B may be weaker when B is a private individual, since B may also be shielded by a fundamental right against A. Equality, for example, the Court has said, needs to be harmonized with freedom of contract (STC 177/1988). The academic freedom of professors in private schools has to be accommodated with the right of the owners of such schools to define their philosophical or religious programme (STC 47/1985). The right to privacy needs to coexist with the right of the employer to control worker performance (STC 98/2000 and 186/2000). An association may have freedom to choose whom to open its doors to, while a governmental entity is forced to deal with everybody, no matter their race or gender. If that association has a monopoly granted by the State, however, its freedom to exclude potential members is reduced (ATC 254/2001). In general, the Court has tried to strike a balance between the interests at stake in each case, in light of the principle of proportionality.[14]

---

[14] For a detailed study of the Constitutional Court's case law on the problem of horizontal effect, see JM Bilbao Ubillos, *La eficacia de los derechos fundamentales frente a particulares* (Madrid, Centro de Estudios Políticos y Constitucionales, 1997).

FUNDAMENTAL RIGHTS IN AN ACTIVIST STATE

A problem that has some connections to horizontal effect, but that is conceptually different, is the role of the State in fostering rights. The Constitutional Court has espoused the idea that the State must actively implement public policies to protect and satisfy rights. It has imported from German law, in particular, the notion that rights have a double dimension: they are subjective rights that their owners can invoke against the government, and they are also objective values of the legal order as a whole that all branches of the State must promote (STC 25/1981). This philosophy fits very well with article 9.2 of the Spanish Constitution, which requires the State to foster the conditions for real liberty and equality.

With this background, it has been relatively easy for the Court to accept the legitimacy of affirmative action programmes, for example. The Court has thus upheld laws that establish quotas for handicapped people in selection processes for public positions (STC 269/1994), as well as measures that grant special benefits to women, to cover nursery school expenses for their children (STC 128/1987). More controversially, it has upheld laws that impose gender parity on the lists of candidates presented by political parties during the elections (STC 12/2008). The Court has thus made it impossible for a feminist party to draw up a list that only comprises female candidates. It has gone so far as to accept the constitutionality of a law that sets a higher penalty on men than it sets on women, for committing the same type of crime in the context of domestic violence (STC 59/2008).

The Court has also held that certain rights that the Constitution grants individuals in the private sphere place the State under the duty to enact the pertinent regulations to ensure protection. The right of workers to a sufficient remuneration, which is guaranteed in article 35, for example, requires the legislature to establish a minimum wage (STC 31/1984).

This governmental duty of protection may require in some contexts the enactment of criminal laws. The Constitution actually includes an explicit duty to criminalize offences to the environment and to cultural goods, as well as to punish officers who abuse their powers to suspend rights in extraordinary cases (articles 45, 46 and 55). The notion that the effective protection of fundamental interests may necessitate in some

cases the employment of the criminal law is well established in the jurisprudence of the European Court of Human Rights. This Court has
held, for example, that rape must be a crime, and that a law that requires
the victim to use physical force to resist a sexual assault violates human
rights.[15]

The most important and controversial example of criminalization in
Spain concerns abortion. The Constitutional Court (STC 53/1985) held
that the foetus is entitled to protection, even though it is not a person.
To ensure this protection against private actors, the law must penalize
abortion. The Court accepted some exceptions, however, concerning
extreme circumstances under which it would be against the woman's
fundamental rights to prohibit abortion. In particular, the Court
accepted as valid the three types of situations where the law under
review had decriminalized abortion (rape, malformation of the foetus,
and health risks for the mother). The Court found that the law was nevertheless deficient, for lack of sufficient safeguards that would guarantee that legally performed abortions fell in practice under one of those
exceptions. The law was modified accordingly, and was in effect for
many years. A new statute was recently passed (in 2010), however,
exempting abortion from the reach of the criminal law, if performed
within the first 14 weeks of pregnancy. The PP (Partido Popular) then in
the opposition, challenged the law on the grounds that abortion can
only be permitted in particular cases, in light of the Court's doctrine.
The Court has not yet rendered its decision at the time of writing. It is
not to be precluded that the Court will revise its earlier doctrine, which
was laid down more than 25 years ago, and will uphold the new law. The
current Government, in any event, has announced its plan to change the
law and go back to the previous system, under which abortion was only
permitted in some exceptional cases.

CONCLUSION

Given the background of Franco's dictatorship, against which the
Spanish Constitution of 1978 must always be read, it is not surprising
that the Bill of Rights included in Title I is a rather long one. The con-

---

[15] See Judgment of 4 December 2003, in the case of *MC v Bulgaria* App no
39272/98 (2005) 40 EHRR 20.

stitutional text tends to be quite generous when it lists the fundamental rights, as well as the social and economic principles, that the State must honour. The structure of Title I, however, is too complicated. Most of the divisions and subdivisions within the sphere of rights and principles are unnecessary, and the classifications are sometimes arbitrary. It would probably be a good thing for the Constitution to be amended in the future, to simplify this Title.

The Constitutional Court, in turn, has produced a very significant case law in this field. Because of its *amparo* jurisdiction, it has had to focus on fundamental rights in many cases. When constructing its jurisprudence, the Court has paid attention to external sources. As was explained in chapter one, the framers of the Constitution sought to connect Spain to the outside democratic world in general, and to European organizations in particular. In the same spirit, the Constitutional Court has been illuminated by judicial opinions from other nations. The case law of the European Court of Human Rights, in addition, has been extremely influential, as was explained in chapter three. It is revealing, for example, that the Court has embraced the proportionality test as the main tool to evaluate restrictions on fundamental rights. The Constitution does not mention the principle of proportionality, but the Court has incorporated it into its jurisprudence, following the example of other European courts. The Court has also endorsed doctrines that had already been developed in other countries, such as the doctrine that extends constitutional rights to the private sphere, and the notion that there is a duty on the State to actively protect fundamental rights, a duty that may even require the criminalization of certain conducts. The Court's case law is thus a good mirror of the general jurisprudential ideas that characterize European constitutional law in the realm of fundamental rights.

FURTHER READING

Alexy, R, *A Theory of Constitutional Rights* (Oxford, Oxford University Press, 2002).

Bernal Pulido, C, *El principio de proporcionalidad y los derechos fundamentales* (Madrid, Centro de Estudios Políticos y Constitucionales, 2003).

Bilbao Ubillos, JM, *La eficacia de los derechos fundamentales frente a particulares* (Madrid, Centro de Estudios Políticos y Constitucionales, 1997).

Díez-Picazo, LM, *Sistema de derechos fundamentales* (Cizur Menor, Aranzadi, 2008).

Ferreres Comella, V, 'Do Constitutional Rights Bind Private Individuals?' SELA paper (2001), available at www.law.yale.edu/intellectuallife/sela2001

González Beilfuss, M, *El principio de Proporcionalidad en la jurisprudencia del Tribunal Constitucional* (Cizur Menor, Aranzadi, 2003).

Jiménez Campo, J, *Derechos fundamentales. Concepto y garantías* (Madrid, Trotta, 1999).

Medina Guerrero, M, *La vinculación negativa del legislador a los derechos fundamentales* (Madrid, McGraw-Hill, 1996).

Rubio Llorente, F, 'Los deberes constitucionales' (2001) 62 *Revista Española de Derecho Constitucional* 11.

Index

www.ingramcontent.com/pod-product-compliance
Lightning Source LLC
Chambersburg PA
CBHW071840270326
41929CB00013B/2055